MATTHEW ARNOLD
and
JOHN STUART MILL

MATTHEW ARNOLD
and
JOHN STUART MILL

by

EDWARD ALEXANDER

LONDON

ROUTLEDGE & KEGAN PAUL

First published 1965
by Routledge & Kegan Paul Limited
Broadway House, 68-74 Carter Lane
London, E.C.4
Printed in Great Britain
by R. & R. Clark, Limited
Edinburgh and London

To the Memory of
My Grandmother
FRADEL LEVY

The author wishes to thank the following publishers for permission to quote from works of which they hold the copyright: The Clarendon Press for R. P. Anschutz's *The Philosophy of J. S. Mill*, E. L. Woodward's *The Age of Reform*, and *The Poems of Arthur Hugh Clough*, ed. H. F. Lowry, A. L. P. Norrington, and F. L. Mulhauser; Macmillan for Michael Packe's *The Life of John Stuart Mill*; Oxford University Press for M. H. Abrams' *The Mirror and the Lamp*, G. M. Young's *Victorian England: Portrait of an Age*, and *The Letters of Matthew Arnold to Arthur Hugh Clough*, ed. H. F. Lowry; and University of Toronto Press for *The Earlier Letters of John Stuart Mill: 1812–1848*, ed. F. E. Mineka.

PREFACE

THE present volume is an attempt to show the confluence of humanism and liberalism by comparing the chief representatives of the two traditions in Victorian England. I have made Matthew Arnold the spokesman for humanism and John Stuart Mill the spokesman for liberalism, but I have also tried to show to what a considerable extent each shared the convictions of the other; how much of a liberal Arnold was and how much of a humanist Mill was. I have tried to discover the causes of past conflicts between liberalism and humanism in order to suggest how they may eventually complement each other, as, indeed, Arnold and Mill hoped they would.

The unifying purpose of the writings of both Arnold and Mill was to prepare their culture for its imminent democratization. Almost alone among their contemporaries in the world of letters, they accepted the inevitability, and urged the desirability, of democracy. But they feared that unless proper preparation were made, all those virtues which were not the inevitable accompaniment of democracy might be lost. Arnold and Mill believed that high cultural ideals, respect for intelligence, love of heroism, the idea of distinction itself, were not natural to the democratic spirit. But they did not believe that these virtues were incompatible with democracy; and although they had very different ideas of how to do it, both were convinced that democracy might be wedded to a high ideal of culture, and that, as Mill wrote in 1836:

> All that we are in danger of losing we may preserve, all that we have lost we may regain, and bring to a perfection hitherto unknown; but not by slumbering, and leaving things to themselves, no more than by ridiculously trying our strength against their irresistible tendencies: only by establishing counter-tendencies, which may combine with those tendencies, and modify them.

EDWARD ALEXANDER

Seattle, Washington.
October, 1964.

vii

ACKNOWLEDGEMENTS

I AM indebted to several persons and institutions for assistance in the writing of this book.

For early encouragement and advice, I am indebted to Professor G. Robert Stange and to Professor Lionel Trilling. For his patience, kindness, and guidance at every stage of the work, I am indebted to Professor J. C. Levenson.

For their support of my work in the form of fellowships and grants, I am indebted to the University of Minnesota, the University of Washington, and the U.S. Educational ('Fulbright') Commission. For a grant in aid of publication, I am indebted to the Agnes Anderson Fund of the University of Washington.

For permitting and helping me to examine manuscript materials, I am indebted to the librarians of King's College, Cambridge, Somerville College, Oxford, and the London School of Economics.

For suggestions and help of various kinds, I am indebted to Miss Ruth Altmann, Miss Muriel Dashwood, Professor Irvin Ehrenpreis, Mr. Peter M. Jackson, Professor Francis E. Mineka, Professor Samuel H. Monk, Professor John M. Robson, Professor Bernard Saffran, Mrs. Arlene Segal.

For her assistance in more ways than I can enumerate, I am indebted to my wife, Leah Alexander.

CONTENTS

I

REPRESENTATIVE MEN

From whom can we more properly derive a general name for
those degradations of Hellenism than from that distinguished
man, who, by his intelligence and accomplishments, is in many
respects so admirable and so truly Hellenic, but whom his dislike for 'the dominant sect,' as he calls the Church of England
. . . seems to transport with an almost feminine vehemence of
irritation? What can we so fitly name the somewhat degenerated
and inadequate form of Hellenism as *Millism*?

MATTHEW ARNOLD

À propos, why does Maudsley charge me with disparaging physi-
ology either in itself or in its application to mind? It is like
Matthew Arnold enumerating me among the enemies of culture.

JOHN STUART MILL

MATTHEW ARNOLD and John Stuart Mill are the representative
figures of the Victorian age because in them the conflicting
forces of the age came closest to attaining a kind of equilibrium.
In their attempts to reconcile the ancient and the modern,
literature and science, above all culture and democracy, Arnold
and Mill were trying to synthesize the partial and diverse
elements of their age into a unified whole which would survive
into the next.

The names of Arnold and Mill were not linked in their age,
and the reasons why this was so are not hard to find. Arnold was
a poet with an avowed distaste for systematic thought and
systematic thinkers, Mill a philosopher whose *System of Logic*
was the basis of scientific and philosophical investigation at
British universities for nearly half a century. Arnold was the

recognized apostle of culture, Mill a disciple of that 'great, dissected master'[1] who had maintained that pushpin was as good as, nay, for the majority of people, better than, poetry. Arnold was the son and pupil of Dr. Arnold of Rugby, Mill the son and pupil of the contentious Scot, James Mill.

Contemporaries of Arnold and Mill seem to have thought of them as the representatives of opposed schools of thought. Victorians who thought of themselves as the defenders of ancient civilization against modern barbarism usually recognized in Arnold their ally, in Mill their enemy. To Ruskin, for example, Arnold probably seemed a fellow seeker, albeit one gone astray, after the meaning of Homer and the Grand Style; but Mill appeared, as we know from Ruskin's furious and ill-advised attacks upon him, the naïve propounder of a system of political economy the inhumane premises of which he dared not follow to their logical consequences. For Newman, Arnold and Mill were the spiritual offspring of two of his greatest enemies, Thomas Arnold and Jeremy Bentham; but whereas Newman had nothing but scorn and words of abuse for Utilitarians,[2] he was flattered by the admiration of Matthew Arnold, whom he was delighted to meet.

Those who championed democracy against genteel aristocratic culture tended, on the other hand, to see in Mill the friend of progress, in Arnold the apologist for the *status quo*. To know the attitude of Walt Whitman towards Arnold and Mill is to know the attitude that was long prevalent among the literate democratic segments of Anglo-American society. Whitman began *Democratic Vistas* with a tribute to John Stuart Mill and an announcement that the major themes of *On Liberty* would provide the subject of his own 'speculations.' He warmly recommended 'Mill's profound essay on Liberty in the future,' in which variety of character and self-development in many, even opposite directions were made the indispensable conditions 'for a truly grand nationality.'[3] Matthew Arnold, on the other hand, was Whitman's abhorrence. Arnold was everything that was not 'people,' and that represented constriction and uniformity and finger bowls. Whitman's usually boundless and indiscriminate tolerance drew up short before Matthew Arnold. 'I accept the world—most of the world—but somehow draw the line on some of those fellows': namely, the 'great army of critics, parlor apostles, worshippers of hangings, laces, and so forth and so forth. . . .'[4] The personal distinction that Arnold exemplified and demanded dealt too highhandedly with the immutable quotidian of life for Whitman's taste.

When one of their contemporaries, Fitzjames Stephen, did associate Arnold with Mill, it was for the purpose of arguing that Mill was responsible for the state of English criticism to which Arnold objected so strongly in 'The Function of Criticism at the Present Time.' 'Mr. Mill,' Stephen wrote, 'has persuaded the English nation that men ought to argue, not from universals to particulars, but from particulars to particulars, and the practical influence of this highly abstract principle is seen in that state of criticism to which Mr. Arnold objects.'[5]

Mill did not connect himself with Arnold any more than his contemporaries did. Yet Mill had elaborated a theory and a set of principles which were intended to justify comparisons between contemporaries as different from each other as Arnold and Mill seemed to be. In 1838, he had asserted that Bentham and Coleridge, men whose names had probably never before been linked, were 'the two great seminal minds of England in their age.'[6] The ideas sown by one or the other of these two, Mill had argued, were present in all the leading minds of the early nineteenth century, and determined to some extent the character of every English publication seriously concerned with ideas.

Mill established the relation between Bentham and Coleridge in order to illustrate how two important thinkers of opposed schools might complement each other. If each of these thinkers was sufficiently comprehensive, Mill maintained, the philosophy of an age might be obtained by combining and harmonizing their methods and doctrines. On the surface, Bentham and Coleridge seemed to be inhabitants of different worlds who had 'scarcely a principle or a premise in common,' each of them capable of seeing little but what the other could not see. Yet, Mill insisted, 'they are connected by two of the closest bonds of association—resemblance, and contrast'; if contraries, they were nevertheless 'farthest from one another in the same kind.'[7]

Mill's lengthy enumeration of the common characteristics of Bentham's and Coleridge's modes of philosophizing cannot serve as a paradigm in which the names of Mill and Arnold can be substituted for those of Bentham and Coleridge. But it does show how opposed doctrines become mutually relevant and even complementary when they are expounded by men who use different tools but agree to use them in accordance with the disinterested spirit of philosophy:

> These two [Bentham and Coleridge] agreed in being the men who, in their age and country, did most to enforce, by precept and example, the necessity of a philosophy. They agreed in making it their occupation to recall opinions to first principles; taking no proposition for granted without examining into the grounds of it, and ascertaining that it possessed the kind and degree of evidence suitable to its nature. They agreed in recognizing that sound theory is the only foundation for sound practice, and that whoever despises theory, let him give himself what airs of wisdom he may, is self-convicted of being a quack. If a book were to be compiled containing all the best things ever said on the rule-of-thumb school of political craftmanship, and on the insufficiency for practical purposes of what the mere practical man calls experience, it is difficult to say whether the collection would be more indebted to the writings of Bentham or of Coleridge. They agreed, too, in perceiving that the groundwork of all other philosophy must be laid in the philosophy of the mind. To lay this foundation deeply and strongly, and to raise a super-structure in accordance with it, were the objects to which their lives were devoted. They employed, indeed, for the most part, different materials: but as the materials of both were real observations, the genuine product of experience—the results will in the end be found not hostile, but supplementary, to one another. Of their methods of philosophizing, the same thing may be said: they were different, yet both were legitimate logical processes. In every respect the two men are each other's 'completing counterpart'; the strong points of each correspond to the weak points of the other. Whoever could master the premises and combine the methods of both, would possess the entire English philosophy of his age. Coleridge used to say that every one is born either a Platonist or an Aristotelian: it may be similarly affirmed, that every Englishman of the present day is by implication either a Benthamite or a Coleridgian; holds views of human affairs which can only be proved true on the principles either of Bentham or of Coleridge.[8]

The notion of two seminal minds dominating the mental life of an age was not wholly original with Mill, who may have gotten it from Carlyle. For in the conclusion of his review of

Croker's 1831 edition of Boswell's *Life of Johnson*, Carlyle
advanced the proposition that Samuel Johnson and David
Hume were the 'two half-men of the eighteenth century.'
Carlyle's symmetrical presentation of the similarities and
differences between the two men foreshadowed Mill's comparison of Bentham and Coleridge; and Carlyle, like Mill after
him, drew his comparison to illustrate a general principle for
the benefit of the succeeding age. He named Johnson 'the father
of all succeeding Tories' and Hume (in spite of his Jacobitism)
'the father of all succeeding Whigs.' Both were spiritual giants,
but 'how unlike in likeness!' Without forgetting the likeness,
Carlyle distinguished the character of both minds. He lamented
that Johnson and Hume had been half-men, alien to one another
spiritually as well as personally; and he prayed over the tombs
of his heroes, as Mill would later over his, for the emergence of
a man who could unite the warring parties of modern life:

> One day, their spirits, what Truth was in each, will be found
> working, living in harmony and free union, even here below.
> They were the two half-men of their time: whoso could combine
> the intrepid Candour and decisive scientific clearness of Hume
> with the Reverence, the Love and devout Humility of Johnson,
> were the whole man of a new time.[9]

Were Arnold and Mill related to the Victorian age in the
way that Johnson and Hume were to the eighteenth century
and Bentham and Coleridge were to the early nineteenth? I
believe that if we think of them as representative figures rather
than as seminal minds, it will not seem presumptuous to accord
to them the central position in English intellectual life of the
mid-nineteenth century that Mill allowed to Bentham and
Coleridge for the earlier period. For the number and variety
of minds penetrated by Arnold and Mill, great as they are, are
less impressive than the number and variety of minds who find
themselves represented in the writings of Arnold and Mill.
Thus Fitzjames Stephen, who was a severe critic of both men
(somewhat as F. H. Bradley later became), held opinions which
cannot be subsumed under the headings of either Arnoldism
or Millism (Arnold's coinage); yet the durable elements of
Stephen's conservative Utilitarianism are represented within
the views of Arnold and Mill, and have more said for them there

than could be said by anyone but an unswerving adherent. The same applies to the philosophies sustaining all positions taken by those Victorians who felt some obligation to summon their actions and opinions before the bar of reason. Parts of the philosophy of Auguste Comte are represented in Mill's work, but it would be difficult to point to any influence of Mill's which penetrated the hermetic enclosure within which Comte sealed his mind against alien spirits. Arnold, similarly, represents a strong strain of Newmanism in his work, but Newman's rigid system cannot encompass Matthew Arnold—as readily appears from a letter of 1872 in which Arnold admits to the cardinal that 'there are four people, in especial, from whom I am conscious of having learnt . . . habits, methods, ruling ideas, which are constantly with me; and the four are—Goethe, Wordsworth, Sainte-Beuve, and yourself. You will smile and say I have made an odd mixture and that the result must be a jumble. . . .'[10] The result, as we shall see, was not a jumble, but a whole greater than any of its parts.

The idea of a pair of representative thinkers who sum up the intellectual life of an epoch has previously been applied to figures of the Victorian age. Leslie Stephen thought that Mill and Newman, 'the two greatest masters of philosophical English in recent times,' were sufficiently alike in their intellectual characteristics—their love of clarity, their corrosive scepticism, their desire for a God outside of nature—to serve as convenient representatives of the two forces struggling for the allegiance of the Victorian world. Emery Neff, in his *Carlyle and Mill*, has attempted to make the division between the mystic and the Utilitarian the representative cleavage of the age. And Louis Bonnerot, in *Matthew Arnold, Poète*, has implied that Arnold and Carlyle are the really central figures.[11]

But the bulk of Newman's work, still more that of Carlyle, has not stood the test of time well. Despite the attraction which the qualities of his mind and thought exercised upon them, Englishmen could not help feeling that, as Matthew Arnold said in his lecture on Emerson, Newman 'adopted, for the doubts and difficulties which beset men's minds to-day, a solution which . . . is impossible.'[12] Carlyle, in his substance and spirit, is now seen to represent a position so extreme that we wonder at the number of Victorians who, albeit briefly, believed themselves to be his followers. Recently, more and more critics have come to support the view that Arnold and Mill are representative, if not *the* representative, figures of the Victorian age.

Several critics and historians of ideas have argued that Arnold and Mill were representative of their age because, by virtue of their eclecticism and their desire to harmonize diverse materials, they reflected so much of it. R. P. Anschutz claims that Mill was 'thoroughly representative of his age' because 'somewhere or other in his writings you can discern traces of every wind that blew in the early nineteenth century.'[13] F. A. Hayek, recalling Leslie Stephen's description of Mill as 'an alien among men of his own class in English society,' asserts that Mill 'is representative of his age only because of his rare capacity of absorbing new ideas made him a kind of focus in which most of the significant changes of thought of his time combined.'[14] Hayek is aware of the paradox, which I shall discuss presently, whereby men isolated from their society are nevertheless representative of it. Similar testimonials are available for Arnold. H. V. Routh calls him 'the most impressionable and responsive mind of his age.'[15] Lionel Trilling maintains that much of Arnold's attraction for 'a large class of cultivated but sorely-tried people' lay in the fact that he represented religion as well as the critical modern spirit, and claims that the essence of Arnold's criticism is 'the reconciliation of . . . rationalism and faith.'[16]

It seems paradoxical that Arnold and Mill, who criticized nearly all the tendencies of their age, should be thought of as representative men typifying those very tendencies on their brighter sides. Yet this is just how they thought of themselves; and this seeming paradox is a key to the richness and complexity of their relation to their epoch.

Arnold and Mill derived a certain typicality from their membership in two great and dominant groups, one political, the other social: for both were liberals, and both were of the middle class.[17] Mill became conscious of the intellectual dominance of the liberals as early as the twenties, when, in trying to organize a debating society, he and his friends discovered that, whatever the composition of parliament might be, the world of ideas was essentially a one-party affair. 'It is curiously illustrative of the tendencies of the time,' Mill recalled in his autobiography, 'that our principal difficulty in recruiting for the Society was to find a sufficient number of Tory speakers. Almost all whom we could press into the service were Liberals, of different orders and degrees.'[18] What was an oddity to Mill in the 1820s had become by the 1860s a widely recognized fact of political life: the only living intellectual tradition in politics, however inadequate it might often have seemed, was the liberal one. Newman wrote, in 1864, that 'the Liberalism which gives a colour to society now, is very different from that character of thought which bore the name thirty or forty years ago. Now it is scarcely a party; it is the educated lay world.'[19]

Arnold was at all times convinced of the need for modern solutions to modern problems. Even though he filled his major works with interminable harangues against liberalism, liberal nostrums, and liberal 'practitioners,' Arnold proclaimed that 'although, like Mr. Bright and Mr. Frederic Harrison, and the editor of the *Daily Telegraph*, and a large body of valued friends of mine, I am a Liberal, yet I am a Liberal tempered by experience, reflection, and renouncement, and I am, above all, a believer in culture.'[20] If, in his letters and in many of his occasional essays, Arnold expressed gratification at Conservative electoral victories, he also made it clear that his gratification was largely due to the fact that the party in whose hands the future lay—the Liberal party—would again have the opportunity to take thought, in order that it might act more wisely and purposefully when it regained power, as it inevitably would.[21]

Arnold's attitude towards his inherited membership in the middle class is difficult to define, yet it enables us to understand what he and Mill meant when they referred to their typicality. Whenever Arnold spoke of the three great classes of England, he liked to single out one man as representative of each class. In Chapter Three of *Culture and Anarchy* he offered himself 'as an illustration of defect in those forces and qualities which make our middle class what it is.'[22] He frequently referred to himself as 'a feeble unit'[23] of the middle class, a Philistine *manqué*. If the middle class was most often the butt of his humor, it was also the class with which he most closely sympathized because, whether he liked it or not, it was his own. 'I myself,' he confessed, 'am properly a Philistine.' He was fond of relating what he called the 'affecting history' of his conversion as a kind of pilgrim's progress from Philistinism to culture which would serve as an exemplary illustration of the truth that one could break with 'the ideas and the tea-meetings' of one's own class without automatically joining one of the other, alien classes.[24] Thus Arnold could portray himself as an exemplary moral figure who proved by his own experience both that progress was possible for the ordinary Philistine and that individual progress consisted not in discarding the peculiarities of one class to adopt those of another but in escaping from class altogether and embracing culture.

The moral *exemplum* that is contained in the tale of Arnold's conversion from Philistinism to belief in culture finds its counterpart in Mill's intellectual and spiritual progress. For Mill was converted from orthodox Benthamism not to mysticism or to Coleridgian transcendentalism but to an eclectic belief combining and harmonizing the best of both possible worlds. Mill usually minimized his originality as a thinker and preferred the role of translator of ideas from original thinkers to the public and from mystics and transcendentalists to Benthamite radicals. As the one man of his age who found himself in sympathy with conservatives and liberals, transcendentalists and empiricists, Mill decided that he was 'much superior to most of my contemporaries in willingness and ability to learn from everybody'[25] and was therefore in duty bound to serve as a mediator between fiercely opposed schools of thought.

Mill read the history of the dialectical development of his own mind back into his account of the development of the London Debating Society in such a way as to show that his own mind represented the composite movement of mind in the age. He referred to the presence of Coleridgians such as Sterling and Maurice at the debates of the once largely Benthamite Debating Society as the entrance into the group of 'a second liberal and even Radical party,' but, above all, a party 'vehemently opposed' to Benthamism. The Debating Society, when once its membership came to include 'philosophic radicals,' 'Tory lawyers,' and Coleridgians seemed to Mill truly representative 'of the movement of opinion among the most cultivated part of the new generation.'[26]

We are thus confronted by the curious phenomenon of two men who prided themselves upon their escape from sectarianism and their ultimate isolation from class and party, and yet described themselves as typical of the mind of a fiercely sectarian and class-conscious age. But we must remember that they conceived of the age and of its mind as being in continuous transition—hence their reiterated emphasis upon the word *movement*. In adopting positions outside the major divisions of class, party, or school of thought; in attempting to fuse and harmonize existing positions (or oppositions) into a new synthesis, they supposed themselves to be representative of a movement which they were, in some sense, initiating. At one and the same time they wished to be representative and exemplary figures.

This doubleness of attitude appears in some of Mill's statements about his life and work. Throughout the *Autobiography*, he gave all the credit for his intellectual powers and accomplishments to the education he received from his father; his natural gifts were but the ordinary ones, and any normal child who received the benefit of a training like his might, he asserted, reasonably expect to reach a comparable level of attainment. He spoke of the resolution of his mental crisis in a similar way. After proposing a philosophy of life based upon Carlyle's 'anti-self-consciousness' theory, Mill justified himself by saying that such a philosophy is suited 'for all those who,' like Mill himself, 'have but a moderate degree of sensibility and of capacity for enjoyment, that is, for the great majority of mankind.'[27]

His self-conscious apologies for some of his writings followed the same pattern, slightly modified by the emphasis upon mental evolution. One of his reasons for writing the *Autobiography*—and he gave it on the opening page of that work—was that a record of the development of a mind like his, ready to consider all the new (and old) ideas put forward in an 'age of transition in opinions' could be peculiarly useful as a miniature representation of the movement of mind in his time.[28] Again, in the Preface to the collection of his miscellaneous writings called *Dissertations and Discussions*, Mill said he had refrained from altering papers written at earlier dates for the purpose of bringing them into line with his present state of opinion and feeling except where they had contained false information or what he now believed to be total untruth. He chose to leave the articles essentially unchanged in order that they might serve as 'memorials of the state of mind in which they were written in the hope that they may possibly be useful to such readers as are in a corresponding stage of their own mental progress.'[29]

Arnold also believed that a large part of the importance of his work resided in its presentation of the stages of growth of his mind, which he thought representative of the evolution of the most important segment of the mind of his age. His writings, he expected, would be valued not for their doctrine but for their ability to show how a capable but not extraordinary mind dealt with problems destined, sooner or later, to afflict all his contemporaries. Arnold was groping towards this idea in a letter of 1856 where he wrote that

> my poems are making their way, I think, though slowly, and perhaps never to make way very far. There must always be some people, however, to whom the literalness and sincerity of them has a charm. After all, that American review, which hit upon this last—their sincerity—as their most interesting quality, was not far wrong. . . . The state of mind expressed in many of the poems is one that is becoming more common, and you see that even the Obermann stanzas are taken up with interest by some.

By 1869, he had unreservedly adopted the idea which was also Mill's:

> My poems represent, on the whole, the main movement of mind of the last quarter of a century, and thus they will probably have their day as people become conscious to themselves of what that movement of mind is, and interested in the literary productions which reflect it. It might be fairly urged that I have less poetical sentiment than Tennyson, and less intellectual vigour and abundance than Browning; yet, because I have perhaps more of a fusion of the two than either of them, and have more regularly applied that fusion to the main line of modern development, I am likely enough to have my turn, as they have had theirs.[30]

The idea of a fusion of intellect and sentiment is also the idea behind Mill's combination of Benthamism and Coleridgianism, or of philosophy and poetry. If we recall that Arnold's intellectual and spiritual uncertainties and his efforts to resolve them constitute the main subject of his poetry, we can see the similarity between his estimate of the possible utility of his poetry and Mill's reasons for presenting the resolution of his own mental crisis as the suitable one for the great majority of men.

Arnold and Mill needed to believe that they were, with whatever hesitations and qualifications, in step with the forward movement of their age, for they both were convinced that, in Mill's words, 'the general tendency [of social and human history] is, and will continue to be, saving occasional and temporary exceptions, one of improvement—a tendency towards a better and happier state.'[31] Mill was proud of having 'sympathized more or less ardently with most of the rebellions, successful and unsuccessful, which have taken place in my time.'[32] It annoyed Arnold to think, in 1887, that such modern spirits as Frederic Harrison and A. C. Swinburne no longer considered him *au courant* in philosophy, or in touch with the opinions of the literary *avant garde*.[33] We shall see, in the next chapter, how their consciousness of being representative men in an age many of whose strongest tendencies they opposed presented Arnold and Mill with the problem of reconciling their absolute preferences in ethics and politics with their professed submission to the relativistic dictates of what Arnold called the *Zeitgeist* and Mill anglicized into the Spirit of the Age.

The representative quality of Arnold and Mill in the Victorian period is inextricably involved with their recognition that the great problem of modern life is the preservation of the ancient humanistic ideal of culture in democratic society. It was this recognition which influenced their conception of the thinker's duty to society, determined their attitude to the reading audience, and inspired their attempts to establish a liaison between the tradition of humane letters and the modern scientific movement.

The division of their allegiance between culture on the one hand and democracy on the other was implicit in the ambivalent attitudes which Arnold and Mill had towards involvement in public life and practical politics. Few philosophers have been less confined in their imaginary closets than Mill; few poets in their imaginary towers than Arnold. These men could not even simulate the physical trappings of solitude, for both were public servants working for their living. Mill was employed by a private arm of the government, the East India Company, from the time that his father, just promoted to second place in the office of the Examiner of Indian Correspondence, took him on at age eighteen until he retired in 1858. Arnold was an inspector of schools from 1851 until his retirement just two years before his death. Mill, to be sure, was less hard-pressed than Arnold by his working duties, and would even justify earning his livelihood by an occupation other than writing with the argument that 'the writings by which one can live, are not the writings which themselves live, and are never those in which the writer does his best.' Mill claimed, moreover, that his position of high responsibility in the India office had taught him 'the necessary conditions of the practical conduct of public affairs' and was thereby of special value to a theoretical reformer of government and society.[34] Arnold, on the other hand, chafed under his work, which became especially tedious and painful after 1862, when the institution of Lowe's system of payment by results transformed Arnold's duties from those of the advisor and friend of the teacher to those incumbent upon the inquisitor of the student in reading, writing, and arithmetic. Friends of his family, when asked for news of Arnold, would reply that he was 'bemoaning his lot as Inspector of Schools, as usual.'[35]

Arnold and Mill both disbelieved in and disapproved of the individual perfecting himself in isolation from society. Arnold had the greatest contempt for poets who judged society solely according to the conditions it provided for art: 'An aristocratical society like ours is often said to be the society from which artists and men of letters have most to gain. But an institution is to be judged, not by what one can oneself gain from it, but by the ideal which it sets up.'[36] Arnold never tired of repeating Senancour's dictum that individual perfection is neither possible nor desirable in the midst of men who suffer. He did not flinch from making simple humanitarianism one of the moving forces of culture:

The love of our neighbor, the impulses toward action, help, and beneficence, the desire for removing human error, clearing human confusion, and diminishing human misery, the noble aspiration to leave the world better and happier than we found it,—motives eminently such as are called social,—come in as part of the grounds of culture, and the main and pre-eminent part.[37]

Mill's mental crisis was, in part, precipitated by an excessive devotion to the social good at the expense of his own development, yet even after he came to recognize the importance of individual development he took it as axiomatic that human life was mean and insignificant when devoted entirely to selfish ends. A recent writer has pointed out that Mill 'realized that one man's freedom to develop and express himself could not be considered apart from the freedom of his fellow men.'[38] Like Arnold, Mill conceived of knowledge as the means to a social as well as an intellectual end. He asserted, in his St. Andrews lecture, that knowledge is primarily useful in 'making each of us practically useful to his fellow-creatures.' The other function of knowledge, he said, is the spiritual one of 'exalting and dignifying our nature.'[39]

For an age like our own, which is distrustful of demands that the writer 'serve' society, and that culture serve 'the people' because it knows that those demands are likely to be made ignorantly and arrogantly by Philistinism in some countries, or deceitfully and brutally by totalitarianism in others, the ideal of public service which prompted Arnold and Mill cannot be insisted upon too strongly. They knew their epoch to be undergoing a tremendous and irresistible revolution, and they felt a moral obligation to use their great gifts to facilitate the transition and to ensure that the great imminent change would be change for the better and not for the worse. Mill noticed how, in his age, 'the quiet surface of routine is as often ruffled by attempts to resuscitate past evils, as to introduce new benefits'[40] and, according to his friend Morley, was habitually warning that 'the future of mankind will be gravely imperilled if great questions are left to be fought out between ignorant change and ignorant opposition to change.'[41] One of the causes which led Arnold to abandon poetry for social criticism is evident in the conclusion of 'Dover Beach,' where the poet laments that

> we are here as on a darkling plain
> Swept with confused alarms of struggle and flight,
> Where ignorant armies clash by night.

14

It also appears in the lines from 'Stanzas from the Grande Chartreuse,' which take note of the fact that

> the best are silent now.
> Achilles ponders in his tent,
> The kings of modern thought are dumb.[42]

Yet, despite their desire to serve the public, Arnold and Mill could never finally settle upon the best means of doing so. They could only serve the public by leading it and not by following it; and to lead they had to criticize old ways and ideas and to inculcate new, even revolutionary ones, for these alone would suit a revolutionary age. But to uproot deep-seated opinions one must do more than criticize or revile those who hold them: one must persuade people, by charm or even cajolery, to exchange their old selves for transformed selves. And of the need to charm and the temptation to flatter, Arnold and Mill were acutely aware.

The theme appears again and again in Arnold's letters. He remarked to his mother, in 1863, upon the widening gulf between himself and a decorous clerical journal, that 'one cannot change English ideas so much as, if I live, I hope to change them, without saying imperturbably what one thinks and making a good many people uncomfortable.' Yet, Arnold at once caught himself up, 'the great thing is to speak without a particle of vice, malice, or rancour.' He sloughed off Fitzjames Stephen's taunting criticism of his refusal—or inability—to argue, for he had taken to heart Voltaire's condemnation of the bitter and contentious inhumanity which is the especial bane of the practitioners of humane letters. He did not want to score points in a debate (though he enjoyed doing so) but to change the way of life of a great nation:

It is very animating to think that one at last has a chance of *getting* at the English public. Such a public as it is, and such a work as one wants to do with it! Partly nature, partly time and study have also by this time taught me thoroughly the precious truth that everything turns upon one's exercising the power of *persuasion*, of *charm*; that without this all fury, energy, reasoning power, acquirement, are thrown away and only render their owner more miserable. Even in one's ridicule one must preserve a sweetness and good-humour.[43]

It is not surprising that what for an infuriated Carlyle was the mob, *canaille*, *Schwärm*, or ragtag and bobtail, was to become, in Arnold's bland and gentle nomenclature, the 'populace.'

Mill was known to even his bitterest enemies as a model of the ethics of controversy. None of his many talents more impressed his disciple John Morley than his 'unrivalled [skill] in the difficult art of conciliating as much support as was possible and alienating as little sympathy as possible for novel and extremely unpopular opinions.'[44] Mill was a warm admirer of Demosthenes (to whom he once was likened) because Demosthenes had the rhetorical wiles with which to prepare his audience for the sympathetic reception of normally unwelcome ideas and because he 'made steal into their minds, gradually and by insinuation, thoughts which, if expressed in a more direct manner would have aroused their opposition.'[45]

Arnold and Mill were both anxious to bring culture, in the form of genuine thought, to bear upon society and fearful that their intellectual integrity could with difficulty survive the demands of practical politics. Culture had somehow to influence democracy without compromising its high standards.

Arnold claimed to be innocent of practical political intentions in order that he might influence politicians all the more effectively. In *Culture and Anarchy*, he said he was addressing the nation at large rather than the House of Commons because the people were more susceptible to ideas than the Parliamentarians were.[46] Besides, he always argued, the man of culture must stay out of public life and refrain from direct political action lest the combatants active in society think that he desires to compete with them for their functions, powers, and privileges. A thinker who attached himself to practical causes was suspect and therefore stripped of the influence he might otherwise have. Who, he asked, would listen to the political criticism of a Cobbett, 'blackened as he is with the smoke of a life-long conflict in the field of political practice,' or of a Carlyle who had written the *Latter-Day Pamphlets*, or of a Ruskin 'after his pugnacious political economy'? Arnold would not make their mistake. 'Where,' pleaded the man who timed *Culture and Anarchy* to appear just before a new Parliament convened, 'shall we find language innocent enough, how shall we make the spotless purity of our intentions evident enough . . . ?'[47] He hoped, by the example of his own contentment with the intellectual life, to stand as a proof that 'the intelligible law of things has in itself something desirable and precious, and that all place, function, and bustle are hollow goods without it.'[48]

But Arnold's profession of reluctance to enter the political arena was not just a form of political strategy; it also expressed a private fear that practical politics almost necessarily corrupted honesty and destroyed intellectual integrity:

> This treatment of politics with one's thought, or with one's imagi-
> nation, or with one's soul, in place of the common treatment of
> them with one's Philistinism and with one's passions, is the only
> thing which can reconcile . . . any serious person to politics, with
> their inevitable wear, waste, and sore trial to all that is best in one.

Though he believed that the perfection of the individual was inseparable from the perfection of society, Arnold was also convinced that 'Plato would have been less perfect than he was had he entered into the stock politics of Athens at his day.'[49]

There was a similar ambivalence in Mill's attitude towards politics. He admitted, in the *Autobiography*, that he had been bitterly disappointed by the total failure of his attempt, lasting from 1832 until 1839, to address himself in his writings to the Radical members of Parliament in order 'to put ideas into their heads, and purpose into their hearts.' He did not, any more than Arnold, give up the hope of immediate political influence, but he too feared that individual culture and involvement in politics were not compatible. While trying to decide whether to accept an invitation to stand for the House of Commons in 1865, Mill wrote to Gomperz:

> I am . . . reduced to wondering whether I shall ever be able to
> resume those quiet studies which are so prodigiously better for the
> mind itself than the tiresome labour of chipping off little bits of
> one's thoughts of a size to be swallowed by a set of diminutive
> practical politicians incapable of digesting them. One ought to be
> very sure of being able to do something in politics that cannot be
> as well done by others, to justify one for the sacrifice of time and
> energies that might be employed on higher work. Time will show
> whether it was worth while to make this sacrifice for the sake of
> anything I am capable of doing towards forming a really advanced
> liberal party; which, I have long been convinced, cannot be done
> except in the House of Commons.[50]

Mill did, as we know, choose to run and was elected in his first candidacy. But he entered politics only on his own terms. A writer promoting Mill's candidacy in 1865 was put to the difficult task of advertising the universality of Mill's culture and the breadth of his sympathies as political virtues:

> It is well that the electors of Westminster have undertaken the task of carrying to the House of Commons one whose eminent philosophy embraces all letters, art, and imagination, combines the ancient and the new, reform and tradition, the principle of permanence and the principle of progression, the practical spirit of Bentham and the reverent ideal politics of Coleridge—is catholic, practical, genial, sympathetic. . . .[51]

Mill's brief political career was a model of integrity. He never minced words in criticizing his countrymen, and never flattered their prejudices when he was running for office. He told his would-be constituents that he would not indulge in logrolling on their behalf; he announced (what was blasphemy at the time) that women had as much right to the suffrage as men did; and he refused to campaign or to incur any of the expenses usually incident upon campaigning. When asked at a rally of workingmen whether he had, in fact, written that workingmen were generally liars, he answered without hesitation, 'I did.'[52] Mill expected that flattery would gain for him not the allegiance of the working class but only its contempt.

The working class epitomized the democracy to which Arnold and Mill were trying to minister with culture. Although Arnold and Mill did not plunge with the enthusiasm of their fathers into schemes for the diffusion of knowledge among the laboring classes, they wanted to address this portion of society and took care that their own works should be available to the poor. Arnold, against his publisher's wishes, insisted on putting out a half-crown edition of *Literature and Dogma* and popular editions of *God and the Bible* and of *St. Paul and Protestantism*.[53] Mill, in 1865, acceded to the requests of many workingmen by arranging for Longmans to publish inexpensive 'People's Editions' of the *Political Economy*, *On Liberty*, and *Representative Government*; and he gave up all of his profits in order that the price could be as low as possible.[54] He also sent at his own expense a number of copies of his works not available in cheap editions to workingmen's clubs and libraries.

Thus Mill and Arnold, two persistent critics of Victorian England, were among its most conscientiously devoted servants. George Jacob Holyoake, a working-class leader, wrote of Mill that 'of all the public men whom I can recall, there have been none, certainly no philosophers, who personally cared for the people as he did, and aided those in their ranks who showed individuality or capacity of self help.'[55] John Morley credited Arnold with 'the deepest, sincerest, and most active interest in the well-being of his . . . countrymen.'[56] Neither Arnold nor Mill would have objected to the application of the criterion of social utility to their work. For their involvement in practical politics and affairs was but the personal reflection of their intellectual endeavor to reconcile the demands of culture with the ambitions of democracy.

Arnold and Mill held that one justification of their claim to the title of representative men was their eclectic and synthesizing habit of thought. The power to select and to combine was essential to men who undertook to perform a task necessary to the preservation of culture in democratic society: namely, the reconciliation of the tradition of humane letters with modern science. Arnold and Mill were among the last men in the Western tradition to move freely and capably between those two worlds now familiarly referred to as 'the two cultures.' They were concerned with the growing rift between the humanistic and the scientific streams of Western culture and with the means of closing it. They thought themselves capable of assimilating and continuing the Western cultural tradition as an integral whole.

Temperamentally, no two men were better suited to the task. We know from his friends that Mill possessed the special qualities of the scientific and humanistic traditions. Morley found that a remarkable and rather French characteristic of Mill was his 'union of stern science with infinite aspiration, of rigorous sense of what is real and practicable with bright and luminous hope.'[57] Bain marveled at Mill's ability to address the feelings and the reason simultaneously.[58] Mill himself thought that Plato had been a great and formative thinker because he possessed both 'moral enthusiasm and logical discipline,' and was capable of instilling in his admirers the disinterested love of virtue not merely by arguing in its favor, 'but by working,' as the artist would, 'on the feelings and imagination.'[59]

Again and again in his works, Arnold preached that the faculty by which modern man must live is the 'imaginative reason'[60]—a faculty which synthesizes the peculiar qualities of the poet and the man of science. He called Goethe the greatest poet of modern times because Goethe understood that the work of interpreting human life afresh was a work not only for poetry but for science as well.[61] Almost as hostile to the pretensions of pure rationalism as he was to the impostures of mysticism, Arnold was specially equipped to mediate between the ignorant armies of the Victorian night. 'Upon the shelves of his study,' observes Lowry, 'is Voltaire in seventy volumes, and near to him Saint Francis of Assisi. One month he studies Locke, and, another, the Benedictine Rule.'[62]

The fact of Arnold's fellow-travelling, in many instances, with the blackest of the mystical reactionaries should not obscure the equally important fact that he recognized reason—even the more formidable 'scientific' reason—as the only reliable and fair means of solving the modern dilemma, whether in the political or spiritual realm. In 1849 he wrote to Clough that 'my dear Tom [his brother] has not sufficient besonnenheit for it to be any *rest* to think of him any more than it is a *rest* to think of mystics and such cattle'; and in 1850 he announced that 'I go to read Locke on the Conduct of the Understanding: my respect for the reason as the rock of refuge to this poor exaggerated surexcited humanity increases and increases.'[63] He copied into his notebook in 1873 Mill's warning that 'the notion that truths external to the mind may be known by intuition or consciousness, independently of observation and experience, is . . . in these times, the great intellectual support of false doctrines and bad institutions.'[64]

If Arnold and Mill were temperamentally suited to closing the breach between the rationalistic or scientific and the humanistic traditions, were they intellectually adequate to the task? Did they know enough? Morley said of Mill that 'he was more widely and precisely informed of the transactions of the day in every department of activity all over the world, than any other person.'[65] The author of a recent book which makes Mill's attitude towards poetry the basis of an inquiry into the relations which may exist between poetry and philosophy justly discerns the Baconian impulse in Mill when he calls him 'one of the last of those philosophers who chose the whole—or a very large part—of knowledge as their province.'[66] Nor can one help being impressed, in poring over Mill's writings, by the thoroughness as well as the breadth of his knowledge, in the physical and biological sciences, as well as in the social sciences and the several branches of the humanities. Yet Morley himself criticized Mill for not giving sufficient weight to Darwin's hypothesis and discoveries;[67] Bertrand Russell has expressed dismay at Mill's inability to grasp the import of the whole trend towards scientific consideration of man as 'one among animals';[68] and Hayek has chastised Mill for not keeping abreast of developments in English economic thought.[69]

Arnold could afford to criticize the Romantic poets for not knowing enough. His own familiarity with, and immersion in, all the major documents of Western culture up to his own day were unsurpassed. Chesterton, seeking the one trait which definitely set Arnold off from his contemporaries, decided that 'Arnold was chiefly valuable as a man who knew things. . . . He simply happened to know certain things, that Carlyle didn't know, that Kingsley didn't know, that Huxley and Herbert Spencer didn't know, that England didn't know.'[70] But Arnold also knew, and lamented, that modern knowledge had outgrown the capacity of any man to assimilate it and—more important— to order it, as Milton had done.

However well-disposed he might have been towards it, Arnold did not know science. Whatever other strange and curious things may have been available in the Oxford of his day, science was not one of them. But Arnold did not make a virtue of his shortcomings, nor did he wish the educational system to perpetuate them. To represent him, because of his position in the controversy with Huxley, as a foe of science or of scientific education, is to misrepresent him. In his official report called *Higher Schools and Universities in Germany*, Arnold provided a rationale for a 'circle of studies' which would include both humanistic and scientific instruction. The aim of education, he declared, 'is to enable a man *to know himself and the world*.' Anyone who wishes to know the world must know science. Because Arnold's case for the humanities is so well known and so often repeated, it is salutary to remember that he also admitted that

> the humanists themselves suffer so much from the ignorance of physical facts and laws and from the inadequate conception of nature, and of man as a part of nature,—the conduct of human affairs suffers so much from the same cause,—that the intellectual insufficiency of the humanities, conceived as the one access to vital knowledge, is perhaps at the present moment yet more striking than their power of practical stimulation.[71]

Arnold refused to become a partisan exclusivist; he wanted humanities and science taught, but above all he wanted them taught as integral parts of a comprehensive and harmonious conception of knowledge.

On the question of curriculum Arnold was in frequent agreement with Mill. In his St. Andrews lecture (which Arnold praised in the work just mentioned), Mill expressed fear that the increasing tendency towards intellectual specialization, unless it was counteracted in some way, would have a damaging effect upon the general quality of intellect:

> Experience proves that there is no study or pursuit, which, practised to the exclusion of all others, does not narrow and pervert the mind; breeding in it a class of prejudices special to that pursuit, besides a general prejudice, common to all narrow specialities, against large views, from an incapacity to take in and appreciate the grounds of them.

As Arnold went out of his way to defend scientific education in the report just mentioned, Mill stressed the importance of literary education in his St. Andrews lecture. But Mill, like Arnold, opposed those who contended for an exclusively scientific or exclusively literary education:

> Can anything deserve the name of a good education which does not include literature and science too? . . . Short as life is . . . we are not so badly off that our scholars need be ignorant of the laws and properties of the world they live in, or our scientific men destitute of poetic feeling and artistic cultivation.[72]

The attempt of Arnold and Mill to reconcile literature and science was an integral part of their attempt to reconcile culture and democracy. Knowledge had already become, in their time, too vast to be mastered by a single individual. But if they were unable themselves to synthesize the materials available to them, they fostered the state of mind which made synthesis and integration seem desirable and possible.

Was their eclectic, representative character the key, as Arnold and Mill hoped and suspected it might be, to influence? Of the deep and broad influence which Arnold and Mill exerted upon subsequent thinkers, there can be little doubt. Leslie Stephen remembered how, in his circle at Cambridge, 'hour after hour was given to discussing points raised by Mill as keenly as mediaeval commentators used to discuss the doctrines of Aristotle.'[73] R. A. Scott-James has maintained that for half a century 'Arnold's position in [England] was comparable with that of [Aristotle] in respect of the wide influence he exercised, the mark he impressed upon criticism, and the blind faith with which he was trusted by his votaries.'[74] If we imagine the reaction against the dominance of Arnold and Mill to have been as violent as was that of the Renaissance against Aristotle's, we can only wonder that their reputations have survived as well as they have. For it was resentment at the extent of their influence which provoked the violent reactions against Arnold and Mill that have characterized many twentieth-century writers, who look upon them, much as Voltaire looked upon Pascal, as evil spirits who must be exorcised before any progress can be made in spheres infected by their influence.

Much of the resentment against Arnold and Mill has been caused, contrary to their expectations, precisely by their eclectic, representative character, and the fact that they worked in so many fields. Many of their contemporary colleagues looked upon Arnold and Mill as renegades from literature and philosophy respectively; and the hopelessly specialized critics of the twentieth century have responded even more unfavorably to what they consider arrogant and amateurish eclecticism.

Tennyson spoke for a sizable number of Victorian literary men when he asked his son Hallam to 'tell Mat not to write any more of those prose things, like *Literature and Dogma*, but to give us something like his "Thyrsis," "Scholar Gipsy" or "Forsaken Merman." '[75] E. L. Hunt's survey of Arnold criticism suggests that the harshest criticisms of Arnold have come from committed specialists with a vested interest of one kind or another to defend: from literary men who thought that Arnold was wasting his powers in abandoning poetry for politics, education, religion, and sociology; and from theologians, philosophers, and social scientists who were offended by Arnold's incursions into their territory.[76] The offended spirit of corporation has contributed as much as anything else to the propagation of the well-known image of Arnold as the epitome of inner conflict desperately seeking to combine mutually exclusive entities and succeeding only in confusing them. Lucas's description of Arnold as 'at war with himself,' a discordant conflict of such pairs of opposites as artist and moralist, Greek poet and Hebrew prophet, and (only think of it!) admirer of Wordsworth and of Byron, is typical.[77]

The offense taken at Mill's defection was more bitter. Bowring was so shocked when Mill fell under the spell of poetry and of the transcendental moonshine of the Coleridgians that he pronounced him a renegade from philosophy. Bowring thought Mill once 'was most emphatically a philosopher, but then he read Wordsworth, and that muddled him, and he has been in a strange confusion ever since, endeavoring to unite poetry and philosophy.'[78] Francis Place, the radical tailor of Charing Cross, was dismayed, after reading the 'Coleridge' essay, to think that Mill was on his way to becoming a German metaphysician, and was sure that 'eccentricity and absurdity must occasionally be the result.'[79] Fitzjames Stephen found himself 'falling foul . . . of John Mill in his modern and more humane mood . . . which always makes me feel that he is a deserter from the proper principles of rigidity and ferocity in which he was brought up.'[80] On the other side of the fence from the Utilitarians, Ruskin thought Mill worth reading only when he forgot, or was inconsistent with, his stated principles. 'He deserves honour among economists,' Ruskin grudgingly admitted, 'by inadvertently disclaiming the principles which he states, and tacitly introducing the moral considerations with which he declares his science has no connection.'[81] Chesterton followed the same line when he described Mill as a pure and delicate flower somehow forced 'to preach a hard rationalism in economics, a hard egoism in ethics'; a creature helplessly torn between the soulless doctrines he had inherited and his own sympathetic and sensitive nature.[82]

Literary critics dealing with Mill's writings on literature have generally been more eager to welcome him as a convert from philosophy to literature than have social scientists and theologians to embrace Arnold as a convert from literature to philosophy.[83] But philosophical critics have treated Mill far more sternly. For Marx, Mill's attempt to join classical political economy with a philosophy sympathetic to the working classes is but a sentimental desire 'to reconcile irreconcilables.'[84] Russell says that 'morals and intellect were perpetually at war in Mill's thought.'[85] Anschutz asserts that Mill looked at things 'from a point of view which had in it something of the moralist but a good deal more of the scientist.'[86]

The ability of Arnold and Mill to represent and to harmonize opposite schools of thought and different realms of experience has not received the acclaim they hoped it would from succeeding thinkers. But it has given them influence over just those modern thinkers who see the need to reconcile the ideals of culture with the ideals of an egalitarian society. Arnold has been the teacher not only of men like Pater and Wilde, but of R. H. Tawney; Mill finds followers not only in men like G. D. H. Cole and Harold Laski, but in F. R. Leavis and Lionel Trilling. It is a striking fact that Leavis and Trilling, the men who are the most obvious heirs and followers of Arnold in contemporary letters, are both deeply influenced by Mill; and both are preoccupied with the relations between literary culture and a democratic society.

The subject of the relationship between Arnold and Mill has a history, albeit a short one. Until fairly recently, as I suggested earlier, the ideas of Arnold and Mill were hardly thought comparable, much less complementary. In the past two decades, however, the collocation of the names of Arnold and Mill has become so common that one who decides to make an extended study of the association soon begins to feel that he is less in the service of an original idea than of the time-spirit. Casual observations of similarities between Arnold and Mill are more frequent than assertions of their general agreement in certain areas of thought, yet the latter also exist.

There is hardly an area of intellectual activity which I shall discuss in which someone has not observed some kind of

similarity between Arnold and Mill. G. L. Nesbitt, in his study
of the early years of the *Westminster Review*, notices that Mill
foreshadowed Matthew Arnold's position on education (as
defined in the debate with Huxley) as well as his attempt to
confound English provincialism.[87] Trilling has several times
associated the two men. In his excellent study of Arnold's
thought, he suggests that Arnold had in mind Mill's advocacy
of 'doing as we like, subject to such consequences as may follow'
when he entitled the second chapter of *Culture and Anarchy*
'Doing as One Likes'; and that Arnold was aiming at Mill's
theory of truth in his onslaught upon British 'atheism' and
British 'quietism.' He argues that the difference between
Culture and Anarchy and *On Liberty* must be viewed with a full
consciousness of the similarity of their outlook upon man's
moral and spiritual goal, upon the idea of human development,
upon Athenian society and American democracy, and upon
the importance of reason. Trilling has also furnished the invaluable insight, in his essay on 'Wordsworth and the Rabbis,'
into the relation between Arnold's 'Memorial Verses' and Mill's
experience of Wordsworth's poetry.[88]

Walter Houghton has followed up Nesbitt's hint of the similarity in Arnold's and Mill's views of education, and has elaborated and refined Trilling's observation of the resemblance
between Arnold's and Mill's conceptions of personal development. He sees how Arnold, when expounding his idea of middle-
class education as the source of personal dignity and nobility,
'joins hands with an ally he never acknowledged (because he
identified him too closely with the Benthamites): John Stuart
Mill.' Houghton agrees with Trilling that Arnold and Mill are
the 'major champions' of the ideal of self-development in the
Victorian age; but once he has acknowledged the broad similarity between their notions of self-development, Houghton
introduces a crucial distinction. For he recognizes the coexis-
tence in this Victorian idea of two different notions of self-
development: the Goethean ideal, seeking 'a complete and
harmonious development of one's nature'; and the Romantic
ideal of developing to their fullest extent 'the individual poten-
tialities that will make the man unique.' He then argues that,
despite the surface similarities between the Puritanism-
Hellenism opposition in *Culture and Anarchy* and in *On Liberty*,

despite even the mutual recognition of Goethe as the modern apostle of self-development, 'Mill's interpretation of this ideal is neither Greek nor Goethean—nor Arnoldian; it is Romantic.'[89]

Other writers minimize the differences between Arnold and Mill which Trilling and Houghton stress. John M. Robson, in an incisive article devoted to a comparison of the two men, argues that Mill's *liberty* and Arnold's *culture* are not so different as they have often been made to seem. He points to similarities between Arnold and Mill in their cosmopolitanism, their idea of transitional and organic ages, and their ideal of culture. Louis Bonnerot and Dwight Culler have, albeit only in passing, noticed similarities in the ethical and religious positions adopted by Arnold and Mill. Bonnerot remarks upon the resemblance between the figure and message of Jesus as they are conceived by Arnold and as they appear to Mill.[90] Culler argues that Mill's mental crisis 'left him at the end pretty much where Arnold terminated in his critical prose' and that although they started from opposite positions they finally converged in 'the Christian Humanist position.'[91]

Two critics, F. R. Leavis and M. H. Abrams, have recently spoken of the connections between Arnold and Mill as not merely chance similarities, but a fundamental relationship and a key to the intellectual life of the Victorian age.

In the view of F. R. Leavis, a student cannot grasp the intellectual environment of Victorian writers until he comes to understand that 'the lines of significant organization—the main lines on which most things in the whole complex field can be most significantly related' move about the foci conveniently named Matthew Arnold and John Stuart Mill. Leavis argues that Arnold, 'because of the peculiar quality of his intelligence and the peculiar nature of his relation to his time, will repay special study in a way no others will,' but that 'a complementary focal line' is needed as well, 'and here it is that Mill presents himself as meeting the case ideally.' Leavis traces the kinship of Mill, through Maurice and Sterling and their Christian Socialism, to Thomas Arnold and thence to his son. He contends that Mill's innumerable connections—through Utilitarianism and the *Westminster Review*, to George Eliot; through his mystical streak (and their personal acquaintance), to Carlyle; and through his spiritual crisis, to the profoundest mental undercurrent of the age—make him as central a figure as Arnold in any study of Victorian intellectual life:

> This, then, is the kind of field that co-ordinates itself round John Stuart Mill. . . . For the other main figure—that to be set over against Mill—I have proposed Matthew Arnold as the obvious choice. . . . For, though he is in so many ways unlike Mill, he too stands for intelligence (as the contrast with Carlyle brings out).[92]

M. H. Abrams, who was the first writer to give serious consideration to Mill as a critic of literature, has arrived at conclusions almost identical with those of Leavis. He says that

> Mill, as much as any Englishman, anticipated and concurred in the central tenets of Arnold's humanism—opposition to English insularity and complacency; recommendation of the best that has been thought and said in all ages; indictment of the brutalizing influence of an industrial and commercial society; and insistence on individual values against the growing pressure toward mass conformity.

There is a compelling resemblance between Leavis' summing up and Abrams' call for further work on Arnold and Mill:

> The parallel between these writers, so different in temper and intellectual training—and by that fact, so widely representative of the main lines of Victorian thinking—can be pursued even farther.[93]

My attempt to carry the pursuit farther will, I hope, show the surprising extent to which the suggestions of Abrams and Leavis are fruitful.

We have now heard what a multitude of people have had to say about Arnold and about Mill, and about both of them together. Did these representative and comprehensive minds contemporary with each other for several decades have something to say of each other? Did they discern something of that kinship which seems so obvious to men of a later age?

The answers to these questions are not what anyone unacquainted with the peculiar ways of Victorian social and intellectual life might expect. So far as we can tell, Arnold and Mill never met. There are two possible explanations for this. Besides the fact that both men, but especially Mill, shunned 'society,' Victorian England suffered from the absence, which Arnold and Mill often lamented, of an intellectual community. The circles of poets, philosophers, and wits that once characterized eighteenth-century England and were still a common feature in France were almost unknown to the Victorians.

An account of the instances in which Arnold and Mill mention each other by name (and not solely by implication) is highly revealing but it is extremely one-sided. While Arnold frequently named Mill in letters and in published works, we find but a single occasion on which Mill, justifiably puzzled by one of Arnold's attacks on him, mentioned Arnold:

> *À propos*, why does Maudsley charge me with disparaging physiology either in itself or in its application to mind? It is like Matthew Arnold enumerating me among the enemies of culture.[94]

Arnold's attitude towards Mill is no easier to define than his attitude towards other complex and many-sided subjects. It was composed of many, often mutually contradictory, impulses and judgments; and it is symptomatic of Arnold's unsettled feelings towards Mill that he once publicly retracted a slur he had cast upon him.

There can be little doubt of Arnold's annoyance with what he thought to be the insensitivity in religious matters of a man of Mill's prominence. 'How short,' he facetiously asked Clough in 1848, 'could Mill write Job?'[95] In other words, the reduction of Job to a skeletal logical outline was all which might be expected from a logic machine devoid of artistic feeling and of human and religious sensibility. How gleefully, again, did Arnold pounce upon what seemed to him the unconscious acknowledgment, in the *Autobiography*, of religion's power from one of religion's confessed enemies:

> Mr. Mill tells us, in a passage where he is adopting his father's words, that his father 'looked upon religion as the greatest enemy or morality.' Eighteen pages farther on, where he is descanting on the lamentable absence, in English society, of any high and noble standards of conduct, he adds that this absence prevails everywhere *'except among a few of the stricter religionists.'*[96]

Arnold also felt called upon to defend the Christian religion in particular from Mill's barbs. His essay on Marcus Aurelius[97] begins by quoting from *On Liberty* Mill's contention that

Christian morality is for the most part a protest against paganism, having a negative and passive ideal which falls far below the best morality of the ancients. The rest of Arnold's essay attempts to refute this contention and, as we shall see, a good many others made in *On Liberty*.

Mill's religious insensitivity was not confined, in Arnold's opinion, to the inward power of religion; it extended also to the realm of religious politics. In what was probably his most vehement and least fair assault upon Mill, Arnold, in the 1870 Preface to *St. Paul and Protestantism*, nearly overwhelmed by the charms of alliteration, named Mill as the representative of Hellenism in its degenerate state, just as Edward Miall was the representative of Hebraism in its degenerate state:

> From whom can we more properly derive a general name for those degradations of Hellenism than from that distinguished man, who, by his intelligence and accomplishments, is in many respects so admirable and so truly Hellenic, but whom his dislike for 'the dominant sect,' as he calls the Church of England,—the Church of England, in many aspects so beautiful, calming, and attaching,—seems to transport with an almost feminine vehemence of irritation? What can we so fitly name the somewhat degenerated and inadequate form of Hellenism as *Millism*? This is the Hellenic or Hellenistic counterpart of Mialism; and like Mialism it has its further degenerations, in which it is still less commendable than in its first form. For instance, what in Mr. Mill is but a yielding to a spirit of irritable injustice, goes on and worsens in some of his disciples, till it becomes a sort of mere blatancy and truculent hardness in certain Millites, in whom there appears scarcely anything that is truly sound or Hellenic at all.[98]

Poor Mill! He is probably the only man in Arnold's gallery of villains who served not only as the representative of degenerate Hellenism, but also as a representative of degenerate Hebraism. For in *Culture and Anarchy*, published a year earlier, he had been accused of being a 'Rabbi' (and Arnold's conception of Rabbinical Judaism was but little higher than that of most who know it only from the picture drawn by its enemies in the Christian gospels):

> Culture tends always thus to deal with the men of a system, of disciples, of a school; with men like Comte or, the late Mr. Buckle, or Mr. Mill. However much it may find to admire in

these personages, or in some of them, it nevertheless remembers the text: 'Be not ye called Rabbi!' and it soon passes on from any Rabbi.[99]

Yet Arnold was not above admitting errors, and in 1874, the year after Mill's death, he forswore the use of the nickname 'Millism.' About to embark upon yet another onslaught on Millism and Miallism in the Preface to his report on continental schools and universities, he was restrained by conscientious misgivings which forced him to admit that the first nickname 'might turn out to be not strictly accurate':

> For Mr. Mill, who was not, perhaps, the great spirit that some of his admirers suppose, but who was a singularly acute, ardent, and interesting man, was capable of following lights that led him away from the regular doctrine of philosophical radicalism, and on no question was he more capable of doing this than in one where the Catholics of Ireland were concerned.[100]

The support of Mill on the Irish question, and particularly on the advisability of establishing a Catholic university in Ireland, even though given, so to speak, posthumously through the written recollections of Morley, meant much to Arnold. He later adduced it as a proof, in 'Irish Catholicism and British Liberalism,' that the best of the Liberals did not share the rigid opposition of their party's spokesmen to the endowment of a Catholic university.[101]

The other concern besides Ireland in which Arnold was conscious—and this during Mill's lifetime—of agreement with Mill was the all-important question of education, especially of what ought to be taught, and how. In the Preface to his *Higher Schools and Universities in Germany*, appearing in 1868, Arnold included Mill, along with Sir James Shuttleworth and Dr. Temple, among the men whose views on education constituted the 'best educational opinion of the country' and who had the undeniable right to be heard on educational topics. In the body of the work, Arnold revealed the reason for this unexpected praise of Mill. At the conclusion of a severe criticism passed upon the old way of teaching the classics primarily by means of composition and linguistics, and after suggesting that people would far sooner gain 'vital knowledge' of classical antiquity by studying Greek and Latin Literature, Arnold expressed his gratification at Mill's agreement with him. In a footnote he confided that

> since the above remarks were in print they have received powerful corroboration from the eminent authority of Mr. Mill in his inaugural address at St. Andrews. The difference of my conclusions on one or two points from Mr. Mill's only makes the general coincidence of view more conspicuous; Mr. Mill having been conducted to this view by independent reflection, and I by observation of the foreign schools and the movement of ideas on the Continent.[102]

Not all of Arnold's praise of Mill came after Mill's death or in connection with specific areas of agreement between himself and Mill. Arnold read *On Liberty* in the year that it appeared and at once decided that it was 'worth reading attentively, being one of the few books that inculcate tolerance in an unalarming and inoffensive way.'[103] In 'Marcus Aurelius,' which more clearly than any other single work reveals his fundamental disagreements with Mill, Arnold called Mill 'a writer of distinguished mark and influence, a writer deserving all attention and respect,' and yet a writer who, for not being sufficiently leavened with some of the truths he has himself perceived, 'falls just short of being a great writer.'[104] In a speech given in Liverpool, Arnold found it one of the saving graces of England that, by some unfathomable mystery, she could still produce 'lovers of free and clear thought such as the late Mr. John Stuart Mill.'[105]

Arnold recognized Mill as a formidable figure whose support was well worth having, and he was therefore greatly pleased to have his opinions corroborated by Mill. He recognized also that Mill was devoted to his own most cherished ideal. Yet he feared that Mill was devoted blindly and doggedly and that his reverence for Hellenism obscured for him the value of Hebraism.

Arnold and Mill never fully comprehended each other personally, but they came close to comprehending each other spiritually. Arnold, when he wrote 'Memorial Verses,' understood the forces which determined Mill's inner life even if he did not understand John Stuart Mill; and Mill, when he drew his portrait of Vigny as the prototype of a conservative poet cast into an age of revolution, comprehended the spiritual dilemma with which Arnold wrestled, even if he did not comprehend Matthew Arnold.

Yet even such comprehension betokens a greater mutual understanding than those other pairs of representative thinkers, Bentham and Coleridge, or Johnson and Hume, ever achieved. Does not this spiritual affinity support the view that Arnold and Mill represent the half-truths which need to be reconciled and combined before the philosophy of a new age can be attained?

II

THE NOISY CONFLICT OF
HALF-TRUTHS

I will write historically as I can write naturally in no other way.
MATTHEW ARNOLD

It has become the aim of really scientific thinkers to connect by
theories the facts of universal history: it is acknowledged to be
one of the requisites of a general system of social doctrine that it
should explain, so far as the data exist, the main facts of history;
and a Philosophy of History is generally admitted to be at once
the verification and the initial form of the Philosophy of the
Progress of Society.   JOHN STUART MILL

IT was a heavy accusation laid against the eighteenth century—
and given its definitive form by Burke—that, in the name of
reason, it had undervalued history, which it supposed to be the
repository of irrational custom and prejudice. Arnold and Mill
partook of only half of the nineteenth-century reaction against
the eighteenth: they attributed a very great importance to
history, but an equal importance to reason. They said, in fact,
that the process of history and the process of reason were inextricably involved with each other.

That agreement about method which was the one kind of
agreement between thinkers which Arnold and Mill thought
intrinsically valuable existed between them. Their method was
at once historical and dialectical. They believed that history
was rational and that sound reasoning was historical, i.e., that
it respected circumstances, was flexible, relative, and explained
things in terms of their development.

They conceived of history as a great, unresolved argument between two antithetical forces which reappeared under different guises through the ages. They did not, like Hegel, declare that thesis and antithesis were invariably resolved into synthesis; yet synthesis was what they desired.[1] Nearly all disagreements between the two men may be explained in terms of their disagreement over how urgently a synthesis of the forces of modern history was needed.

Arnold and Mill could assimilate the process of history to the process of reason because they believed history to have a rational, meaningful pattern, and to exhibit the interaction, in a tangled yet ultimately comprehensible web, of cause and effect. It was, for them, neither a tale told by an idiot, sound and fury signifying nothing, nor a nightmare from which men were trying to awake. Mill thought history amenable to scientific investigation, and Arnold could still discern in it the manifestations—the regular and rational manifestations—of a guiding Providence. When he advised the students at St. Andrews to study history with a view to discerning the causes or laws which determine stasis or progress, Mill showed that his conception of history was at once scientific, dramatic, apocalyptic, and—like his father's and like Thomas Arnold's—essentially Manichean. He urged each student to look upon history as

> a chain of causes and effects still unwinding itself before his eyes, and full of momentous consequences to himself and his descendants; the unfolding of a great epic or dramatic action, to terminate in the happiness or misery, the elevation or degradation, of the human race; an unremitting conflict between good and evil powers, of which every act done by any of us . . . forms one of the incidents; a conflict in which even the smallest of us cannot escape from taking part, in which whoever does not help the right side is helping the wrong, and for our share in which . . . no one of us can escape the responsibility.[2]

Arnold was certainly no Bossuet, but he claimed to see the will even of his empirically and scientifically constructed God working itself out in history. 'Look a little deeper,' he said, 'and you will see that one strain runs through it all [the history of the world]: nations and men, whoever is shipwrecked, is shipwrecked on *conduct*. It is the God of Israel steadily and irresistibly asserting himself; *the Eternal that loveth righteousness*.'[3]

Arnold and Mill believed that to adapt the method of history to the process of reasoning—whether on politics, ethics, or art—was to acknowledge that truth is relative, that what may be good and true at one time can be harmful and false at another. The just reasoner who would follow the historical method, they said, cannot play favorites but must, like history itself, admit that for every thesis there is an equally valid antithesis; and, instead of riveting himself to what has long seemed a true position, be flexible enough to swing to the opposite position when a changed historical situation makes it the true and desirable one. But Arnold and Mill also believed that a historically disciplined thinker must desire and work for the ultimate reconciliation of giant adversaries, and the resolution of historical thesis and antithesis, one half-truth and the half-truth which denies it, into synthesis, into the whole truth.

Thus history seemed to issue conflicting orders to the reasoner who would obey it. On the one hand, it dictated relativism and flexibility; on the other hand, it suggested the desirability of an ideal which would harmonize and synthesize hitherto opposed forces. I shall try, in this chapter, to show how the attempt to mediate between fidelity to the historical process of incessant conflict on the one hand and the historical ideal of harmony on the other is the underlying principle of the works of Arnold and Mill. In subsequent chapters I hope to show how the disagreements which exist between Arnold and Mill are attributable to their differing estimates of the conflicting claims of the historical process on the one hand and the historical ideal on the other.

Arnold connected his theory of history with his theory of criticism and reasoning in the essay, 'The Function of Criticism at the Present Time.' The historical relativism of Arnold's approach is implicit in the last four words of the title: though it may not be true for all times and places, it is certainly true that for Victorian England—for what Arnold calls an 'epoch of expansion'—the function of criticism is to preoccupy itself with thought and to eschew practice; to seek the best that is known and thought in the world, unfettered by considerations of any other kind.[4]

Mill's theory of history was first outlined in a series of articles appearing in *The Examiner* during 1831, thirty-four years before the appearance of 'The Function of Criticism.' Like Arnold, Mill defined his method of criticism in terms of his theory of history. If 'disinterestedness' was justified by the requirements of what Arnold called an epoch of expansion, so were free discussion and the willingness to hear all sides of a question— things which in the 1830s Mill did not value for their own sake— justified by the needs of what Mill called an age of transition or a critical age. Like Arnold, he was at once led by the discussion of history into a consideration of 'those mental processes which are necessary to the investigation of truth.'[5]

What are the theories of history which prescribed to Arnold and Mill their theories of reason? In his autobiography, Mill described the influence which the Saint-Simonian school of French thinkers began to have upon him in 1829 and 1830. At this stage of his acquaintance with them, the Saint-Simonians had not yet plunged either into socialism or into the excesses of secular religiosity, which later possessed them. The most important Saint-Simonian idea which took hold of Mill, and which—as we shall see presently—impelled him to write *The Spirit of the Age*, was an idea of history. According to it, history is a series of oscillations between 'organic periods' and 'critical periods.' During the former, a firm and nearly universal adherence to some belief guides the thoughts and rules the lives of the people; when this belief stagnates and loses its authority, the inevitable period of 'criticism and negation,' during which men search in multifarious ways for a new creed, succeeds. When applied to the history of modern Europe, the theory makes Christianity the creed of the organic period which commenced with the dissolution of the 'skeptical period of the Greek philosophers' and which was itself supplanted by the critical period inaugurated by the Reformation and, at the time Mill wrote, not yet superseded.[6]

The series of articles called *The Spirit of the Age*, which Mill said he wrote in order 'to point out in the character of the present age the anomalies and evils characteristic of the transition from a system of opinions which had worn out, to another only in process of being formed,'[7] can almost be said to constitute a Saint-Simonian tract.[8] Mill expounded the Saint-Simonian conception of history; and yet he altered the customary emphasis of Saint-Simonian doctrine. For, in Mill's restatement of the doctrine, the theory of history becomes inextricably linked with a theory of the proper method of seeking the truth.

In the first article of the series, Mill argued that the age of transition (an alternative term for the Comtian 'critical' period) in which he lived had managed to dissipate the superstitions and chimeras of past ages by its greater engagement in continuous free discussion of the most important subjects. But if discussion has the power of destroying ancient beliefs and institutions by excavating the erroneous opinions on which they were built, it can also discover and spread new truths—though Mill admitted that in 1831 it had not yet completed the second half of its task as the catalyst of change. Should his contemporaries forget that free discussion and not their improved understanding had enabled them to progress beyond their predecessors, they would try, Mill warned, to cling to their newly found conviction as if it were the complete truth. Yet it would, in all likelihood, be only the complement of what had gone before:

> Whether men adhere to old opinions or adopt new ones, they have in general an invincible propensity to split the truth, and take half, or less than half of it; and a habit of erecting their quills and bristling up like a porcupine against anyone who brings them the other half, as if he were attempting to deprive them of the portion they have.[9]

The connection has been made between a theory of history and a theory of truth: it is in ages of transition, Mill argued, that the tendency to cling to but one half of the truth is greatest.

Mill's age, because it was an age of 'transition,' was also an age of 'intellectual anarchy,' a state of affairs which struck into the young Mill the kind of terror which later drove Matthew Arnold to propose the official establishment of right reason. It was, for Mill, characteristic of his transitional age that, with the exception of the physical sciences, all disciplines of knowledge failed to impress upon the layman the necessity of his deferring to the judgments of those who devoted themselves to the pursuit of knowledge. In such an age, the layman was convinced that his opinion, blind and uninformed as it might be, on any particular subject, was as good as that of anyone else— nay, better, for in such times 'it is rather the person who *has* studied the subject systematically that is regarded as disqualified. He is a *theorist*: and the word which expresses the highest and noblest effort of human intelligence is turned into a bye-word of derision.'[10] Anyone acquainted with Arnold's writings will at once see that Mill has here carried us into the milieu which preoccupied Arnold in 'The Function of Criticism at the Present Time.'

The unsettled state of the intellectual world, Mill argued, is reflected in the condition of society at large. In the third installment of *The Spirit of the Age*, Mill classified societies past and present according to the way power was wielded in them. He defined two categories: the natural state of society and the transitional or artificial state. In the first, power rests with those members of society best fitted to exercise power; in the second, the correspondence between power and fitness for power has disappeared and society at large contains among its members 'persons fitter for worldly power and moral influence than those who have hitherto enjoyed them.'[11]

Inevitably, Mill had to find a place for England in this scheme of things. What ought to have been the ruling body in England, the upper class, did not, like its ancestors, make itself worthy of the powers it inherited. Great as had been the role of the aristocracy in civilizing England, Mill held, it now was little better than an atrophied limb of a fast growing body, for 'the higher classes, instead of advancing, have retrograded in all the higher qualities of mind.' In his simultaneous praise of the past work of the aristocracy and denial of its capacities for making further contributions to society; still more in his demand that English 'institutions [be] adapted to the present state of civilization, and made compatible with the future progress of the human mind,' Mill foreshadowed some of the major themes of Arnold's work.[12]

The real importance of this series of essays, however, lay in the connection it established between history and reason, between a theory of history and a method of seeking truth. Mill summarized the meaning of the essays when he recalled, later in life, that

the chief benefit which I derived from the trains of thought suggested by the St. Simonians and by Comte, was, that I obtained a clearer conception than ever before of the peculiarities of an era of transition in opinion, and ceased to mistake the moral and intellectual characteristics of such an era, for the normal attributes of humanity. I looked forward, through the present age of loud disputes but generally weak convictions, to a future which shall unite the best qualities of the critical with the best qualities of the organic periods; unchecked liberty of thought, unbounded freedom of individual action in all modes not hurtful to others; but also, convictions as to what is right and wrong, useful and pernicious, deeply engraven on the feelings by early education and general unanimity of sentiment, and so firmly grounded in reason and in the true exigencies of life, that they shall not, like all former and present creeds, religious, ethical, and political, require to be periodically thrown off and replaced by others.[13]

Knowledge of the way history works will, Mill believed, determine the attitude of a sound reasoner. He will recognize that a transitional period of history warrants and even demands fresh, critical, and independent thought; but his sense of historical perspective will enable him to see that ultimately doubt, scepticism, and analysis must issue in resolution, faith, and synthesis.

The Saint-Simonian conception of history which Mill adopted finds a parallel in Arnold's theory of history as an alternation between epochs of concentration and epochs of expansion. Arnold employed this notion in 'The Function of Criticism at the Present Time' without any acknowledgment of indebtedness to Saint-Simon. Bonnerot has, indeed, observed the similarity between Arnold's theory and Saint-Simon's;[14] but by 1865 the idea may have become current coin even in laggard England. George Eliot, for example, used it familiarly in a letter of March, 1848, when, after hearing of the French Revolution of that year, she breathed a sigh of relief that, perhaps, her epoch was not after all 'what St. Simon calls a purely critical epoch' but was, in some sense, organic.[15] So casually does Arnold introduce the phrases *epoch of concentration* and *epoch of expansion* that we are obliged to form our own definitions of the terms from the ways in which he uses them. He says that the French Revolution 'created in opposition to itself,' by its excesses and also by its failure to establish a new and universally acceptable order of ideas, 'what I may call an epoch of concentration.' Europe was led into the epoch of concentration by England, 'and the great voice of that epoch of concentration was Burke.'[16]

In this essay, Arnold took pains to praise Burke, for a number of reasons. Yet he implied that Burke's virtues emerged not because of, but in spite of, the fact that he was the spokesman for an epoch of concentration. Such epochs, he asserted, are characterized by tenacious attachment to old, and fierce resistance to new, ideas. Burke's extraordinary genius could make his epoch's resistance 'rational instead of mechanical' and could keep aloft not only an epoch of concentration but also the dead weight of English Tory politics.[17] In a private letter, where he could afford to be less careful of his hero's reputation, Arnold even admitted, in 1880, that Burke 'did harm as well as good, for he made concentration too dominant an idea with us, and an idea of which the reign was unduly prolonged. The time for expansion must come, and Burke is of little help to us in presence of such a time.'[18]

If epochs of concentration are characterized by uniformity, constriction, clinging to old and familiar forms and ideas, and hostility to new and alien—in both senses of the word—forms and ideas, epochs of expansion are characterized by receptivity to a multitude of new and foreign ideas. With the opening of a new epoch of expansion in England—for 'epochs of concentration cannot well endure for ever'—'all danger of a hostile forcible pressure of foreign ideas upon our practice,' Arnold observes, 'has long disappeared; like the traveller in the fable, therefore, we begin to wear our cloak a little more loosely. Then, with a long peace, the ideas of Europe steal gradually and amicably in, and mingle, though in infinitesimally small quantities at a time, with our own notions.'[19]

The idea of expansion, sometimes abstracted from its chronological setting, was to become a vital one for Arnold. It was, as he said in the Preface to *Mixed Essays*, the dominant idea behind all the essays in that collection. Upon the instinct of expansion, man's effort to civilize himself by developing all the powers of human nature rests; and this instinct cannot thrive— here is an important corrective to the impression given by *Culture and Anarchy*—without liberty and equality. To attempt to arrest expansion, Arnold argued, is to attempt to arrest nature, always a dangerous proceeding. The chief means to the end of humanizing man in society—to the end of civilizing him —is expansion, the instinctive and necessary principle of human growth; and the most important manifestation of the instinct for expansion is the love of liberty. As in Mill's historical scheme an age of transition makes liberty of expression a necessity, so in Arnold's theory an epoch of expansion demands liberty, because 'man is not to be civilised or humanised . . . by thwarting his vital instincts.'[20]

It must not be thought that whereas Mill was willing to give equal weight to organic and to transitional ages Arnold was prejudiced in favor of epochs of expansion. For Arnold believed as firmly as Mill that the combination of the best characteristics of both kinds of historical epoch constituted the elements of a whole and civilized life. Thus, in 'The Future of Liberalism' he accused the Liberal party, somewhat as Mill had accused the *philosophes*, of lacking a comprehensive view of what constitutes a civilized human and social existence because Liberals had grasped but a single element of civilization, the instinct for expansion (especially as manifested in demands for liberty and free trade), and had given scant attention to those powers of human nature—like knowledge and beauty—which flourish in epochs of concentration.[21]

Nevertheless, Arnold knew that he lived in an epoch of expansion, and was as fully conscious of the peculiar conditions imposed by such an age as the writer of *The Spirit of the Age* had been. Arnold could not take seriously Père Lacordaire's castigation of the nineteenth century as an age which did not know how to obey, for 'this is not so absolutely a matter of reproach as Lacordaire made it; in an epoch of transition [apparently the term was interchangeable with epoch of expansion] society may and must say to its governors, "Govern me according to my spirit, if I am to obey you."'[22] What Mill, in 1831, had called the outstanding peculiarities of the age—namely, that 'mankind have outgrown old institutions and old doctrines, and have not yet acquired new ones,' and that 'the old order of things has become unsuited to the state of society and of the human mind'[23]—struck Arnold even more forcibly in 1863 when he proclaimed:

> Modern times find themselves with an immense system of institutions, established facts, accredited dogmas, customs, rules, which have come to them from times not modern. In this system their life has to be carried forward; yet they have a sense that this

system is not of their own creation, that it by no means corresponds exactly with the wants of their actual life, that, for them, it is customary, not rational. The awakening of this sense is the awakening of the modern spirit. The modern spirit is now awake almost everywhere; the sense of want of correspondence between the forms of modern Europe and its spirit, between the new wine of the eighteenth and nineteenth centuries, and the old bottles of the eleventh and twelfth centuries, or even of the sixteenth and seventeenth, almost every one now perceives; it is no longer dangerous to affirm that this want of correspondence exists; people are even beginning to be shy of denying it. To remove this want of correspondence is beginning to be the settled endeavour of most persons of good sense. Dissolvents of the old European system of dominant ideas and facts we must all be, all of us who have any power of working; what we have to study is that we may not be acrid dissolvents of it.[24]

For Arnold and Mill, the theory of history led directly to a theory of the right method of pursuing truth. Mill had complained that the theorist is looked upon with contempt in a transitional and critical age, just when nothing is so much required as theory and willingness to grant fair hearing to all ideas. Now Arnold, in 'The Function of Criticism,' lamented the dislike of his practical countrymen for ideas and for criticism— and this in an epoch of transition, a time when a 'free play of the mind' was needed to prevent the English national spirit from dying of intellectual starvation. Mill's belief that he lived in a 'critical' period of history, when men were prone to cling to one or the other half of truth, dictated his insistence upon unfettered liberty of discussion and his eclectic, conciliatory approach towards intellectual controversy. Arnold's consciousness that he lived in an epoch of expansion dictated his insistence upon a free play of the mind and a disinterested devotion to ideas—the only proper devotion during that period of criticism which is the necessary precursor of a period of creation.[25]

Arnold and Mill recognized that one unfortunate yet inevitable accompaniment of the intellectual anarchy which characterized an age of transition and expansion was intellectual sectarianism. Recognizing no established standard by which opinions might be judged, the individual thinker came to believe that loyalty to his own sect or party was a valid standard, and that all opinions might be judged according to whether they confirmed or denied the ideas of his sect.

England had a long history of sectarianism, largely as a result of her deep religious divisions. Voltaire, though tolerant, disliked sectarianism with as vehement a passion as his intolerant contemporary, Swift; yet his beloved England, the land of progress and enlightenment, seemed to him 'le pays des Sectes. Un Anglais, comme homme libre, va au Ciel par le chemin qui lui plaît.' One reason why, in Voltaire's opinion, England had failed to produce distinguished or even creditable historians, was that 'l'esprit de parti, qui fait voir trouble, a décrédité tous leurs historiens: la moitié de la nation est toujours l'ennemi de l'autre.'[26] According to Mill, 'the spirit of philosophy in England, like that of religion, is rootedly sectarian.'[27] In the nineteenth century, party spirit found its ideal expression and most lethal weapon in the periodical reviews which had burgeoned since the beginning of the century. Peacock had described the reviews and the reviewers in unflattering terms:

> If periodical criticism were honestly and conscientiously conducted, it might be a question how far it has been beneficial or injurious to literature; but being as it is merely a fundamental and exclusive tool of party, that it is highly detrimental to it none but a trading critic will deny. . . . Personal or political bias being the only passport to critical notice, the independence and high thinking that keeps an individual from all filthy subdivisions of faction makes every several gang his foe.[28]

Arnold's and Mill's estimation of the spirit which animated the periodicals was not much higher than Peacock's.

Mill, as the living example of the applied doctrines of the Benthamite sect, was inevitably plunged into the war of the periodicals. Since the Tories had the *Quarterly Review* as their mouthpiece and the Whigs had the *Edinburgh Review* as theirs, the Benthamite Radicals decided, in 1824, to make their ideological presence felt by means of a new organ—the *Westminster Review*. In the early numbers of the new review, Mill and his father undertook the mammoth task not of merely attacking the positions taken by the *Quarterly* and the *Edinburgh* but of refuting, in detail, nearly everything that those journals had asserted in their pages since their commencement. Yet even in this largely unpromising start, at age eighteen, Mill revealed the philosophical impulse which led to his attempt, when he ran the *London and Westminster Review* from 1835–40, 'to free philosophic radicalism from the reproach of sectarian Benthamism.'[29]

In the second number of the review, he wrote a long criticism of the *Edinburgh*, a quarterly which exemplified the 'vices to which we have shown periodical literature to be liable.' He attacked not simply the opinions of the *Edinburgh* but its reasons for adopting them. He maintained that the position of compromise which the Whig party was obliged to assume in politics consistently showed itself in the opinions of the Whig organ, the *Edinburgh*, 'in so much that there is scarcely a question of any importance, of which it has not either given up half, or preached alternately, first on the one side and then on the other.'[30]

More and more, Mill found sectarianism the besetting intellectual sin of the age. In 1829, after having sketched what he thought the gravest errors of Auguste Comte in a letter to one of Comte's proselytizing Saint-Simonian admirers, Gustave d'Eichthal, Mill warned his friend that

if the proselytes of Saint Simon insist upon forming a sect, which is a character above all to be avoided by independent thinkers [,] & imagine themselves under a necessity, if they belong to the sect, to take all its dogmas without exception or qualification, they will not only do no good but I fear immense mischief.[31]

Knowing that sectarianism could warp literary as well as political judgments, Mill, in his 1835 review of Tennyson's poems of 1830 and 1832, accused the *Quarterly Review* of greeting every new work by a creative writer, 'unless forced upon it by the public voice, or recommended by some party interest,' with surly and sneering contempt.[32]

When Mill assumed control of the *London and Westminster Review* (as it was called for a time after 1836 when its amalgamation with Mill's own *London Review*, founded in 1835, took place), at once he opened its pages, as he said in the *Autobiography*, 'to all writers who were in sympathy with Progress as I understood it.'[33] His management was said to have 'aimed at a wider comprehension than had ever been allowed before in any periodical representing a sect.'[34] As might have been expected, the sectarians complained. In 1838, at a time when Radical friends like the Grotes and Roebuck were upbraiding Mill for opening the pages of the *Westminster* to a reactionary hysteric like Carlyle and an ordained clergyman like John Sterling, he was being blamed by Albany Fonblanque for being a tool of the Radical clique led by the Grotes. He gave an angry disclaimer:

> What is the meaning of *your* insisting upon identifying me with Grote or Roebuck or the rest? . . . Have you forgotten . . . that my Radicalism is of a school the most remote from theirs, at all points, which exists? *They* knew this as long ago as 1829, since which time the variance has been growing wider & wider. I never consented to have anything to do with the London Review but for the sake of getting together a body of writers who would represent radicalism more worthily than they did . . . but in proportion as I did find such persons I have been divesting the review of its sectarian character. . . .[35]

The corruption of criticism by its association with practical ends which Arnold deplored in English life was, for him, equivalent to that subordination of the free play of ideas to the interests of a party which was the standard practice of the leading periodicals. Each periodical, he charged, would allow only as much free play of mind as suited the interests of the party it represented. The *Edinburgh Review* allowed as much free play of mind as was compatible with Whiggery; the *Quarterly* as much as was compatible with Toryism; the *British Quarterly* as much as was compatible with Dissent; the *Dublin* as much as was compatible with English and Irish Catholicism; and so on down the line. 'It must needs be,' Arnold snapped,

> that men should act in sects and parties, that each of these sects and parties should have its organ, and should make this organ subserve the interests of its action; but it would be well, too, that there should be a criticism, not the minister of these interests, not their enemy, but absolutely and entirely independent of them.

Burke was, for Arnold, the rare English example of loyalty to truth rather than to party. Arnold extolled the famous passage near the end of Burke's *Thoughts on French Affairs*, in which the arch-foe of the French Revolution admitted that if the world had irrevocably set its head in the direction of the path charted by the Revolution, it was not only useless but perverse and almost wicked to resist it. This about-face, Arnold held, was a notable example of living by ideas and of being able

> when one side of a question has long had your earnest support, when all your feelings are engaged, when you hear all round you no language but one, when your party talks this language like a steam-engine and can imagine no other,—still . . . to think, still to be irresistibly carried ∴ . . by the current of thought to the opposite side of the question, and like Balaam, to . . . speak [nothing] *but what the Lord has put in your mouth*.[36]

There was, in addition to their concern for the disinterested pursuit of truth, a more personal reason for the hypersensitivity of Arnold and Mill to sectarianism. The disputatiousness which was almost demanded by the age in which they lived was alien to their characters, and they never ceased to be repelled by it, even as necessity more and more drew them to it.

We know that Arnold stayed clear of the theological controversies which had rent Oxford when he was a student there. When he visited the university many years later, in 1861, he found things worse than ever:

> All the world here seems more perturbed and exacerbated than of old. If I was disposed to fly for refuge to the country and its sights and sounds against the rather humdrum life which prevailed here in old times, how much more am I disposed to do this now, convinced as I am that irritations and envyings are not only negatively injurious to one's spirit, like dulness, but positively and actively.

Even as he was working on one of the argumentative Homer lectures, Arnold confessed a desire to 'live in a purer air than that of controversy' and vowed that, after two more polemical articles, one on middle-class education and one on Academies, he would 'leave this region altogether and . . . devote myself wholly to what is positive and happy, not negative and contentious, in literature.'[37] Needless to say, this was a pleasure Arnold never came to allow himself.

Mill, though he had more faith in argument than Arnold did, did not himself like to argue. Henry Adams recalled his surprise when, at the age of twenty-three, he found himself at an after-dinner conversation 'instructing John Stuart Mill,' whom

Adams knew as 'his Satanic free-trade majesty,' in, of all things, the special merits of the American system of protection.

> In spite of all the probabilities, he [Adams] convinced himself that it was not the Duke's [Argyll's] claret which led him to this singular form of loquacity; he insisted that it was the fault of Mr. Mill himself who led him on by assenting to his point of view. Mr. Mill took no apparent pleasure in dispute. . . .[38]

Not only did he take no apparent pleasure in dispute—he positively abhorred it. In a letter of 1830 in which he outlined what he hoped would be his course of intellectual conduct throughout life, Mill promised that he would never be degraded into a sectarian, expending strength and spirit in a waste of controversy. He would read the books written by those from whom he differed and try to examine patiently and sympathetically the views of opponents before reaching his own conclusions. In dealing with persons he thought in error, he would avoid the great evil of controversy (which only forces people to cling to their opinions out of pride more than conviction). By first seeking out the portion of truth in his opponent's ideas and then hinting at an idea which would put that opponent in the right path, Mill hoped to serve the cause of truth without offending personal sensibilities:

> And when this is done, or at least if it were universally done, no one's offended *amour propre* would make him cling to his errors; no one would connect, with the adoption of truth, the idea of defeat; and no one would feel impelled by the ardour of debate & the desire of triumph, to reject, as almost all now do whatever of truth there really is in the opinions of those whose ultimate conclusion differs from theirs. In short, I do not insist upon making others give up their own point of view & adopt mine, but I endeavour myself to unite whatever is not optical illusion in both.[39]

Mill resolved to eschew sectarianism not only because it was unpleasant, but because it hindered the recognition that the truth is more often divided between two parties to a controversy than monopolized by one of them.

The Englishman's inability to see more than one side of a question was, Arnold and Mill believed, the result of his sectarianism. That was why they objected to the letter as well as to the spirit of sectarianism; they hated not only its rancour, but its incompleteness. They proposed to substitute for the spirit of sectarianism the spirit of synthetic reason, which recognized the complex, many-sided nature of truth. Arnold's European mouthpiece in 'My Countrymen' told Arnold and his countrymen that

> you can never see the two sides of a question; never perceive that every human state of things, even a good one, has its inconveniences. We can see the inconveniences of your state well enough, and the inconveniences of ours; of newspapers not free and prefects over-busy; and there are plenty of us who proclaim them. You eagerly repeat after us all we say that redounds to your own honour and glory; but you never follow our example yourselves.[40]

Arnold's prejudice against systematic thinkers may, in part, be explained by the dialectical disposition of his mind, which necessarily saw systematizers as blinkered, narrow-minded dogmatists. For Mill, seeing all sides of a question became so much a way of life and an article of faith that it could determine his friendships. When he feared that John Sterling's resignation from the London Debating Society might deprive him of a friend, Mill explained to Sterling that he highly valued their intimacy 'for this reason among many others that it appears to me peculiarly adapted to the wants of my own mind; since I know no person who possesses more, of what I have not, than yourself.'[41] In his essays on Bentham and Coleridge, Mill elaborated the theory that opposing modes of thought are not only tolerable but desirable, because necessary to the discovery of the whole truth on any subject. In arguing that it was too soon for Coleridge to be justly estimated as a thinker, Mill put it to his readers that

> a true thinker can only be justly estimated when his thoughts have worked their way into minds formed in a different school; have been wrought and moulded into consistency with all other true and relevant thoughts; when the noisy conflict of half-truths, angrily denying one another, has subsided, and ideas which seemed mutually incompatible have been found only to require mutual limitations.[42]

Such a theory of controversy is the opposite of that of sectarianism; for whereas sectarianism precludes completeness, the theory of the necessity of opposing modes of thought claims to be the only guarantee of completeness.

G. M. Young has said that 'the function of the nineteenth century was to disengage the disinterested intelligence, to release it from the entanglements of party and sect . . . and to set it operating over the whole range of human life and circumstance.'[43] Surprised as they would have been at such a tribute, Arnold and Mill would have been extremely gratified to know that their isolation from party sectarianism had been justified by posterity.

The attacks on intellectual sectarianism and the proposed substitution of the spirit of synthetic reason for the spirit of sect were but the application to controversy of what Arnold and Mill thought the method of history. As, on the one hand, neither the epochs of transition nor the epochs of concentration could make up the whole of history, so, on the other, neither could one opinion in a controversy nor its opposite make up the whole truth. As history would not be complete without both kinds of epoch, so truth would not be complete until the doctrine accepted as truth had encountered its adversaries.

But, in seeking to allay the narrowness of their sectarian contemporaries by recommending the synthetic view of truth implicit in the historical method, Arnold and Mill forgot that the dialectical process which they admitted to be the law of history was itself a justification for the one-sidedness of their contemporaries in an age of transition. They overlooked the fact that the argumentative process of history which they defined was finally incompatible with the synthetic, harmonious ideal of human nature and society which they also derived from history. The attempts of Arnold and Mill to reconcile the demands of the dialectical historical process with the demands of the ideal of perfection they extracted from this process form the subject of the rest of this chapter.

When Arnold and Mill came to employ their theory of history as a weapon in controversy, they deserted the abstract terms 'organic,' 'critical,' 'concentration', 'expansion,' and substituted the more concrete and highly charged Hebraism and Hellenism, Christianity and Paganism, Benthamism and Coleridgianism; it is by the latter group of labels that the historical counters of Arnold and Mill are usually designated. These historical definitions, it must be remembered, were essentially polemical weapons; they were employed to persuade not discover, to reform not reveal. They were less historical designations than the constituent elements of a complete human nature.

Arnold's conception of Hebraism and Hellenism is his theory of the dialectic of history transformed into a theory of the completeness of human nature and society. The conflicting elements of history become the constituent elements of a complete view of human nature and of society—so that a lack of respect for history must produce a partial and incomplete view of man and society.

Arnold conceived of the dialectic of history as equivalent to the growth and development of the human spirit:

> Hebraism and Hellenism are, neither of them, the *law* of human development, as their admirers are prone to make them; they are, each of them, *contributions* to human development. . . . The nations of our modern world, children of that immense and salutary movement which broke up the Pagan world, inevitably stand to Hellenism in a relation which dwarfs it, and to Hebraism in a relation which magnifies it. They are inevitably prone to take Hebraism as the law of human development, and not as simply a contribution to it, however precious. And yet the lesson must be learned, that the human spirit is wider than the most priceless of the forces which bear it onward, and that to the whole development of man Hebraism itself is, like Hellenism, but a contribution.
>
> .   .   .   .
>
> By alternations of Hebraism and Hellenism, of a man's intellectual and moral impulses, of the effort to see things as they really are and the effort to win peace by self-conquest, the human spirit proceeds; and each of these two forces has its appointed hours of culmination and seasons of rule.[44]

His theory of the two elements which constitute history and human character was the keystone of Arnold's thought. In the year of the publication of *Culture and Anarchy*, he predicted that 'the chapters on Hebraism and Hellenism are . . . so true that they will form a kind of centre for English thought and speculation on the matters treated in them'; and in the following year he called his distinction between Hebraism and Hellenism 'a distinction on which more and more will turn, and on dealing wisely with it everything depends.'[45]

The definition of Hebraism and Hellenism supplies a distinction upon which everything in Arnold's work, at any rate, does indeed depend. 'The uppermost idea with Hellenism,' he said, 'is to see things as they really are; the uppermost idea with Hebraism is conduct and obedience. Nothing can do away with this ineffaceable difference.' True, he admitted, both the Hebrew ideal of right action and the Greek ideal of right thinking spring from the desire to be at one with the universe, that noblest of desires, which is, in effect, the love of God. But, if their goal is the same, they seek it by different paths. Hellenism is guided by '*spontaneity of consciousness*,' Hebraism by '*strictness of conscience*.' Arnold did his best, as the balanced phrasing suggests, to maintain an equilibrium between the two adversaries. He reproached writers like Frederick Robertson, who used Hellenism merely as a foil to Hebraism, or like Heinrich Heine, who used Hebraism merely as a foil to Hellenism. But he could not help letting the cat out of the bag. Hellenism, after all, represented all of Arnold's hopes for the perfection of mankind, and Hebraism his scepticism about the capacity of men for perfection and his consciousness of their inherent weakness. Whereas Hellenism is a positive ideal, investing human life 'with a kind of aerial ease, clearness, and radiancy [Hebraism] has always been severely pre-occupied with an awful sense of the impossibility of being at ease in Zion; of the difficulties which oppose themselves to man's pursuit or attainment of that perfection of which Socrates talks so hopefully, and, as from this point of view one might almost say, so glibly.' Hebraism and Hellenism are committed, ultimately, to opposite conceptions of human nature. For the ideal of culture as a harmonious human perfection which Arnold espoused throughout *Culture and Anarchy* was the ideal of Hellenism; and just as culture, in Arnold's theory, ultimately encompasses religion, so is Hellenism ultimately to encompass Hebraism.[46] But not before Hebraism has done its work. For Hebraism alone can supply the 'devout energy' needed to live one's ideal, to translate knowledge into conduct. So long as righteousness is needed, so long will the religious experience of Israel, its unique source, be relevant, for in spite of all which in them [the Hebrew people] and in their character is unattractive, nay, repellent,—in spite of their short-comings even in righteousness itself and their insignificance in everything else,—this petty, unsuccessful, unamiable people, without politics, without science, without art, without charm, deserve their great place in the world's regard, and are likely to have it more, as the world goes on, rather than less.[47]

Yet Arnold knew that he often talked up Hellenism at the expense of Hebraism, and he justified doing so by saying that, as he wrote, Hellenism was generally being unfairly and excessively subordinated to an ascendant Hebraism. He justified himself, that is, by appealing to the historical process, which shows that each side of the great historical argument has always had to overstate its own case in order to survive, much less flourish. Yet his ideal of a complete and harmonious human nature requires nothing less than the negation of the historical process, which only oscillates between two incomplete views of human nature. If his opponents are forbidden to justify the overstatement of *their* case by appealing to historical precedent, why should Arnold be allowed to justify *his* excesses by such an appeal? Arnold was at one and the same time blaming those who retarded the ultimate fusion of Hebraism and Hellenism by praising one at the expense of the other and admitting that he himself was forced to conform to the wearisome historical process by overstating the case for that part of human nature which had most recently been undervalued. He advocated seeing things as they really are and then excused his failure to do so by pleading that the circumstances of time and place required him to distort and exaggerate.

If the ideal of harmonious perfection espoused by the ancient Greeks was sound, why did it fail to establish itself upon a lasting basis? It failed, Arnold said, because religion had not yet succeeded in strengthening the moral fiber of mankind, and the noble effort of the Greeks was therefore premature. Here was the prototype of the pattern which Arnold saw pervading Western history. Was not the failure of the ancient Greeks, for example, repeated in the Renaissance? Was not the sixteenth century (for Arnold the time of the English Renaissance) the second great attempt of Hellenism to rule the world and the spirit of man? And like the first wave of Hellenism, this one receded too; for it carried with it a strong tendency to flout Hebraism and ignore morality. (And also, one must add, though Arnold did not, that even after fifteen hundred years of Christianity, morality had still not done its work.) Just as primitive Christianity was the reaction to a Hellenism fallen short of its ideal, so the seventeenth-century Puritanism of the English people was a reaction to the moral laxness of the Elizabethan age.[48]

Arnold thus saw all history in terms of this process of interaction. Ultimately, however, he wanted historical oscillation to cease and give way to fixity. He would join alternating elements of past history into a stable and unified whole, and would, in effect, cause history to cease. Yet when he was confronted with a system of law and ethics which pretended to absolute and eternal validity he rejected it—precisely on the grounds of its pretended fixity.

Arnold thought of Christianity as being like Judaism in its obsession with conduct but unlike Judaism insofar as it had been leavened with the Hellenism that undermined what Arnold, following Paul, called a fixed and mechanical law. He defined Christianity as a Hebraism reformed by Hellenism out of its adherence to the law. His quarrel with the law was based upon two premises. One was that immorality is attributable not to human depravity but to the existence of a moral law. The other was that a law which is fixed and permanent, shut off from 'a free play of thought'[49] and consciousness, must inevitably become mechanical and ineffectual.

Once again, Arnold was guilty of special pleading. He resorted to the necessary working of the historical process to explain and justify the demise of a system he disliked. He proceeded on the assumption, supported by the theory of historical oscillation, that no synthesis is ever so perfect and complete that it leaves no room for further development. But he categorically rejected this very assumption when he was fashioning his own synthesis of the elements of perfection under the aegis of a state which would be the expression of a humanity 'not manifold, and vulgar, and unstable, and contentious, and ever-varying, but one, and noble, and secure, and peaceful, and the same for all mankind.'[50]

Arnold's attack upon the fixity of Hebrew law resembles

Mill's complaint about 'the Hebrews' in *Utilitarianism*. Mill held them primarily responsible for the equation frequently made between law and justice and for the widespread supposition that justice consists in conformity to law. This equation was to be expected in 'a people whose laws attempted to embrace all subjects on which precepts were required, and who believed those laws to be a direct emanation from the Supreme Being.' The Greeks and Romans, on the other hand, released mankind from this bondage because they knew that laws were made by men and, as such, might be bad laws which conflicted with true principles of justice.[51] In the later 'Utility of Religion,' Mill noted a positive danger in 'ascribing a supernatural origin to the received maxims of morality': namely, the assumption that these commandments comprise a perfect and complete morality closed to further discussion.[52]

But Mill was not the insensitive Hellenizer—or, for that matter, the rigid Hebraizer—that Arnold often thought him. Running through *On Liberty* is Mill's own version of Hebraism and Hellenism; and, in its application to human character, it is not significantly different from Arnold's. Mill said that so-called Christian ethics needed to be complemented by ethics from other sources if mankind's 'moral regeneration' was to be achieved. Christian morality, Mill asserted, is essentially the formulation of the early church fathers, who knew that the New Testament documents were not in themselves a complete system of morality. But this morality, according to Mill, even though specifically intended to fill out the inadequacies of the Gospels, is

in many important points, incomplete and one-sided, and . . . unless ideas and feelings, not sanctioned by it, had contributed to the formation of European life and character, human affairs would have been in a worse condition than they now are. Christian morality (so-called) has all the characters of a reaction: it is, in great part, a protest against Paganism. Its ideal is negative rather than positive; passive rather than active; Innocence rather than Nobleness; Abstinence from Evil, rather than energetic Pursuit of Good; in its precepts (as has been well said) 'thou shalt not' predominates unduly over 'thou shalt.' In its horror of sensuality, it made an idol of asceticism. . . .[53]

For his ideal of a complete human perfection, Mill, like Arnold, resorted to ancient Greece. He concluded a sharp criticism of

Calvinism, which, he said, is bent on rooting out most of the natural human impulses, by asserting that

> there is a Greek ideal of self-development, which the Platonic and Christian ideal of self-government blends with, but does not supersede. It may be better to be a John Knox than an Alcibiades, but it is better to be a Pericles than either; nor would a Pericles, if we had one in these days, be without anything good which belonged to John Knox.[54]

When he sought to win over English Puritans to the true ideal of human completeness, Mill spoke in terms of the Christian and the Pagan ideals. But when he tried to cure the narrowness of his own school of Utilitarians, he used the images of Bentham and of Coleridge to represent the constituent elements of history, and of human perfection. Once again, a theory of history gave rise to and then merged with a theory of society and of human nature. Mill assumed that the laws of human society are really the laws of history, and that they are only to be discovered there. He associated the success of the Coleridgians and the failure of their adversaries in discovering the requisites of civil society with the respect shown by the former and the contempt by the latter, for history. As Hebraism and Hellenism are but contributions to human development, so the men of Bentham's type and the men of Coleridge's type, who 'seem to be, and believe themselves to be, enemies, are in reality allies. The powers they wield are opposite poles of one great force of progression.' The rhythm of interaction between Hebraism and Hellenism is apparent in the reaction of the nineteenth century, of which Coleridge was made the representative, against the eighteenth century, which Bentham (in spite of the fact that he carried on well into the nineteenth century) represented. The nineteenth-century or Coleridgian philosophy, Mill maintained, was ontological because the Benthamite philosophy was experimental, 'conservative, because that was innovative; religious, because so much of that was infidel; concrete and historical, because that was abstract and metaphysical; poetical, because that was matter of fact and prosaic.'[55]

As Arnold chided champions of Hebraism who used its opposite merely as a foil, and advocates of Hellenism who used Hebraism as a foil, Mill blamed—though, as we shall see, not so severely as Arnold—each reaction for abusing its deserved victory over that which preceded it. Again, historical adversaries are analogous to the diverse elements of human character and society. Benthamism stands for the rational element in man, and Coleridgianism for the poetical and emotional elements. As the excess of eighteenth-century rationalism was its belief in the infallibility of the 'reasoning elements,' the answering excess of the nineteenth-century belief in emotion was its belief in the infallibility of 'the unreasoning elements in human nature.'[56]

The names Bentham and Coleridge meant for Mill not just two particular men but two types of philosophical men. Mill believed that in societies, like that of England in the eighteenth century, which rested on their old foundations but no longer believed in their solidity, two types inevitably arose: 'one demanding the extinction of the institutions and creeds which had hitherto existed; the other, that they be made a reality; the one pressing the new doctrines to their utmost consequences; the other reasserting the best meaning of the old. The first type attained its greatest height in Bentham; the last in Coleridge.' Like Arnold placing Hebraism and Hellenism in the scales, Mill tried to give a semblance of equality and symmetry to his treatment of Bentham and Coleridge. Bentham represented the interest of the state in progression, Coleridge its interest in permanence:

> To Bentham it was given to discern more particularly those truths with which existing doctrines and institutions were at variance; to Coleridge, the neglected truths which lay *in* them.

. . . .

> By Bentham . . . men have been led to ask themselves, in regard to any ancient or received opinion, Is it true? and by Coleridge, What is the meaning of it?

Mill even pretended to discover that the laissez-faire doctrines which Bentham—with some qualifications—supported and which Coleridge bitterly opposed were half true and half false. Yet there is nothing in Mill's discussion of Coleridge comparable in its ferocity to the harsh strictures which he passed upon Bentham, and, in fact, nothing that is negatively critical of Coleridge at all, aside from the remark that his opinions on political economy are not worthy of an educated man.[57] Mill knew and admitted that his essays had been weighted unfairly. But he defended his action by pointing out that he was writing for Benthamites, who for the most part had never heard anything but praise spoken of Bentham, or dispraise spoken of Coleridge—if indeed they had heard of Coleridge at all.[58] That is to say, he defended himself, as Arnold did, by invoking the doctrine of historical relativism.

Mill's attack on his old friend and teacher, Jeremy Bentham, took place on several fronts. Mill, by 1838, had become a partial adherent to the organic theory of society and was in full revolt against Bentham's mechanistic theory of society as a mere conglomeration of warring selfish interests; he had become conscious of the importance of poetry and the cultivation of the feelings—and was understandably estranged from the philosopher who, in Hazlitt's words, 'had struck the whole mass of fancy, prejudice, passion, sense, whim with his petrific, leaden mace . . . had "bound volatile Hermes," ' and reduced the theory and practice of human life to a *caput mortuum* of reason, and dull, plodding, technical calculation.'[59] Only one aspect of Mill's assault upon the great foe of ipsedixitism, however, need concern us here: namely, his criticism of Bentham's subjectivism and narrowness, his complete reliance upon the resources of his own mind and experience.

There are, Mill asserted, two necessary prerequisites for the philosopher who would deal adequately with human nature and life: a nature and a personal experience broad enough to be fairly representative of common human nature and common experience; and the ability to learn from other minds. But Bentham was nothing if not eccentric. He knew little of the common experiences, joys and sorrows, of human life; like James Mill, he was an empiricist with very little experience. The natural gift required of an ethical philosopher—that which, one is tempted to reply to Mill, Bentham can hardly be blamed for being born without—was wanting in Bentham, who seemed condemned to remain relatively ignorant of 'many of the most natural and strongest feelings of human nature.'[60]

Bentham also lacked the requisite which is the product not of nature but of art. For Bentham 'begins all his inquiries by supposing nothing to be known on the subject, and reconstructs all philosophy *ab initio*, without reference to the opinions of his predecessors.' The Bentham Mill described was like the spider of Bacon's treatise or of Swift's fable who worked without any material but what his own entrails could supply; or like the Romantic poets whose ignorance and subjectivism Arnold would later attack in the 1853 Preface to his poems. But, Mill urged, originality is not more necessary to the philosopher than 'a thoughtful regard for previous thinkers, and for the collective mind of the human race.'[61]

Rarely did Mill disapprove so strongly of subjectivism as he did in the Bentham essay; or so fervently urge the importance of the common as opposed to the peculiar, the public as opposed to the private, the general as opposed to the particular. The common or general opinion of mankind, Mill maintained, is of importance to the thinker because it is an average of all minds, without sublimity but also without eccentricity:

> . . . a net result, in which everybody's particular point of view is represented, nobody's predominant. The collective mind does not penetrate below the surface, but it sees all the surface; which profound thinkers, even by reason of their profundity, often fail to do: their intenser view of a thing in some of its aspects diverting their attention from others.

It was precisely the original thinkers with whose infirmities Mill was concerned. Though it does all thinkers good to know what their predecessors and the common run of people have thought, it is 'the hardiest assertor . . . of the freedom of private judgment —the keenest detector of the errors of his predecessors, and of the inaccuracies of current modes of thought' who, most of all, should 'fortify the weak side of his own intellect, by study of the opinions of mankind in all ages and nations, and of the speculations of philosophers of the modes of thought most opposite to his own.'[62]

The vehemence of Mill's reaction against Bentham carried him to the point where he was working at cross-purposes with one of the primary intentions of the essays on Bentham and Coleridge. Certainly, his denigration of Bentham differs from that of Arnold, who took the opportunity, in *Culture and Anarchy*, publicly to free himself from the obligation to consider Bentham's ideas because Bentham had not considered anyone else's ideas. Arnold mentioned Bentham's disdain for Socrates and Plato, who 'were talking nonsense under pretence of talking wisdom and morality' and concluded—with a noticeable sigh of relief: 'I am delivered from the bondage of Bentham! the fanaticism of his adherents can touch me no longer, I feel the inadequacy of his mind and ideas for supplying the rule of human society, for perfection.'[63] Mill had been disturbed by the same passage, in the *Deontology*, where Bentham expressed his scorn for Socrates and Plato 'in terms,' Mill groaned, 'distressing to his greatest admirers'; and he thought the entire work (only a small part of which was known to be by Bentham) might with profit to Bentham's reputation be omitted from the collected edition of his works. Yet, and almost at the beginning of his evaluation of Bentham, Mill, who knew Bentham's shortcomings far better than Arnold did, warned that 'to refuse an admiring admission of what he [Bentham] was, on account of what he was not, is a much worse error [than to overpraise him], and one which, pardonable in vulgar, is no longer permitted to any cultivated and instructed mind.' At the completion of the most devastating part of his attack on Bentham, and, in fact, at the completion of nearly every stage of the attack, Mill, as if in recompense, qualified (and, in one sense, disqualified) all he had said by insisting on the usefulness and even indispensability of 'one-eyed men.' In spite of the fact that Bentham entirely overlooked all those truths which did not suit his philosophy, Mill warned, he should be unhesitatingly praised for his ability to 'hunt half-truths to their consequences and practical applications, on a scale both of greatness and minuteness not previously exemplified.' At a point in the essay where Mill claims (erroneously, as it turns out) to have completed the 'unpleasing part' of his work, which dwells on Bentham's errors, he turns around and says we ought not to judge Bentham's accomplishments of small worth, because 'man has but the choice to go a little way in many paths, or a great way in only one. The field of Bentham's labours was like the space between two parallel lines; narrow to excess in one direction, in another it reached to infinity.'[64]

But in spite of Mill's noble attempts to conceal them, the contradictions of his essay remain. The essay contains two conflicting impulses of thought, one opting for the vigorous

pursuit and development of that half of the truth especially
needed at some particular time, the other anxious for synthesis
and harmony. Both spring from the historical method, which
dictates eclecticism and relativism on the one hand, and synthesis on the other. The resulting contradiction runs through all
the work of Arnold, as well as Mill, and determines the complex nature of their personal relation to the historical process,
which is the subject of my next, and concluding, section in this
chapter.

We have seen how, in spite of his censure of Bentham's narrowness and blindness, Mill was forced to admit that the synthesis
of half-truths cannot be performed by individual men, but only
by history itself:

> For our own part, we have a large tolerance for one-eyed men,
> provided their one eye is a penetrating one: if they saw more, they
> probably would not see so keenly, nor so eagerly pursue one course
> of inquiry. Almost all rich veins of original and striking specula-
> tion have been opened by systematic half-thinkers: though
> whether these new thoughts drive out others as good, or are
> peacefully superadded to them, depends on whether these half-
> thinkers are or are not followed in the same track by complete
> thinkers. The field of man's nature and life cannot be too much
> worked, or in too many directions; until every clod is turned up
> the work is imperfect; no whole truth is possible but by combining
> the points of view of all the fractional truths, nor, therefore, until
> it has been fully seen what each fractional truth can do by itself.[65]

Harmony and synthesis, Mill warned, must not come too soon,
or they will leave out materials necessary for completeness.

In *On Liberty*, Mill showed even less hope of imminent harmony and synthesis than he had in the Bentham essay, where
at least each successive historical oscillation seemed to bring
men a little bit closer to the balance at the center of the pendulum's swing. Does not history, he asked, demonstrate that
one-sidedness is the rule and many-sidedness the exception?
Popular opinion always tries to present its portion of truth as
the whole truth, while heretical opinion, instead of seeking to
supply the 'suppressed and neglected truths' which form the
necessary complement to the accepted ones, sets itself up 'with
similar exclusiveness, as the whole truth.' Thus, Mill lamented,

there is no discernible progress towards a harmonious synthesis. Epochs can only hope to satisfy the demands of the *Zeitgeist* by making available the fragment of truth which is more needed at a particular time than the part of truth it is displacing. Nor does there seem to be any alternative to this wearisome struggle, for 'so long as popular truth is one-sided, it is more desirable than otherwise that unpopular truth should have one-sided assertion too.'[66]

Mill never ceased to warn against premature synthesis. It was all very well for Bentham to propound the synthetic method —it was his own as well—but Bentham's raw materials were woefully incomplete, and 'nobody's synthesis can be more complete than his analysis.'[67] Mill applied the same criticism to a thinker whose materials were fewer and whose passion for harmony and synthesis was greater than those of Bentham: Auguste Comte.

Auguste Comte had adopted a rule of mental health or '*hygiène cérébrale*' which proscribed the reading of almost everything not written by himself, and allowed him to pursue exclusively and with absolute concentration a particular line of thought. He, of all thinkers, Mill maintained, should have been the readiest to 'resign the pretension of arriving at the whole truth on the subject, whatever it may be, of his meditations.' Mill was liberal enough to admit that a hygienic thinker like Comte might make a contribution 'towards the elements of the final synthesis,' but severe enough to disbar him from the serious business of synthesizing his small particle of truth with the innumerable other particles.[68]

The pretensions of Auguste Comte, however, were as grand as his sympathies were narrow. When he had laboriously traced the slow development of the natural and physical sciences from the theological through the metaphysical and finally into (and within) the positive stage, Comte leapt to the conclusion that 'the mere institution of a positive science of sociology [was] tantamount to its completion.' All differences of opinion on the subject, he decided, had arisen from the fact that it was formerly studied in the theological and metaphysical modes. The time had arrived, he believed, for the final truths of sociology to be formulated. Sociological phenomena no longer required to be analyzed, but only to be synthesized. Human nature, similarly, no longer required to be developed but only to have its existing powers harmonized. For Mill, however, the millennium was not yet in sight, and Comte's work sharpened his fears lest a synthesis be attempted before all the available materials had come under analysis:

> The period of decomposition . . . is not yet terminated: the shell of the old edifice will remain standing until there is another ready to replace it; and the new synthesis is barely begun, nor is even the preparatory analysis completely finished.[69]

But despite Mill's repeated warnings against a premature synthesis of the forces of history and the powers of human nature, he continued to be annoyed and even angered by the incessant action and reaction of history, the tendency of each age to overlook that half of the truth possessed by the age it was superseding; and he continued to believe in the synthetic method.

The same contradictory pattern pervades Arnold's work. On the one hand, he was a critic of narrow and exclusive advocates either of Hebraism or of Hellenism, he seemed to have little tolerance for one-eyed men, and he was annoyed by the unwillingness of the historical pendulum to balance in dead center:

> Hebraism and Hellenism,—between these two points of influence moves our world. At one time it feels more powerfully the attraction of one of them, at another time of the other; and it ought to be, though it never is, evenly and happily balanced between them.

He was sure that dialectic, whatever its uses, is ultimately inadequate to man's needs, which are for balance and harmony. He said of the oscillation between Hebraism and Hellenism that

> sooner or later it becomes manifest that when the two sides of humanity proceed in this fashion of alternate preponderance, and not of mutual understanding and balance, the side which is uppermost does not really provide in a satisfactory manner for the needs of the side which is undermost, and a state of confusion is, sooner or later, the result.[70]

On the other hand, Arnold wished to postpone literary creation—which was to him what philosophical synthesis was to Mill—until his own epoch of criticism had adequately analyzed the materials available to it. The great work of literature, Arnold said, is a work 'of synthesis and exposition, not of analysis and discovery.' It can arise only in eras which have already collected and refined all their raw materials; and so have afforded the artist that 'national glow of life and thought' without which great art is impossible.[71] Arnold, like Mill, resorted to a ploughing metaphor to extract the implications of the theory of the alternation of historical epochs of analysis and synthesis:

> After the fall of the Roman Empire the barbarians powerfully turned up the soil of Europe—and after a little time when the violent ploughing was over and things had settled a little, a vigorous crop of new ideas was the result. Italy bore the first crop—but the soil having been before much exhausted soon left bearing. The virgin soils of Germany and England went on longer —but they too are I think beginning to fail.[72]

No more than Mill could Arnold totally and irrevocably commit himself to the synthetic rather than the dialectic method —though both had been dictated by history. He was caught in Mill's dilemma. For him, as for Mill, two theories derived from a single source issued contrary directives. The consciousness that they lived in a transitional or critical era encouraged Arnold and Mill to insist on analysis, discovery, and free development; but the knowledge that transitional eras usually go astray by ignoring the elements of wholeness and order which were present in the preceding age made them cling to the ideal of synthesis, harmony, and stability.

Bonnerot, commenting upon Arnold's reluctance to arrive at synthesis, says that 'le douteur désire donc la synthèse, mais ne veut pas pour cela renoncer à son éclectisme, au relativisme . . . bien qu'il sache pertinemment que qui dit relativisme, dit scepticisme.'[73] It was precisely relativism, as expressed in the historical notion of the *Zeitgeist*, that warred against synthesis. Whenever Mill and Arnold consented to overpraise one element of human perfection or one half of the truth at the expense of the other in order to rectify a supposed historical imbalance, they were espousing relativism. The idea of cultural and intellectual relativism, which is often supposed to distinguish the Victorians who flourished after 1870 from their immediate predecessors,[74] pervades the writings of Arnold and Mill. When Arnold overpraised the virtues of Hellenism after having called Hebraism and Hellenism equally necessary to human perfection, he justified his apparent inconsistency by saying that 'whether at this time or that time, and to this or that set of persons, one ought to insist most on the praises of fire and strength, or on the praises of sweetness and light, must depend, one would think, on the circumstances and needs of that particular time and those particular persons.'[75] Arnold, who was so conscious of the difficulty of being disinterested, failed to see not only that this doctrine of circumstances contradicted the spirit of disinterestedness (which makes truth and not a man's own notion of what is needful to others the sovereign power) but that it was fraught with temptations of every kind—and especially the temptation to sacrifice principle to expediency. Mill espoused the doctrine of relativism when he said, in *On Liberty*, that if, on such questions as the contest between property and equality, aristocracy and democracy, cooperation and competition, one opinion is to be encouraged more than another, 'it is the one which happens at the particular time and place to be in a minority.' This opinion needs to be affirmed not because it is true but because it 'represents the neglected interests, the side of human well-being which is in danger of obtaining less than its share.'[76]

The relativistic doctrine of circumstance supported many of Arnold's and Mill's judgments of thinkers and ideas. I have already noted how Mill justified the favoritism shown in the 'Bentham' and 'Coleridge' essays by saying that, when writing in a Radical journal, he was under less of an obligation to defend opinions which he held in common with most of his audience than to acquaint that audience with whatever of value the representative of a different school of thought might have to offer it. He explained his early praise and his subsequent vehement dispraise of Comte by arguing that 'while a writer has few readers, and no influence except on independent thinkers, the only thing worth considering in him is what he can teach us.' His errors, so long as they are not capable of doing harm, should be overlooked, in public at any rate. Once the time has come (as Mill thought it had, in 1865, for Comte), when a thinker is of sufficient repute so that his errors can be injurious to the world but the exposure of them not fatal to his reputation, it becomes one's duty to expose them.[77]

The attempt to modify his opinions in accordance with time and to allow his criticism to be determined by what he supposed to be the needs of the public, could land Mill in some embarrassing situations. He often was obliged to impede the too thorough acceptance of ideas he had himself first proposed. Thus, many years after he had argued in favor of the right of the state to interfere with endowments and divert them from their original purposes, he wrote an article in the *Fortnightly Review* to combat the magnification of this idea into the doctrine that private parties ought to be permitted no discretion whatever in designating endowments for public interests. Mill even apologized for the one-sidedness of his occasional writings:

> Where what I had written appears a fair statement of part of the truth, but defective inasmuch as there exists another part respecting which nothing, or too little is said, I leave the deficiency to be supplied by the reader's own thoughts; the rather, as he will, in many cases, find the balance restored in some other part of this collection. Thus, the review of Mr. Sedgwick's Discourse, taken by itself, might give an impression of more complete adhesion to the philosophy of Locke, Bentham, and the eighteenth century, than is really the case, and of an inadequate sense of its deficiencies; but that notion will be rectified by the subsequent essays on Bentham and on Coleridge. These, again, if they stood alone, would give just as much too strong an impression of the writer's sympathy with the reaction of the nineteenth century against the eighteenth: but his exaggeration will be corrected by the more recent defence of the 'greatest happiness' ethics against Dr. Whewell.[78]

Arnold also tempered his opinion of men and ideas to the requirements of time and place. He discounted France's lubricity in the 1850s and 1860s when England was still in the throes of a kind of Puritanism, but exaggerated it in the 1880s when the Aesthetes and idolators of France like Swinburne had become prominent on the English scene. He acknowledged, and even detailed, the dangerous practical implications of Emerson's most impressive maxims (especially the philosophically optimistic ones); yet he maintained that such criticism was essentially invalid because Emerson's maxims were, in a certain ideal sphere, true, and, more important, because Emerson was right to state his doctrines in an absolute and general way, without circumstantial limitations, at the particular time he appeared on the intellectual horizon.[79] The demands of the *Zeitgeist* formed a sufficient excuse, Arnold thought, for excess on one side of the truth.

The relativism of Arnold and Mill depended, in large part, upon their belief that it was foolhardy to cling to absolute values when they went against nature itself. The seeming rationality of history led them to equate its movements not with the working out of the divine will, as earlier thinkers had done, but with the course of nature. They invested history with all the rights and dignities of Providence, and they submitted not to the will of God but to the law of nature.

History often appears in the works of Arnold and Mill as a mysterious natural force which makes the absolute preferences of men for certain beliefs and institutions quixotic and absurd. Arnold spoke of 'the inevitable transitoriness of all human institutions' and warned those who cling desperately to established ideas and institutions that 'human thought, which made all institutions, inevitably saps them, resting only in that which is absolute and eternal.'[80] Mill congratulated the nineteenth-century French political philosophers for recognizing that 'underneath all political philosophy there must be a social philosophy—a study of agencies lying deeper than forms of government, which, working through forms of government, produce in the long run most of what these seem to produce, and which sap and destroy all forms of government that lie across their path.'[81]

In the view of both Arnold and Mill, Tocqueville had recognized better than anyone history's insistence upon relativism and flexibility. Tocqueville had affirmed that since 'the gradual and progressive development of social equality is at once the past and future of history,' then 'to attempt to check democracy [is] to resist the will of God.'[82] Mill agreed with Tocqueville, and praised the Frenchman because his ideas for the future were based firmly upon his analysis of the past. Having observed history's unmistakable evolution towards social and political equality, Tocqueville proved, according to Mill, 'that to smooth this transition, and make the best of what is certainly coming, is the proper employment of political insight.'[83] In his second review of *Democracy in America*, Mill devoted considerable effort to expounding Tocqueville's assertion of the irresistible tendency towards democracy. For he recognized that English readers, as distinguished from French, had 'less faith in irresistible tendencies, and . . . while they require for every political theory an historical basis, are far less accustomed to link together the events of history in a connected chain.'[84] Arnold learned from Tocqueville the same lesson that Mill did. Arnold proclaimed that, whatever arguments might be urged in favor of inequality, 'the one insuperable objection to inequality is the same as the one insuperable objection to absolutism: namely, that inequality, like absolutism, thwarts a vital instinct, and being thus against nature, is against our humanisation.'[85] He warned against the rigid adherence to traditions, customs, and prejudices 'because it renders us very liable to be found fighting against nature, and that is always calamitous.'[86]

Arnold always argued that equality was the will of the *Zeitgeist* or of '*the modern spirit*,' and that the demands of the modern spirit were no less imperious than those of nature itself. The modern spirit, he said, is an 'irresistible force, which is gradually making its way everywhere, removing old conditions and imposing new, altering long-fixed habits, undermining venerable institutions, even modifying national character.' Arnold's admiration for Burke's willingness to submit to the time-spirit as if it were Providence itself stemmed from his conviction that 'to recognise a period of transformation when it comes, and to adapt themselves honestly and rationally to its laws, is perhaps the nearest approach to perfection of which men and nations are capable.'[87]

How successfully did Arnold and Mill adapt themselves to the historical 'laws' of the transitional epoch in which they lived? Did they consistently view ideas and institutions as relativists? Were they always able to suppress absolute personal preferences in deference to the time-spirit and the stream of history? The evidence suggests that they were not so far removed spiritually from their contemporaries that they could effect the transition from more traditional habits of thought to historical relativism without much difficulty. Indeed, they often defiantly and

consciously transgressed against relativism and set themselves
against seemingly irresistible natural forces.

In a letter written in July, 1848, Arnold expressed to Clough
his great fondness for the relativity of judgment allowed by the
theory of the *Zeitgeist* as Goethe defined it. For example, Arnold
told his friend: 'This view . . . causes me, while I confess that
productions like your Adam and Eve are not suited to me at
present, yet to feel no confidence that they may not be quite
right and calculated to suit others.' But, in a remarkable letter
written to Clough just a few months later, Arnold spoke of his
heroic efforts to keep from being submerged in the Time Stream.
He had been at Oxford among a group of acquaintances who
were generous in their praise of Clough's *Bothie*, and he had
been revolted by them, the age, the poem, and even Clough:

> Yes I said to myself something tells me I can, if need be, at last
> dispense with them all, even with him [Clough]: better that, than
> be sucked for an hour even into the Time Stream in which they
> and he plunge and bellow. I became calm in spirit, but uncom-
> promising, almost stern. More English than European, I said
> finally, more American than English: and took up my Obermann,
> and refuged myself with him in his forest against your Zeit Geist.[88]

Violent indeed must have been Arnold's revulsion from the
time-spirit if he could call it not only English but American!
The same man who advised individuals and even whole
nations to comply with the laws of the *Zeitgeist* and to swim with
the stream often reconciled himself to membership in 'a very
small circle' of stubborn people who insisted upon seeing things
as they are:

> It is true that the critic has many temptations to go with the
> stream, to make one of the party movement, one of these *terrae
> filii;* it seems ungracious to refuse to be a *terrae filius*, when so many
> excellent people are; but the critic's duty is to refuse, or, if
> resistance is vain, at least to cry with Obermann: *Périssons en
> résistant.*[89]

Mill also encountered difficulties in subordinating his
absolute standards and preferences to the requirements of
historical relativism. On the one hand, he justified dictatorships
in backward countries like India or Malaya because all political

truths—like the principles of liberty or democracy—are 'corre-
lative [to] a given state or situation of society.'[90] On the other
hand, he could condemn the most benevolent despots for failing
to foster the *sine qua non* of human perfection: individual development.[91] He sacrificed a good deal of influence over the dominant
forces of his age and country in order to be what Sterling called
'a private in the army of Truth.'[92] He conceived *On Liberty* as
an impediment to be placed in the path which all the reform
movements of the age were taking.[93]

But even if Arnold and Mill had been temperamentally
capable of a rigorous adherence to the relativistic historical
method, it is doubtful that, as social and political reformers,
they would have wished to be irrevocably fettered by a method
that has necessitarian and conservative implications of the most
extreme kind. The belief that institutions and opinions should
be suited to the spirit and culture of an age encourages the
belief that such correspondence must have existed in the past;
the surrender to necessary, irresistible, and inevitable movements or tendencies is accompanied by the conviction that
whatever was, in the past, was right, because it must have been
established by some irresistible force, call it nature or Providence.

The historical method often led Arnold and Mill to accept
conservative and necessitarian conclusions which were ultimately contrary to their deepest convictions. Mill, in *The Spirit
of the Age*, held that 'human nature must proceed step by step,
in politics as well as in physics,' and so unwittingly deified
certain stages of civilization as necessary and indispensable
links in a long chain of causation.[94] He admired Coleridge for
asserting that 'long duration of a belief' is an adequate sign that
it was capable of satisfying 'some natural want or requirement
of human nature'; and he forgot that the true reformer can
hardly accept the idea of an intractable human nature which
needs to have certain permanent, morally neutral, needs
satisfied. He castigated the philosophers of the eighteenth
century who criticized existing institutions because their icono-
clasm 'threw away the shell without preserving the kernel';
and he overlooked the fact that institutions which are the product of natural growth are subject to inalterable natural laws
and can nowise be meddled with by the rationalistic reformer.[95]

The historical method—as well as his own volition and preferences—brought Arnold into similar difficulties. He was full of gratitude to Constantine for having prevented Christianity from dissipating itself in a multitude of 'hole-and-corner churches' during the early period when it was divorced from the two great traditions of human life (Hebraism and Hellenism), and for having placed it in the mainstream of history. Yet he also asserted that the world was saved from both Hellenism in its dying throes and Hebraism in its unenticing original form, by the introduction of early Christianity. Arnold's theology told him that the best moment of Christianity was the moment in which it was not in either mainstream of human life; but his view of history asked him to rejoice that Christianity was rescued by a Roman emperor. The historical method also allowed Arnold to say that 'if Hellenism was defeated, this showed that Hellenism was imperfect, and that its ascendancy at that moment would not have been for the world's good.'[96] Yet two thirds of Arnold's writing was devoted to the overthrow of a Hebraic ascendancy that had already endured almost two hundred years.

Arnold and Mill adopted the historical method because they thought it might favor social progress and individual development; they believed it could serve ends other than those it had served in the hands of Burke or Coleridge. If the historical and relativist approach sometimes inclined them to a conservative acceptance of some of the worst enormities of history, Arnold and Mill usually were aware that, as the elder Arnold Toynbee has said,

> the historical method is often deemed conservative, because it traces the gradual and stately growth of our venerable institutions; but it may exercise a precisely opposite influence by showing the gross injustice which was blindly perpetrated during this growth. The historical method is supposed to prove that economic changes have been the inevitable outcome of natural laws. It just as often proves them to have been brought about by the self-seeking action of dominant classes.[97]

Arnold and Mill employed the historical method in both ways, and never really resolved the conflict between them. If, on the one hand, Mill assumed an almost organic inevitability about the suitableness of past institutions to the cultural epochs they served, then, on the other, he frequently called history a dismal record of concessions won by classes of men through raw power—the vindication not of the rule of Providence but of the rule of force. 'History gives a cruel experience of human nature,' he said in *Subjection of Women,* 'in showing how exactly the regard due to the life, possessions, and entire earthly happiness of any class of persons, was measured by what they had the power of enforcing.'[98] If, on the one hand, Arnold believed that whatever was, was right, and was ordained by powers beyond the reach of man, on the other hand he called the belief that one powerful, governing class is able to represent the interest of other classes without power and representation 'the last left of our illusions.'[99] Mill called human nature 'a tree, which requires to grow and develop itself on all sides, according to the tendency of the inward forces which make it a living thing';[100] and Arnold said that 'all tendencies of human nature are in themselves vital and profitable; when they are blamed, they are only to be blamed relatively, not absolutely.'[101] But Mill also maintained that some instincts require not merely to be regulated but to be rooted out, and that the 'artificially created or at least artificially perfected nature of the best and noblest human beings, is the only nature which it is ever commendable to follow';[102] and Arnold sought to rescue men from their natural taste for the bathos by persuading them that 'man must begin . . . where Nature ends.'[103]

The more Arnold and Mill applied their historical method to the problems of their own age, the more the contradictory implications of the method came to the fore. Whereas everything that was established in the past must have been transitory, relative, partial, the perpetual recurrence of the same conflicting forces throughout history tempted the devotee of the historical method to believe that he could once and for all put an end to historical oscillation by forming into a complete synthesis all those partial elements which historical analysis had revealed, and establishing it on an absolute and permanent foundation. The dialectical theory of history suggested to Arnold and Mill both a process and an ideal: but the process of oscillation between alternative extremes was incompatible with the ideal of a harmonious fusion of those extremes. The desire to analyze came into conflict with the desire to synthesize; the insistence on development was contradicted by the insistence on harmony;

the wish to submit to the historical process in the guise of nature or the *Zeitgeist* was contradicted by the will to resist it in behalf of human perfection.

Much of the writing of Arnold and Mill must be viewed as an attempt to mediate between the claims of the historical process and those of the historical ideal. Arnold and Mill shared the same theory of historical process, and they derived from it similar ideals of human and social perfection. But they differed from one another in estimating the conflicting claims of the historical process on the one hand and the historical ideal on the other. When Arnold thought the time had come for synthesis, Mill demanded further analysis; when Arnold was ready for harmony, Mill insisted on more development; when Arnold demanded perfection, Mill still wanted freedom. I shall try to show, in subsequent chapters, how this disagreement over timing is at the root of all other disagreements between Arnold and Mill.

III

FATHERS AND SONS

It will be a curious problem for the critics of another age to work at, and, if they can, to work out, this influence of men more or less imbued with the savour and spirit of Philistia upon the moral Samson who has played for our behoof the part of Agonistes in the new Gaza where we live. From the son of his father and the pupil of his teacher none would have looked for such efficient assault and battery of the Philistine outworks. . . . A profane alien in my hearing once defined him as 'David, the son of Goliath.'   A. C. SWINBURNE [on Matthew Arnold]

How the sweet, ingenuous nature of the man has lived and thriven out of his father's cold and stringent atheism is wonderful to think, and most so to me, who during fifteen years have seen his gradual growth and ripening.

       JOHN STERLING [on John Stuart Mill]

I am falling foul . . . of John Mill in his modern and more humane mood . . . which always makes me feel that he is a deserter from the proper principles of rigidity and ferocity, in which he was brought up.   FITZJAMES STEPHEN

'I WOULD give James Mill as much opportunity for advocating his opinion,' Dr. Arnold once declared, 'as is consistent with a voyage to Botany Bay.'[1] What dire offense could have provoked such an outburst from the normally tolerant and liberal Dr. Arnold? Was not James Mill, like himself, a social reformer, a historian, an ordained minister of religion, a supporter of the nonsectarian education to be offered by the new London University?[2] Did not Arnold subscribe to the doctrine, announced by Bentham and propagated by James Mill, of the greatest happiness of the greatest number?[3] Did not a leader of the Oxford Movement accuse Arnold of having formed his system, in large part, upon 'the radical and destructive principles of the school of Mill'?[4]

The affirmative answers which must be given to these questions conceal almost as much as they reveal. Dr. Arnold was certainly a reformer, and the founder of a highly influential school of reformers; but he imbibed his principles of reform from the Bible and from Greek and Roman civilization. James Mill, as an adherent of scientific or philosophic radicalism, as it was called, derived his political principles from a school of thinkers who had their roots in the Enlightenment. No two historians could have set about their work with more different intentions than those of Thomas Arnold and James Mill. As for religion, Mill retained only the *odium theologicum* and a zealous and conscientious temper from his training for the Scottish Kirk; and nothing more clearly reveals the difference between his conception of sectarianism and Dr. Arnold's than the latter's resignation from the Board of Examiners of the London University when it decided to countenance the admission of Jews. If Arnold concurred in the Benthamite devotion to the greatest happiness principle, it was largely because he thought it an obvious corollary of Christian principles, which, he believed, should preponderate over all others. What the Oxford Movement, never very apt in discriminating among its enemies, took to be the destructive influence of the Utilitarians upon the Arnoldians was in reality the influence of more general forces working upon everyone in the age, Tractarians not excepted.

Yet the affirmative answers do reveal something; and it will help much towards our understanding of Matthew Arnold and John Stuart Mill if, without minimizing the contrasts between their fathers, we can underline the significant similarities between them, especially as educational theorists, as teachers, and as fathers.

It is hardly surprising that John Mill knew little of his father's early life, and nothing at all of James Mill's career in the Scottish Church until after his father's death.[5] For there is, perhaps, no more incongruous episode in the history of philosophic radicalism than that of James Mill's preparation for, and entry into, the Scottish Church.

The son of a shoemaker, James Mill, by his precocious intellectual acumen, won the favor of one of the local worthies, Sir John Stuart, whose habit it was to endow a few promising young men with the wherewithal to prepare for a career in the Church. Mill pursued a course of study in divinity at the University of Edinburgh from 1794 to the beginning of 1797. During his stay at the university, he was employed in the capacity of private tutor to the daughter of Sir John and Lady Jane Stuart. This was the first of his many involvements with the business of education.

In the course of his examination for the Presbytery, he delivered a homily on the text, 'Blessed are the pure in heart, for they shall see God.' He also gave several lectures on the fourteenth chapter of John's Gospel and the text, 'I am crucified with Christ.'[6] Is it any wonder that James Mill concealed his youthful waywardness from his son? Might not John Mill, had he known of the saddle bag full of sermons which his father kept in the attic of the family house in Queen Square, been reminded of Parson Adams?

According to the scanty evidence which is available, Mill was no great hand at preaching, and soon reverted to supporting himself as a private tutor to the children of several families. His son, however, seems to have been under the impression that his father did not follow a career in the church for which he had been ordained solely because of his disbelief in 'the doctrines of that or any other Church.'[7] Whatever the reason, James Mill, like so many of his countrymen before him, left Scotland to make his name and fortune in London.

Mill does not appear to have left all his religion behind him in Scotland. His translation from Edinburgh to London was not contemporaneous with his transition from clericalism to radicalism. Thus, shortly after his arrival in London, he remarked (somewhat in the vein, as will appear later, of Dr. Arnold's famous counterblast at Tractarian principles) that 'religion without reason may be feeling, it may be the tremors of the religious nerve, but it cannot be piety towards God, or love towards man.' He attacked Voltaire in one of his early periodical articles, where he wished for a general abatement of the public admiration for that writer. He reproved someone who had not been 'sufficiently respectful' of the Bible.[8]

It would not be long before Mill, immersed in the world of radical journalism[9] and fallen under the influence of Bentham, substituted an almost completely new set of opinions for those he had brought with him from Scotland. But I am now concerned with his character more than with his positive doctrines; and therefore more interested in what remained in him of the religious temper even after he had relinquished the doctrines of religion. For the force and uniqueness of James Mill's political influence—to say nothing of his influence upon his son—depended upon his ability to join a religious zeal to the doctrines of philosophic radicalism.

Benthamism was an eighteenth-century philosophy. Bentham's masters were Helvétius, Beccaria, and Hume; and Bentham himself had lived fifty-two years of his life in the eighteenth century. As John Mill wrote, Bentham's lot was cast 'in a generation of the leanest and barrenest men whom England had yet produced, and he was an old man when a better race came in with the present century.' Mill complained, in his essay on Coleridge, that the spirit of the eighteenth century was unable to instill emotion in its meditative or philosophical men, who wanted 'earnestness,' and that the era was one of 'compromises and half-convictions.'[10] Bentham, who was of a playful, almost boyish nature throughout his life, could only with great difficulty be prevailed upon to prepare his writings for publication. Even after they were published, Bentham was far better known, more influential, and more honored in the remote republics of Latin America than he was in England.[11]

But the prophet was not to die before he had found an apostle who would bring him honor in his own country. 'I have often reflected upon it as a very fortunate coincidence,' James Mill wrote to Bentham, 'that any man with views and propensities of such rare occurrence as mine, should happen to come in toward the close of your career to carry on the work without any intermission.'[12] Mill was justified in believing that no man was so fit as he to sustain the oral tradition after the master had departed. He had an unequaled capacity for staunch, unflagging devotion to a predetermined end. Leslie Stephen has remarked upon the extraordinary physical and mental vigor which were required for Mill to survive the struggle of his early years in London when he was simultaneously toiling over the writing of his *History of British India* and exercising rigorous control over the education of his children.[13] He was the ideal disciple because his handsome personal appearance, his great conversational power, and his ability to impress all who met him did not interfere with ready submission to his master and to the exigencies of his master's cause. Halévy holds that

> in Bentham he [James Mill] had found a great man, *his* great man, and he set it before himself as the purpose of his own life to give Bentham an influence in his own time and in his own country. In his relations with Bentham he was systematically docile, and determined, without ever abdicating his own personal dignity, never to allow any whim on Bentham's part to cool or extinguish a friendship which he considered necessary to the good of humanity.[14]

The earnest religious zeal which could no longer be commanded by the doctrines of Scottish Presbyterianism attached itself to the doctrines of Utilitarianism. Though John Mill, when he wrote of Bentham, belittled the eighteenth century for its want of earnestness, he called it, when he sought a niche in it for his father, 'an age of strong and brave men,' of whom James Mill was the last representative, a Voltaire living on into the nineteenth century. For the younger Mill could see that to the propagation of the best doctrines of the eighteenth century his father brought the peculiar qualities of the nineteenth—earnestness and zeal. Halévy calls James Mill the type of the religious man in his absolute devotion to the Utilitarian cause and his rigid maintenance of the bond between his personal existence and his ideas.[15] Stephen underlines the analogy to religious devotion when he says that Mill, once he adopted Bentham's doctrines, never swerved from a single one of what he took to be orthodox views, but accepted them 'as a mathematician might accept Newton's *Principia*.'[16] A more recent critic, recognizing the way in which Mill's training for the Church was reflected in the peculiarly Spartan flavor which he gave to the Utilitarian creed, says that, in Mill's hands, Utilitarianism 'becomes as stern a code of personal conduct as any Evangelical could wish, and as sharp a spear-point for a political crusade as the most ardent reformer could desire.'[17]

Indeed, no one ever gave the lie more thoroughly than James

Mill to the popular conception of the Utilitarian philosophy, with its felicific calculus, as an extended apology for hedonism. John Mill showed remarkable insight into his father's character when he said that James Mill's Utilitarian and epicurean moral standard, which took the resultant pleasure or pain as the chief criterion for judging an action, was contradicted by his disbelief in pleasure itself—moderation in the indulgence of pleasure being a watchword with the elder Mill.[18] Suspicious of emotion, indifferent to poetry,[19] James Mill was the prototype of the active, earnest, self-assured, single-minded reformers who were to change the face of England during the nineteenth century.

Along with the admirable traits of righteous religious devotion, there appeared in James Mill the unpleasant characteristics of the dedicated religious zealot. Even his acknowledged master, Bentham, was irked by Mill's severe manner, and complained that 'when he differs, he is silent. . . . He expects to subdue everybody by his positiveness. His manner of speaking is oppressive and overbearing. He comes to me as if he wore a mask on his face.'[20] Nothing provided more ammunition for James Mill's enemies than Bentham's remark (reported in Bowring's biography, called by Stephen the worst in the language) to the effect that James Mill's sympathy for the oppressed many was attributable to his antipathy for the oppressing few. George Grote, though convinced, after his first meetings in 1818 with the newly famous historian of India, that Mill was a profound thinker, disliked his 'cynicism and asperity,' and the readiness with which he depicted the faults of even the greatest men. So prevalent was the belief in Mill's hardness that the grief into which he fell after the death of his close friend, Ricardo, was received with as much incredulity as relief by his Utilitarian comrades.[21]

Nothing, finally, could be more unlike the doubt and hesitation and divided purpose which we shall observe in John Stuart Mill than the self-assured, active, energetic temperament of his father, who could consciously direct his powers to the attainment of a few supremely important ends, instead of dissipating them in doubt and distraction.[22] Morley recalled that many men who had known both of the Mills held the son inferior to the father 'in stoical tenacity of character, as well as in . . . concentrated force of understanding.'[23] John Stuart Mill thought his claim to the ability to contribute something to the science of method verged on audacity. His father unabashedly announced the intention of writing a book which would 'make the human mind as plain as the road from Charing Cross to St. Paul's.'[24] No biographer would dare to sum up John Mill's purpose in life by the simple—and accurate—account that Alexander Bain gave of James Mill's:

> Mill had formed for himself, at an early age, his ideals of pursuit. He conceived a certain ambitious future in the employment of his high intellectual powers; and, he combined with this, a wish to contribute something to the welfare of mankind.[25]

Thomas Arnold was born in 1795, in the Isle of Wight, the son of a postman and collector of customs. At age twelve he went to Winchester, where he remained until age sixteen. Four years at the famous public school influenced him so deeply that some of his polemical articles written later in life in defense of various public-school practices were defiantly signed, 'A Wykehamist.' Arnold was known to his classmates at Winchester as Poet Arnold because of his passion for reading, and propensity for writing, poetry. But already his temperament seemed to some less that of the poet than the sectarian. One of his schoolmates called him 'stiff in his opinions, and utterly immovable by force or fraud, when he had made up his mind, whether right or wrong.'[26]

Justice Coleridge (a nephew of the poet) who knew Arnold at Corpus Christi College in Oxford, described him as 'in argument bold almost to presumption and vehement; in temper easily roused to indignation, yet more easily appeased, and entirely free from bitterness.' We also learn from Coleridge that Arnold's chief interests at Oxford were the philosophers and historians of antiquity (especially Aristotle and Thucydides) rather than its poets.[27] In fact, Poet Arnold scarcely seems to have survived Winchester. He acquired very soon those earnest characteristics which caused his son to say of Dr. Arnold, 'Ah, my poor Father! he had many excellencies, but he was not a poet.'[28]

While he was a fellow at Oriel College, and before taking

orders, Thomas Arnold was afflicted by doubts about certain of
the doctrines contained in the Thirty-Nine Articles, and began
to fear lest he suppress his conscientious doubts in order to
secure a living. Justice Coleridge described the Arnold of this
period as possessed of 'an anxiously inquisitive mind, a scru-
pulously conscientious heart.' Keble, hearing of his friend's
difficulties, reproved him for excessive inquisitiveness on matters
of doctrine, and recommended that Arnold deaden his malady
not by reading and controversy, but by action of a certain kind,
by 'holy living.'[29]

The story of Arnold's malady and Keble's remedy for it
might serve as a parable of the rift which was to develop between
the liberal and the reactionary wings of the Anglican Church.
Strachey intimates that Arnold had no difficulty in applying
the remedy, which gave him 'perfect peace of mind, and a
settled conviction' (and left him with but one other problem—
his inability to rise at an early hour).[30] Yet Arnold insisted,
long after this early crisis, in his many battles with Newman
and the Oxford Movement, that 'faith without reason, is not
properly faith, but mere power worship; and power worship
may be devil worship.'[31] Contemporaries said of Arnold that he
awoke each morning 'with the conviction that everything was
an open question.'[32]

The truth probably lies somewhere in between Strachey's
opinion that Arnold quickly and easily suppressed any doubts
about doctrine, and the view which holds him to have been
conscientiously rationalistic about religious questions. In Arnold,
the spirit of inquiry was inseparable from a foundation of
belief. If he was conscientious, he nevertheless had a built-in
corrective to the corrosive effects of speculative analysis which
was wanting in men like Clough and his son Matthew, in
whom, as I shall try to show, he could instill conscientiousness
and even religiosity but not belief. If, on the one hand, he
found irrational power worship characteristic of Newmanism,
he also believed that the love of paradox and scepticism about
moral and intellectual questions which he observed in the
young men of 1838 led to Newmanism:

First, directly, as it leads men to dispute and oppose all the points
which have been agreed upon in their own country for the last

two hundred years . . . and then, when a man gets startled at the excess of his scepticism, and finds that he is cutting away all the ground under his feet, he takes a desperate leap into a blind fanaticism.[33]

Arnold was ordained in 1818 and married two years later. Marriage necessitated surrender of his Oriel fellowship and removal with his wife to Laleham, where he supported himself for ten years—as he had for a short time at Oxford—as a private tutor to young men preparing for the universities. During these years he formulated his ambition; and he was, as he admitted to a Rugby pupil, 'one of the most ambitious men alive.' Three objects he considered worthy of his ambition: 'to be the prime minister of a great kingdom, the governor of a great empire, or the writer of works which should live in every country.'[34] He would have been highly pleased could he have heard the young master who exclaimed, in *Tom Brown's Schooldays*: 'What a sight it is . . . the Doctor as a ruler. Perhaps ours is the only little corner of the British Empire which is thoroughly wisely and strongly ruled just now.'[35]

Eminently political ambitions in an ordained minister of religion seemed to Arnold no contradiction but almost the natural order of things. Whereas James Mill harnessed a religious zeal to the secular doctrines of social and political reform, Thomas Arnold tied the impulse for reform to the doctrines of religion. 'The world, as he conceived it,' writes G. M. Young, 'needed new rulers, and the rulers needed a new faith, which was to be found in the historical record, in the Bible, doubtless, most of all, but in the Bible . . . interpreted not by tradition, but by science, scholarship, and, above all, political insight.'[36]

Arnold wanted to make Christianity the law of the land. In 1828 he wrote that his views of things were becoming 'daily more *reforming*,' and that what he wished for above all else was 'a close union between Christian reformers and those who are often . . . falsely charged with being enemies of Christianity.' If he blamed reform movements which lacked a religious basis, then he also often blamed irreligion upon the church's indifference to political reform. He feared that many cases of irreligion were political in origin: men who disapproved of the existing social system frequently came to despise the church which was officially connected with it, supported by it, and almost invariably a staunch supporter of it.[37] Tocqueville was to make precisely the same observation in *Democracy in America,* but where Tocqueville concluded that religion can survive only if it separates itself from the state,[38] Arnold concluded that neither church nor state could thrive unless they were not merely united, but identical.

Even more literally than for James Mill, politics was for Thomas Arnold a matter of religious devotion. He never had to bother about transferring the earnest, evangelical zeal of his temperament from the religious to the political realm because he saw no difference between the two. He applied the Manichean philosophy (which he shared with James Mill[39]) to the material world of social and political forces more literally and directly than Mill would have dared. To Arnold, the world appeared to be approaching 'a greater struggle between good and evil' than had ever been seen; and men appeared to be 'dividing more and more into two divided [*sic*] parties of good and evil.' Since the true end of the Christian Church is 'the putting down of moral evil,'[40] how can it neglect the opportunity—rather, avoid the obligation—of making the state its arm for subduing the forces of evil? His conception of the political world as divided, like the spiritual world, between the powers of light and of darkness led Arnold to identify his foes with antichrist. He therefore had little difficulty, in any political controversy, in deciding between black and white, colors to which his uncertain pupils were often blind. His task, at any rate, was clear.

Like James Mill, Thomas Arnold brought the earnestness, the energy, the certitude and some of the rancor of the religious zealot to the business of political reform. As James Mill, working in the shadow of Bentham, founded a school of political reformers who subjected every institution to the test of utility, Dr. Arnold headed another school of reformers who were ready to measure every existing institution against the high standard of the moralists of Israel and Greece.

We must now see how the founders of the two most powerful traditions of nineteenth-century reform sowed the seeds of that dissension in the reform movement which was only checked, insofar as it was checked at all, by the intellectual influence of their sons.

It was from their fathers as much as from the spirit of their age that Matthew Arnold and John Stuart Mill learned the historical method. Both Thomas Arnold and James Mill were historians whose works created a considerable stir in their own day, however eclipsed they may be now. But with what different presuppositions did the Churchman and the Utilitarian approach the task of writing history!

For Dr. Arnold history was pre-eminently religious work. The significance of history lay in its revelation of God, and it was the historian's task both to define that revelation and to make it prevail, especially at a time when the forces of good and evil seemed to be gathering for a great final collision. Modern history, Arnold told an Oxford audience in his inaugural lecture as Regius Professor of History in 1841, gave signs of being the last step in civilization: 'It appears to bear marks of the fulness of time, as if there would be no future history beyond it.' The modern nations might well be the 'last reserve of the world'; if they are, the world's fate is in their hands, and the historian will ignore at his peril the strong possibility that 'God's work on earth will be left undone if they do not do it.'[41] Arnold undertook his most important work, the *History of Rome*, impelled by the sense of an immediate moral obligation to discredit the irreligious treatment of the crucial subject for which Gibbon had been responsible.[42]

Stanley was puzzled by his master's having turned to so engrossing a labor as the Roman history in 1833, just when he was in the midst of political and theological controversies; and he explained the action as an escape from the hectic broils of the present into the quiet refuge of the past.[43] But a simpler explanation lies ready to hand. Everything in Arnold's political and religious system which does not come from the Bible—and there is a great deal—comes from the ancient civilizations of Greece and Rome. His strong sense of the immediate relevance of the ancient writers lay behind his defense of the Rugby regimen of classical studies. 'Aristotle, and Plato, and Thucydides, and Cicero, and Tacitus,' he wrote, 'are most untruly called ancient writers; they are virtually our own countrymen and contemporaries.'[44] In teaching the classics at Rugby, he would insist (as his son would later) that the ancient authors belonged to a period of modern civilization like his own and that ancient Greece and Rome could afford men of the nineteenth century practically useful examples of ways to settle political questions, or, at the very least, to discuss them freely, eloquently, and profoundly.[45]

Arnold sensed that modern England was more akin spiritually to the ancient civilizations of Greece and Rome than to the feudal barbarism of that Middle Age which he so thoroughly despised. He therefore attempted, in his historical writing, to communicate to his readers the emotional proximity to ancient history which he himself possessed. He once wrote that it was indispensable for someone who wished to write a history of Rome to absorb himself as much as possible in the life of the ancient Romans, to live 'in a manner amongst them, and [have] them and their life distinctly before [his] eyes.' Stanley recalled how Arnold (who thus foreshadowed a habit of his son and of the younger Mill) used to throw himself into the Periclean age, and observe with all the emotion of an eyewitness the disastrous expedition to Syracuse.[46] John Stuart Mill (who mentioned Thomas Arnold far more frequently than he did Matthew Arnold) held that, although Dr. Arnold had barely perceived the possibility of scientific historical investigation, which is the highest stage of historical writing, he had nevertheless 'completely realized the second stage [historical investigation which attempts to see past civilizations as they really were and to recreate them faithfully]; and to those who have not yet attained that stage, there can scarcely be more instructive reading than his Lectures.'[47]

Mill could not have paid the same tribute to his father. For if Dr. Arnold, by an exercise of sympathy and imagination, tried to live as a Roman in order to write Roman history, James Mill, who really could have lived in and seen the India of which he was to write a vast history, declared that it was of the greatest advantage to him in writing the history of British India that he had never lived in the country or seen the people he was dealing with, and did not know their language. He argued that emotional submersion in a particular milieu and reliance upon the partial impressions of the senses were the greatest obstacles to impartiality. Even the most conscientious observer could not, after all, survey all the facts of Indian life. Consequently, those few objects of which he had received a strong sensual impression would obtain undue preponderance over phenomena of which he had only the second-hand knowledge of testimony. A serious historian knows that

> whatever is worth seeing or hearing in India, can be expressed in writing. As soon as everything of importance is expressed in writing, a man who is duly qualified may obtain more knowledge of India in one year in his closet in England than he could obtain during the course of the longest life, by the use of his eyes and ears in India.[48]

As Dr. Arnold brought to the writing of history the ideals of imaginative sympathy contributed to English sensibility by the Romantic movement, James Mill brought the censorious rationalism of the Enlightenment to his treatment of the superstitions and traditions of an 'uncivilized' society. J. S. Mill called his father 'the historian who first threw the light of reason on Hindoo society.'[49] Where Arnold brought heat, Mill brought light; where Arnold sought revelation, Mill sought reformation.

Macaulay, whose ideological quarrels with James Mill are notorious, called the *History of India* 'the greatest historical work which has appeared in our language since that of Gibbon,' and Bentham called it 'a work from which more practically applicable information on the subject of government and policy may be derived . . . than from any other as yet extant.'[50] But the judgment of the work—more particularly of the intellectual premises of Mill's approach to his subject—which was to prevail was that of William Hazlitt.

In an essay called 'On Reason and Imagination,' Hazlitt attacked the leading premises of eighteenth-century Neoclassical aesthetics. To the eighteenth-century awe for the grandeur of generality Hazlitt opposed his strong respect for the particular and concrete. Joshua Reynolds had defined the ideal in art as an abstract, generalized entity: the ideal tree, for example, does not exist except in the mind, for it is composed entirely of those characteristics which all trees have in common; the ideal becomes, in effect, the mean, and the mean is sought by eliminating the extremes, truth being reached by a process of subtraction. For Hazlitt the great weakness of art which tries to depict a generalized abstraction is that it deals with something that does not exist, a rationalistic conception and not a concrete reality. The 'general man' of whom eighteenth-century literature was so fond does not, after all, exist; he is only what is left when all the differences between men are subtracted and we are left with a 'common humanity.' Hazlitt's argument is moral as well as aesthetic. Since men are creatures of feeling as well as reason, their sympathies can only be fully aroused when appeal is made to their senses as well as their minds—and such an appeal can only be made by the artist or historian who shows particular men and real sufferings, and not by him who refuses to look at nature (to keep his eye, as Wordsworth said, on the object) and depicts only a generalized rationalistic conception:

> The aspect of a moral question is to be judged of very much like the face of a country, by the projecting points, by what is striking and memorable. . . . Millions of acres do not make a picture; nor the calculations of all the consequences in the world a senti-ment. We must have some outstanding object for the mind, as well as the eye, to dwell on and recur to—something marked and decisive to give a tone and texture to the moral feelings. Not only is the attention thus roused and kept alive; but what is most important as to the principles of action, the desire of good or hatred of evil is powerfully excited.[51]

Hazlitt's argument is that of a social reformer perhaps even more than it is that of an aesthetician. It is therefore all the more important that he should find James Mill's boast that he could write a better history of India from never having seen it than if he had been swayed from his rational detachment by particular and immediate impressions a flagrant example of the absurdity of the abstracting, generalizing habit. If what James Mill says were true, Hazlitt continued, then 'an artist would paint a better likeness of a person after he was dead, from description or different sketches of the face, than from having seen the individual living man.'[52]

Hazlitt's criticism of Mill's method of writing history was to become a commonplace. Leslie Stephen, criticizing Mill's rationalistic premises, called it a characteristically Utilitarian error 'to assume that a sufficient knowledge of fact can always be obtained from bluebooks and statistics. Some facts require imagination and sympathy to be appreciated, and there Mill was deficient.'[53] G. P. Gooch criticizes Mill's history for its lack of 'sympathy and imagination.'[54] Hazlitt, trained in abstract philosophy, insisted that suffering and injustice required imagination and sympathy to be appreciated. Eventually, John Stuart Mill, too, was to recognize that this want of sympathy and imagination in the Utilitarian ethos was a grave weakness in a philosophy of reform, and he would supplement the light of his father's school by the heat of Thomas Arnold's.

If the opposition between their fathers' ideas of history was far more absolute than the opposition—if indeed there was any—between the historical theories of Matthew Arnold and J. S. Mill, so too was the gulf between Dr. Arnold's and James Mill's conceptions of social and political reform wider and deeper than that which separated the social and political philosophies of their sons.

It was of the greatest importance to politics as well as religion that a man generally allowed to be 'one of the greatest and holiest men whom [his] generation [had] produced,'[55] and one whom G. M. Young has called the most influential figure, after Newman and Pusey, during the 1830s in the English Church, was a professed liberal.[56] When Dr. Arnold was not finding antichrist in the person of John Henry Newman, he was busy locating it in the spirit of conservatism, or aristocratic Toryism. Far less amiable and conciliatory towards the Tory aristocracy than his son was to be, Dr. Arnold saw in it the reincarnation of the Jewish aristocracy denounced by the prophets, and anything tinged with Jewishness was sufficient to make Arnold breathe fire: 'The wickedness of Toryism,' he proclaimed, is 'that spirit which crucified Christ himself.' Along with his fierce hatred of Toryism went an intense dislike of the High Church party, which, he said, had by and large been, throughout English history, opposed to improving measures of any kind. However great the sins of the Dissenters might be, those of the High Churchmen were less excusable because the latter had received the benefit of Aristotle and Thucydides, and the former had not.[57]

But conservatism, Stanley recalled, was not, for Arnold,

simply the characteristic of a party. Rather, it was 'the symbol of an evil, against which his whole life, public and private, was one continued struggle, which he dreaded in his own heart no less than in the institutions of his country.' He thought it folly to rely upon the works and ways of ancestors when we had the benefit of a greater amount of experience. Conservatism in the abstract he attacked as the most dangerously revolutionary of principles because (and here he provided the foundation for his son's attitude towards democracy)

> there is nothing so unnatural and so convulsive to society as the strain to keep things fixed, when all the world is by the very law of its creation in eternal progress; and the cause of all the evils of the world may be traced to that natural but most deadly error of human indolence and corruption, that our business is to preserve and not to improve.[58]

No one could doubt Arnold's liberalism. But there was less certainty about the precise nature of his liberalism. In a letter of 1831, J. S. Mill sent to d'Eichthal a list which included the names of those few Englishmen who might read the Saint-Simonian journal, the *Globe*, with interest and profit:

> Perhaps the Reverend Dr Arnold, Head Master of Rugby School near Birmingham, would be a proper person. He is one of the most enlightened and liberal of our clergy; but I am not sufficiently acquainted with his turn of mind to be able to judge in what manner your doctrines would affect him.[59]

A letter written by Thomas Arnold to Chevalier Bunsen a year and a half later suggests that Mill was more hopeful of Dr. Arnold's liberalism than he had any right to be. For antichrist, in Arnold's view, had lodged not only in the head of Newman, and in the heart of Toryism, but in the body of the Utilitarians. 'I detest Jacobinism,' he wrote, 'in its root and in its branches, with all that godless Utilitarianism, which is its favourite aspect at this moment in England. . . . They hate Christ, because he is of heaven and they are of evil.'[60]

For Arnold, reform had to go hand in hand with religion; democracy had to be allied with a powerful state and an established church. Arnold is often represented, by contrast with Newman, who had the effrontery publicly to doubt whether Arnold was even a Christian, as a latitudinarian tolerant of religious diversity. It is certainly true that he was far more tolerant than his son of Puritan Dissenters, but then his tastes were more in line with Puritanism than his son's, and he preferred Bunyan's *Pilgrim's Progress* to 'the rubbish of the theologians,' and Milton's tracts to the false shows of learning of the Anglican divines. He said that he preferred liberty to uniformity, but only 'where no principle is concerned.'[61] Arnold's pamphlet on church reform angered High Churchmen by its latitudinarianism and proposals for internal reform of church organization, but it also offended liberals by its defense of the idea of a national religious establishment which would be identical to the state. Perhaps it offended them still more by its attempt to wean Dissenters away from their association with secular reform movements, and to free them from the baneful influence of what Arnold called the 'antichristian party.'[62]

For all his vaunted latitudinarianism, Thomas Arnold remained a sectarian. He boasted, in a letter of 1834, that he had 'one great principle which I never lose sight of: to insist strongly on the difference between Christian and non-Christian, and to sink into nothing the differences between Christian and Christian [though he urged that Newman be denied the right to preach at Oxford even before Newman had gone over to Rome].'[63] Here was surely an arbitrary stopping at the halfway house between High Church exclusivism and deistic Voltairian tolerance. Did not the deist have as much right to call Arnold a sectarian as he did to apply the label to a Strict and Particular Baptist?

The split which occurred in the English reform movement over the religious question was foreshadowed by the different kinds of relations which Thomas Arnold and James Mill had with two educational projects of the second and third decades of the century. Both men were deeply interested in the Society for the Diffusion of Useful Knowledge, formed in 1827, and in the London University, begun as University College in 1828 and chartered as an examining board under a chancellor and a senate in 1836. Arnold's interest in the first project evaporated when he discovered that he was incapable of giving to the Society a religious tone; Mill continued as a member of the

Society's committee. Arnold and Mill participated in two different stages of the development of the London University. Mill, as a member of the council of the original London University, staunchly supported the principle of religious neutrality. Arnold was a member of the first senate of the new (chartered) London University until, in 1838, after many months of wrangling, he found himself unable to persuade his colleagues of their Christian duty to keep Jews out of the university.[64]

Opposition to church establishment was one of the cardinal principles of the Utilitarian wing of the reform movement. The Utilitarians generally, but not always, thought of the state and the church as the antitheses of democracy. In 1836, James Mill, in an article in the *Westminster Review*, came out against all ecclesiastical establishments, including, of course, the Church of England. He called ecclesiastical establishment 'essentially antichristian'[65] and maintained that religion is endangered unless it is left wholly free to individual choice. The evils wrought by the spirit of corporation in religion are traced in the article from the time of the Nicene Council onward. The English Church is shown by Mill to possess, no less than the Roman, the spirit of persecution natural to priestly corporations; and it has, moreover, affected not only religion and morality adversely, but also corrupted education, government, and national character.

But if the Utilitarians' hostility to church establishment was repulsive to Arnold, how much more revolting must have been their idea of what to put in place of the church. For Utilitarianism was not necessarily liberal and would entertain any idea or institution, including an establishment, which could stand the test of utility. In an essay of 1835 called 'The Church and its Reform,' Mill proposed to replace the Church of England Establishment with a genuine state church admitting all, regardless of opinion, to its services. Mill, in his ideal Sunday service, would have sermons delivered not only upon moral subjects but also upon science and useful knowledge, particularly government and political economy. After the instructional sermons, there would follow social amusements: sports, music, dancing (but with special care given to having none but proper and elevating dances). The acts of theistic worship would be capped by a grand communal dinner, at which—Mill had not discarded all Presbyterian views—no intoxicating liquors would be served.[66]

Mill's philosophy of reform was as far removed as it could well be from Thomas Arnold's. He belonged to, and may even be said to have founded, the school of those who came to be called the scientific as opposed to the sentimental reformers. John Stuart Mill pointed out that the cardinal principle of his father's political faith—his absolute and unswerving adherence to democratic suffrage—was based not upon sentimental or humanitarian grounds, 'not on the ground of liberty, Rights of Man, or any of the phrases . . . by which democracy had usually been defended,' but as an indispensable guarantee of good government.[67] Starting from such a premise, it was inevitable that James Mill should arrive at a conception of government very different from Thomas Arnold's. How startled one is, indeed, after dwelling upon Arnold's elaborate conception of government, drawn from the experience of Israel, Greece, and Rome, as the embodiment of the highest secular and religious powers united to mould the destiny of man, to turn back to James Mill's naked, seemingly truncated view of government, in his famous essay on the subject, as coming into existence by virtue of the joining together of a number of men who wish to protect themselves.[68]

The thinness of Mill's idea of government is partly due to his deductive approach to the whole problem. Though Mill, according to his biographer, 'knew as much history as any man of his time,' he found the empirical method unreliable here (for historical experience speaks with many contradictory voices on the question of which form of government is best), and placed almost complete reliance upon deducing forms of government from laws of human nature. From such laws he readily deduced that the only security for good government is the representative system.[69] The lack of historical depth in Mill's essay prompted Macaulay to label him a fifteenth-century Aristotelian schoolman born out of his time, and to remark that the essay was 'an elaborate treatise on Government, from which, but for two or three passing allusions, it would not appear that the author was aware that any governments existed among men.'[70]

The differences between Thomas Arnold and James Mill,

both of them fervent democrats and reformers, multiply the more we study and compare their expectations from reform.

In the first of a series of letters on the condition of the working classes addressed to the *Sheffield Courant* in 1831, Arnold, at a time when James Mill was feverishly pressing his efforts for passage of the Reform Bill, wrote of his impatience when he thought of the moral and physical condition of English working-men in conjunction with 'those long discussions upon the Reform Bill, which are engrossing the time, if not the attention, of Parliament.' In another letter to the paper, he doubted whether a reformed Parliament could do much to improve the economic situation. Pursuing a line of argument diametrically opposed to the Utilitarian ethos of enlightened self-interest, he said that the best plan of representation could do no more than enable people to choose those who could best represent them. But if those who possessed the suffrage voted merely on the basis of selfish or class considerations and not in the public interest, then the reformed Parliament would be as corrupt as the unreformed one.[71]

Mill anticipated reform with vastly different expectations. For all of his radicalism and his acidulous contempt for Whigs as well as Tories, he was still a man of the middle class; and in his essay on government he looked forward to the institution of popular representation because it would ensure the pre-ponderance of the middle classes, who are 'the chief source of all that has exalted and refined human nature.' The fact that Mill could put such faith in middle-class rule sufficiently indi-cates that for him the question of reform was still primarily political and not, as for Thomas Arnold, social and economic. In 1832, James Mill wrote to his good friend Lord Brougham (who later incurred John Mill's hostility and contempt) on the sub-ject of the mischievous antiproperty doctrines which were being sown among the people. With the millennial enfranchisement of the wealthy middle classes imminent, Mill looked with horror upon those agitators who defiled the movement for political reform by confusing it with social or economic questions. He berated Thomas Attwood, of the Birmingham Political Union, for giving 'an exaggerated description of the misery of the people, from low wages,' and alluded to the 'mad nonsense' of those who suggested that the whole produce of the country rightfully belonged to laborers. He urged it upon Brougham—the Lord Chancellor at this time—that the spread of anti-property doctrine 'would be the subversion of civilised society; worse than the overwhelming deluge of Huns and Tartars.'[72]

For Arnold, the real economic danger lay not in antiproperty doctrines, but in the rigid adherence of the middle classes to the Utilitarian doctrine of *laissez faire*. He described the doctrine as 'one of the falsest maxims which ever pandered to human selfishness under the name of political wisdom,' and called it the negation of the social bond.[73] More and more the economic question appeared to him to supersede all others, even (he could imply in 1839) the religious questions.[74] He showed no more hesitation than his son was to do in proposing government interference with property 'rights' when such interference seemed useful.[75]

We can recognize in the positive doctrines of Thomas Arnold and James Mill the germs of those two factions of the reformist or liberal movement whose opposition to each other did so much to retard reform and liberalism in the nineteenth century. On the one side, we see the now familiar doctrine which holds that there is no incompatibility between democracy and a strong state; on the other, the belief that *laissez faire* is the natural accompaniment and the necessary guarantee of democracy; in the case of Dr. Arnold, we recognize the liberalism which has little concern with liberty, and is obsessed by questions of social welfare; in the case of Mill, the liberalism which cherishes liberty, and is convinced that economic reform is inimical to it.[76]

It has been pointed out by many—including the principals involved—how Matthew Arnold and John Stuart Mill inherited the political and social philosophies of their fathers, and then, without rejecting the basic premises of these philosophies, modified them in the direction of greater comprehensiveness and broader sympathy. The two traditions of reform and liberalism whose opposition I have been observing were, when reformulated by the sons of Thomas Arnold and James Mill, to soften their mutual antagonism and come closer together. Otherwise the traditions could not have survived.

Even the rigid, self-assured Dr. Arnold sometimes sensed, towards the end of his life, that he had reached a dead end;

that his philosophy was not adequate, and that it needed to be completed by something which he could not supply. In 1839, he wrote of a morose conviction that it was 'too late' to reform society in England, and that 'we are engulfed ... inevitably, and must go down the cataract.' As his earlier militancy about social reform began to give way to a morbid fatalism about the condition of England, so, too, according to Stanley, his enthusiasm for the establishment of a reformed, comprehensive, national Church waned as he became convinced that the divisions in the Church were irreparable.[77] Perhaps, too, Arnold had come to see the justice of Bentham's incisive criticism of his most cherished doctrine—the ideal of a Christian State. For Bentham had said of the doctrine that Christianity is the law of England that, if it is true, disobedience of any single precept of the New Testament ought to be an indictable offense.[78] Arnold came to suspect—though perhaps he never seriously doubted—the perfect soundness and perfect Christianity of his guiding idea of the identity of church and state. Some conscientious scruple forced him to admit, in the course of a sermon, that

> I am myself so much inclined to the idea of a strong social bond, that I ought not to be suspected of any tendency to anarchy; yet I am beginning to think that the idea may be overstrained, and that this attempt to merge the soul and will of the individual man in the general body is, when fully developed, contrary to the very essence of Christianity. After all, it is the individual soul that must be saved, and it is that which is addressed in the Gospels.[79]

Despite their accomplishments as historians and as theorists of reform, it seems likely that Thomas Arnold and James Mill will be best remembered as educators. Generally, what first springs to mind at the mention of Arnold's name is the Rugby public-school education; the likeliest thing to be immediately associated with the name of James Mill is the peculiar kind of education which he gave his son, who has been called James Mill's most permanent and successful work.[80] Widely different as were their ideals of reform, Arnold and Mill were so deeply imbued with them that they conceived of education as the business of producing social reformers, and so devised, each of them, a special and peculiar kind of education the effects of which were to reverberate throughout the nineteenth century.

Thomas Arnold's biographer has drawn a striking picture of the way in which the Doctor managed Rugby with at least one eye trained upon the great world outside the school and upon what he thought its exigencies. 'Whatever interest he felt,' Stanley recalled, 'in the struggle of the political and ecclesiastical world, reacted on his interest in the school, and invested it in his eyes with a new importance.' His consciousness of the social evils of the time led him to check just those impulses in his public school boys which if left alone would serve to aggravate existing evils. Whenever he looked at English society, he thought of the roles which his own boys might be called upon to fill in it. Stanley marveled that 'even in the details of the school, it would be curious to trace how he recognised in the peculiar vices of boys the same evils which, when full grown, became the source of so much social mischief.'[81]

Education, as Arnold saw it, was not intended to prepare young men to accommodate themselves to life as it was, but to instill in them a devotion to an ideal of life as it ought to be. Their duty was not to accept life, but to question it. His hatred of conservatism, of the doctrine of letting things alone, or of letting them slide, made it incumbent upon Arnold to impress his students with the urgency and seriousness of the task that lay before them: for they were to be deprived of the comfort of indulging in the customary practices and believing in the inherited prejudices of the community.

Arnold had preached the doctrine of earnestness and of the duty to work even before coming to Rugby. Thomas Arnold the Younger recalled that all the Arnold children were brought up under the aegis of the precept ' "Work." Not, work at this or that—but, Work.'[82] A man who had been Arnold's pupil in the days at Laleham said that 'Dr. Arnold's great power as a private tutor resided in this, that he gave such an intense earnestness to life. Every pupil was made to feel that there was a work for him to do—that his happiness as well as his duty lay in doing that work well.'[83] Naturally, then, when he came to Rugby, Dr. Arnold preached to the boys, regarding the meaning of life, 'that it was no fool's or sluggard's paradise into which [they] had wandered by chance, but a battle-field ordained from of old, where there are no spectators, but the youngest must take his side, and the stakes are life and death.'[84]

Arnold's renovation of the inherited classical curriculum was not motivated simply by a desire to replace philology with history and literature. Would-be social reformers could hardly be expected to waste time over studies which made no contribution to their stock of ideas about social, political, and religious institutions. Arnold defended the study of Greek and Roman literature and history—perhaps this is why John Stuart Mill called him the most eminent of the reformers of the public schools[85]—precisely because he thought that Greek and Roman ideas, especially ideas of the state, were immediately relevant to the social problems bedeviling England. He minimized the importance of the physical sciences precisely because knowledge of them was of no use in political struggles:

> Rather than have physical science the principal thing in my son's mind, I would gladly have him think that the sun went round the earth, and that the stars were so many spangles set in the bright blue firmament. Surely the one thing needful for a Christian and an Englishman to study is Christian and moral and political philosophy. . . .[86]

No physical science was taught at Rugby.

In his primary object, that of producing social reformers, Dr. Arnold was successful. According to G. M. Young, the credit for the early Victorian reforms belongs largely to 'the Arnoldians,'

> a new type issuing from the Universities and public schools, somewhat arrogant and somewhat shy, very conscious of their standing as gentlemen but very conscious of their duties, too, men in tweeds who smoke in the streets, willing hearers of Carlyle, passionate for drains and co-operative societies, disposed to bring everything in the state of England to the test of Isaiah and Thucydides. . . .[87]

But the Arnoldians played a less happy role in the mental and spiritual history of the Victorian age than they did in its social and political history. For there was something in Dr. Arnold's course of education for social reformers which unintentionally produced, along with social reform, by-products of individual confusion and despair. Although John Stuart Mill praised Arnold's reform of the public schools, and even Lytton Strachey admitted that Arnold had purified and moralized the atmosphere of public-school life, the 'uncle' of Arthur Hugh Clough insisted, in the Epilogue to *Dipsychus*, that Arnold 'spoilt the public schools':

> 'Not that I mean to say that the old schools were perfect, any more than we old boys that were there. But whatever else they were or did, they certainly were in harmony with the world, and they certainly did not disqualify the country's youth for after-life and the country's service.'
>
> 'But, my dear sir [replies the poet], this bringing the schools of the country into harmony with public opinion is exactly—'

Exactly, we can add, what Arnold opposed. But for Clough's staunchly conventional uncle, the true purpose of education is 'simply to make plain to the young understanding the laws of the life they will have to enter.'[88]

To free the Rugby student from the trammels of custom and the yoke of public opinion and to burden him instead with the obligation of forming, or at least adopting, for himself his principles of action was Arnold's goal. 'The real servility which exists in England, whether amongst men or boys,' he wrote in an article on the public schools, 'is not an excessive deference for legal authority, but a surrender of individual judgment and conscience to the tyranny of public opinion.'[89] To protect the individual young man from this tyranny, the teacher had to remove him from the outside world to the confines of Rugby, and then, if possible, from the influence of his fellow Rugbeians to the influence of the master. Even in the days when he was a private tutor, Arnold showed 'a strong sense of the duty of protecting his charge, at whatever risk to himself, from the presence of companions who were capable only of exercising an evil influence over their associates.' He was never to lose his hypersensitivity to the influence of the many bad pupils over the few good, and he often wondered whether the child who had been removed from the influence of his family was really better off in the public schools, which were cursed by 'the spirit . . . of combination, of companionship, of excessive deference to the public opinion prevalent in the school.'[90]

But the teacher anxious to protect his pupil from the tyranny of public opinion by isolating him from outside influences was liable inadvertently to become a tyrant in his own person. Dr. Arnold certainly appears as the domineering tyrant in *Tom Brown's Schooldays*. At various points in the book he is seen as 'a terrible stern man,' a martinet who boxes the ears of young men who commit errors in Latin translation, a 'great, grim man' whom students fear 'more than anybody on earth.' Hughes describes, almost as if it were a Gothic horror, a scene in which Tom and his friend East are called into 'the awful presence' of Dr. Arnold.[91]

For Tom Brown and his schoolmates Dr. Arnold is also the man 'who knew everything,' and when he dies the hero of the novel feels 'completely carried off his moral and intellectual legs, as if he had lost his standing-point in the invisible world.'[92] Yet the physical conditions of the Rugby School prevented Arnold from exercising the influence he might have desired over his students, and obliged him to delegate much of his power to the sixth-formers. At home, on the other hand, his sway was uncontested, and Stanley recalled how, upon his death,

> the first thing which struck [Matthew] when he saw the body was the thought that [his and his family's] sole source of *information* was gone, that all that they had ever known was contained in that lifeless head. They had consulted him so entirely on everything, and the strange feeling of their being cut off for ever one can well imagine.[93]

Arnold knew that neither his influence nor that of Rugby could retain undivided sway over the minds of the young forever. Perhaps that is why he put so much stress on the importance of boys hastening as quickly as possible to the state of manhood, when the mind and character would be fully formed and less susceptible to new and foreign impressions than they had been in boyhood. Clough's uncle would later complain that the young men coming out of Arnoldian public schools were not young men at all but 'a sort of hobbadihoy cherub, too big to be innocent, and too simple for anything else.'[94] Arnold was always inveighing against 'moral childishness.'[95] In his defense of corporal punishment, he showed himself to be the very opposite of a Wordsworthian by discovering an 'essential inferiority in a boy as compared with a man.' Since children were by nature sinful it was not possible, at Rugby, to form Christian boys but only Christian men.[96] Little wonder, then, that the Rugby magazine should have described the school as a society whose members 'act and live not only as boys, but as boys who will be men.'[97]

But many of Arnold's pupils, when they became men, and left Rugby, began to suffer the ill effects of that liberation from custom, tradition, and public opinion which Arnold had granted them. Clough's old-fashioned uncle must have sympathized with the Rugby boys who cried out against the new Doctor who tore old customs up, and urged their comrades to 'stand up for the good old ways, and down with the Doctor!'[98] Another old-fashioned conservative, Edmund Burke, had insisted that men cannot live and act without the unquestioning acceptance of custom, prejudice, and the doctrines of a party. Without prejudice and ready-made opinions and ideas, Burke had argued, no one would be able to act unless he reverted to first principles and erected a new philosophical system for each decision he was forced to make.[99] But Thomas Arnold defied the spirit of conservatism and sectarianism. He ignored Burke's warning, and prayed that 'God grant to my sons, if they live to manhood, an unshaken love of truth, and a firm resolution to follow it for themselves, with an intense abhorrence of all party ties, save that one tie which binds them to the party of Christ against wickedness.'[100] In the following chapter, I shall examine the results of Dr. Arnold's inculcation of the habit of conscientious moral and intellectual independence in some of his students.

In the educational theories and practices of Thomas Arnold, we have seen the antecedents of some of the better-known spiritual crises of the Victorian age. We must now return to James Mill to examine the antecedents of the most famous mental crisis of all those which occurred in the nineteenth century, that of John Stuart Mill.

James Mill presented his theory of education in an article probably written in 1818, and published in the Supplement to the fifth edition of the *Encyclopedia Britannica*. An acquaintance with the article is as necessary to the understanding of Mill's conception of education as a knowledge of his son's autobiography; and the full significance of the education described in the autobiography cannot be grasped without reference to James Mill's essay.

Education was, for the elder Mill, a means to the dual end of rendering the individual an 'instrument of happiness' to himself and to his society (in this order). He therefore defined it, in his awkward way, as 'the best employment of all the means which can be made use of, by man, for rendering the human mind to the greatest possible degree the cause of human happiness.' He scoffed at the suggestion that knowledge is often sorrow, and said that to ask whether people ought to be educated is to ask whether they should be happy or miserable.[101]

Exhibiting that self-assured completeness of the limited man which so infuriated the opponents of Utilitarianism, Mill starkly defined knowledge by classifying it into the knowledge of events and the knowledge of the sequence in which events occur. The first kind of knowledge is expressed by history; the second kind by philosophy. The philosophy of mind, or psychology, reveals that 'the character of the human mind consists in the sequences of its ideas.' Upon this simple principle of the associationist psychology which he had inherited from Hartley, Mill rested his entire educational philosophy. The teacher, he said, can apply his knowledge of the order in which human feelings or thoughts take place to the training of individual minds in such a way that beneficial (rather than harmful) sequences of feelings or thoughts take place.[102]

John Stuart Mill claimed that the doctrine which holds that character is formed by circumstance through the principle of association gave to James Mill and his friends a scientific foundation for their willed belief in the perfectibility of mankind through education.[103] The Enlightenment's faith in reason and its belief in perfectibility were expressed in James Mill's theory of education as consisting in the skillful manipulation of sequences of thoughts or impressions. Since all differences between individuals and between classes of men result entirely from differences of education, it is education which is the sovereign remedy for individual or class inferiority, and the means for raising the whole human race to the level of its noblest individuals. 'What a field for exertion!' exclaimed Mill.

'What a prize to be won!' All that need be done to apply the science of education to the perfection of human life, he argued, is to decide what are the objects of human desire, to select the morally best means of attaining them, and 'to accustom the mind to fill up the intermediate space between the present sensation and the ultimate object, with nothing but the ideas of those beneficent means.'[104]

Since sequences of impressions begin to occur as soon as a child is born, it becomes extremely important to commence the child's education even while he is still in the cradle. James Mill attacked the general failure of educationists (excepting his beloved Helvétius and Rousseau) to recognize that education properly begins long before the age of six or seven when the child enters school. It begins in the cradle and perhaps (one cannot help thinking of Walter Shandy) even earlier. Because they grossly underestimate the domain of life which is subject to education, people in general underestimate the (in actuality unlimited) power of education. The educator must not for a moment relax his vigilance over his pupil, because 'if education does not perform every thing, there is hardly anything which it does not perform.' Moreover, Mill maintained, universal experience seems to confirm that the earliest sensations of life produce the greatest effects and that the earliest sequences of mental associations become the most ineradicable habits. It is therefore all the more important that education—and of the most vigilant kind—begin as soon as sensation itself begins.[105]

The 'trains' or sequences of thought which education should produce in the child ought to be not only beneficent but 'natural.' The child is to be habituated in trains that mirror nature rather than custom, which is supposed to be its opposite. As resolutely as Thomas Arnold, Mill flouted Burke's dictum that it is essential for man to submit to inherited prejudices of family, party, and nation if he is to retain the power of action. For Mill said that children should be trained to think and feel in accordance with the stringent dictates of reason rather than the easy prejudices of custom:

> If indication is given to children that ideas of disgust, of hatred, and detestation, are passing in the minds of those about them, when particular descriptions of men are thought of; as men of different religions, different countries, or different political parties

in the same country; a similar train becomes habitual in the minds of the children; and those antipathies are generated which infuse so much of its bitterness into the cup of human life.[106]

Mill felt quite as strongly as Arnold that sound education ought to be in conflict and not in harmony with public opinion. He maintained that the trains or habits which are ingrained in the child during the time of his domestic (parental and pre-school) education and then of his technical (school) education can and should serve to reduce greatly 'the influence of a vicious and ignorant society.' Yet the rewards and punishments which are at the disposal of social education (i.e., custom and communal traditions) are so great as to prevent all but a few individuals from following a path which runs counter to the direction in which society is disposed to move.[107] When we consider that James Mill held most of the social education made available by the England of 1806—the year of his eldest son's birth—to be debilitating and demoralizing in the highest degree, we understand why it was incumbent upon him to make the domestic and technical education of his son as rigorous as possible, so that John Mill might be prepared to withstand the contrary influences he would inevitably encounter in the non-Benthamite world at large.

Mill concluded his essay on education by calling political education the 'key-stone of the arch' of the educational system.[108] For his plan of education, like Thomas Arnold's, was a program for producing social and political reformers. Every step in the education of his eldest son found its justification in political terms. In 1815, he explained to Francis Place that he and his children would live for some time in France, Germany, and Italy, in order that they might learn the language and manners of different nations, and return to England with 'plenty of knowledge, the habit of living upon little, and a passion for the improvement of mankind.'[109]

His education of his son is the most famous and most important of James Mill's involvements in educational experiment, but not his only one. His first active exertion in public affairs was his co-sponsorship, with the Quakers Joseph Lancaster and William Allen, and with Francis Place, of Lancastrian schools, highly economical institutions in which students were to teach one another. He then joined with the same men under the benevolent guidance of Bentham himself, in the attempt to establish Chrestomathic schools, which, it was hoped, would spring up in the form of small Panopticons in Bentham's garden. The Lancastrian schools foundered on the question of religious teaching, the Chrestomathic scheme on matters of finance.[110]

As an educator, Mill was destined to be more successful on a smaller scale. Looking upon the improvement of the institution of government as the highest act of human virtue,[111] he attempted to imbue his son with the same kind of earnest, dutiful, almost religious devotion to the public good that Dr. Arnold preached at Rugby and in his home. James Mill tried to inculate in John what he thought of as the Socratic virtues:

> justice, temperance (to which he gave a very extended application), veracity, perseverance, readiness to encounter pain and especially labour; regard for the public good; estimation of persons according to their merits, and of things according to their intrinsic usefulness; a life of exertion in contradiction to one of self-indulgent sloth.[112]

The younger Mill's memory did not exaggerate the importance which his father attached to Spartan temperance as a political virtue: James Mill had announced in the essay on education that the two qualities of mind which education should seek to produce are intelligence and temperance, or 'a perfect command . . . over a man's appetites and desires.'[113]

The aura of religiosity haunts John Stuart Mill's account of his education. He recalled how, after his first reading of Bentham's magnum opus, the *Traité de Législation*, the principle of utility had unified all he had formerly thought and known, and given him 'a creed, a doctrine, a philosophy; in one among the best senses of the word, a religion; the inculcation and diffusion of which could be made the principal outward purpose of life.'[114] When he left the faith, John Mill had a strong sense of his apostasy from Bentham. David Masson recalled how, in 1843, Mill, while discussing Bentham's remaining disciples, suddenly remarked: 'And I am Peter, who denied his Master.'[115]

James Mill's notions of education resembled Thomas Arnold's in another particular: the desire to protect the student from alien and corrupting influences, whether of public opinion or of evil companions or of wrong-headed instructors. So zealous was Mill for the right training of young minds that, when he heard from his friend Napier that a rigid conservative stood a good chance of obtaining the Edinburgh University chair of Moral Philosophy, whence he might corrupt the minds of 'the unfortunate youth,' he (Mill) was ready to give up his great opportunities at India House, and his cherished London residence, in order to take the professorship himself.[116]

With the education of his eldest son, James Mill would take no chances whatever. He assumed sole charge of John's education from the very beginning, and when opportunities arose in 1821 and 1823 for John to go to Cambridge, James Mill told the interested parties that his son already knew more than he could ever be taught at Cambridge.[117] The young Mill hardly ever consorted with other children, who might have set going maleficent trains of associations. Nearly all the adults he met were his father's political associates who visited the house from time to time. When he went abroad to France, he was put in custody of Jeremy Bentham's brother. We get a good indication of how closely the Benthamites guarded their special prodigy (almost their secret weapon) from a letter written by Bentham to James Mill in 1812. Mill had fallen ill, and Bentham, fearing the worst, at once offered his services in the education of the budding social reformer in the event James Mill did not remain to complete his task:

> If you will appoint me guardian to Mr. John Stuart Mill, I will, in the event of his father's being disposed of elsewhere . . . by whipping or otherwise, do whatsoever may seem most necessary and proper, for teaching him to make all proper distinctions, as between the Devil and the Holy Ghost, and how to make Codes and Encyclopedias, and whatsoever else may be proper to be made, so long as I remain an inhabitant of this vale of tears.[118]

No wonder, then, that John Mill said he had been 'brought up more exclusively under the influence of a peculiar kind of impressions than any other person ever was.'[119] His father, like Thomas Arnold, rescued his pupil from the tyranny of public opinion only to place him under a more immediate and irresistible subjection. Utterly devoted to his son's education as he was, it is not surprising that James Mill should have become intellectually intolerant of John's perverse aberration. The son recalled in his autobiography how he refrained from seeking a mutual understanding with his father when he had wandered a sizable distance from orthodox philosophic radicalism because 'my father was not one with whom calm and full explanations on fundamental points of doctrine could be expected, at least with one whom he might consider as, in some sort, a deserter from his standard.'[120] The testimony of contemporaries reveals that James Mill was looked upon by his children, as was Thomas Arnold by his pupils, as a fearful tyrant.[121]

There is one more resemblance between the programs for educating social reformers advocated and carried out by Dr. Arnold and James Mill. James Mill, like Dr. Arnold, had no patience with the state of boyhood nor any respect for what Henry Adams ironically called its inalienable rights. He provided his son neither with children's books nor children's playthings. John Stuart Mill complained in later life that he had never really been a boy; and the intellectual head start of twenty-five years which he enjoyed over his contemporaries is partly attributable to his having skipped boyhood.[122] It was the opinion of Clara Mill that her brother had been made to think 'prematurely' and had consequently missed the enjoyments of life specially reserved for boyhood.[123] John Stuart Mill spoke as much from personal experience as from accurate general observation when he told Gustave d'Eichthal that, whereas the French are eternal children, 'with us even children are care-hardened men of fifty.'[124]

James Mill was as successful in his educational venture as was Thomas Arnold. He produced a social reformer whose influence may have been greater than that of all the Arnoldians put together. But his system of education also produced unexpected and undesired by-products in his son. Could it have been otherwise with a system which, though it insisted that happiness was the end to which education was devoted, confessed itself unable to define happiness? The title of the third section of Mill's 'Education' reads as follows:

Happiness, the End to which Education is devoted.—Wherein it consists, not yet determined.[125]

IV

A SMACK OF HAMLET

Hence we see in Hamlet a great, an almost enormous, intellectual activity, and a proportionate aversion to real action, consequent upon it, with all its symptoms, and accompanying qualities. . . . He vacillates from sensibility, and procrastinates from thought, and loses the power of action in the energy of resolve.

Hamlet's character is the prevalence of the abstracting and generalizing habit over the practical. He does not want courage, skill, will, or opportunity; but every incident sets him thinking; and it is curious, and, at the same time strictly natural, that Hamlet, who all the play seems reason itself, should be impelled, at last, by mere accident to effect his object. I have a smack of Hamlet myself, if I may say so.

SAMUEL TAYLOR COLERIDGE

JOHN STUART MILL, in a state of apparently unmotivated depression, was suddenly stricken, in the autumn of 1826, with the consciousness that the achievement of all the social, intellectual, and political reforms to which his education had dedicated him would not give him happiness. In what has become a *locus classicus* of the literature of confession, Mill described the moment in which the futility, as it then seemed, of his life revealed itself to him:

It occurred to me to put the question directly to myself: 'Suppose that all your objects in life were realized; that all the changes in institutions and opinions which you are looking forward to, could be completely effected at this very instant: would this be a great joy and happiness to you?' And an irrepressible self-consciousness distinctly answered, 'No!'

107

The Benthamite religion which he had adopted just four years earlier seemed to have exhausted its motive power, and Mill found himself with 'nothing left to live for.'[1]

Even at the height of his affliction, Mill did not seriously consider consulting his father about his emotional quandary. The question he imagined he ought to have put to his father was the question which a bitter Macbeth had posed for his physician: 'Can'st thou not minister to a mind diseas'd?' But James Mill was hardly the physician who could cure his son's disease.

> My education, which was wholly his work, had been conducted without any regard to the possibility of its ending in this result; and I saw no use in giving him the pain of thinking that his plans had failed, when the failure was probably irremediable, and, at all events, beyond the power of his remedies.[2]

Mill explained his mental and spiritual crisis in terms of his father's philosophy of education. His account, given in the *Autobiography*, of the genesis and the underlying cause of his ordeal rests upon the assumption that there is an inevitable, endless conflict between feeling and analysis, between the human power which moves to action and the power which resists action. The habit of analysis, according to Mill, has 'a tendency to wear away the feelings' even in normal circumstances; but its corrosive force doubles when it works in an individual who has been brought up on the principles of association to be a social reformer.[3]

James Mill's associationist psychology relied heavily upon education to undo the customary or traditional (but not necessarily natural) associations between pleasure or pain and particular actions and beliefs. It sought to replace old and harmful associations (say, for example, between pleasure and high social rank) with 'associations of pleasure with all things beneficial to the great whole, and of pain with all things hurtful to it.' But the effectiveness of such a heterodox education, John Stuart Mill now argued, will depend upon the strength it can give to the associations formed early in the lives of would-be reformers. The same habit of analysis which has served to wear down traditional associations or trains of thought will work even more swiftly and destructively upon those associations which have been newly formed in opposition to the inertia of custom and tradition. James Mill, in educating his son, failed to discover the means of securing and maintaining the newly formed associations between pleasure and the ultimate objects of Benthamite reform:

> My education had failed to create these feelings in sufficient strength to resist the dissolving influence of analysis, while the whole course of my intellectual cultivation had made precocious and premature analysis the inveterate habit of my mind.[4]

So pervasive did young Mill's *ennui* and spiritual indifference become that he began to regret even the loss of the attraction he once felt towards certain petty vices of personality. He saw that the life of the will is often dependent upon the ability to will what is evil, or, at least, morally reprehensible. He regretted that 'the fountains of vanity and ambition seemed to have dried up within me, as completely as those of benevolence.'[5] His attitude recalls Milton's tribute to Fame as that last infirmity of noble mind; and it resembles, as will appear later, Matthew Arnold's attachment to superficial vices of personality as a shield against his father's conscientious fervor.

The first step in Mill's recovery from the mood of depression and futility came with his reading of Marmontel's *Mémoires d'un père* and not, as is often thought, after his reading of Wordsworth. In reading a scene in which Marmontel describes his father's death and his own subsequent resolution to fill his father's place, Mill felt overcome by a lively imagination of the event and a deep impression of its emotional force, 'and . . . was moved to tears.' From this time forward, in spite of occasional relapses, Mill felt less heavily burdened, and even entertained hopes that he still possessed the power to feel.[6] This particular literary experience in Mill's life helps to account for the emphasis, in his critical theory, upon literature's power to make people feel.

In the slow course of recovery from his mental crisis, Mill came to adopt what he called Carlyle's 'anti-self-consciousness' theory. This says that happiness is properly not an end consciously pursued but a by-product of other pursuits. Mill did not become, like Carlyle (and Shaw after him), a Thersites railing against happiness, for he still held that 'happiness is the test of all rules of conduct, and the end of life.' Only it could not be pursued directly:

> The only chance is to treat, not happiness, but some end external to it, as the purpose of life. Let your self-consciousness, your scrutiny, your self-interrogation, exhaust themselves on that; and if otherwise fortunately circumstanced you will inhale happiness with the air you breathe, without dwelling upon it, without either forestalling it in imagination, or putting it to flight by fatal questioning.

Mill did not, in adopting Carlyle's theory, become, like its propounder, a believer in action for its own sake; he did not seek an escape from thought. On the contrary, he followed his remarks on Carlyle with an account of the experiences which had taught him that life was not coextensive with action, and that 'there was real, permanent happiness in tranquil contemplation.'[7]

Mill's recovery from the state of mental anguish was to be completed by his experience of the poetry of Wordsworth. But before Mill could seek a cure he had to understand his illness; and he was aided in his diagnosis by another Romantic poet: Samuel Taylor Coleridge. In those very pages of the *Autobiography* where John Stuart Mill lamented his father's emotional obtuseness, he resorted, on two separate occasions, to the poetry of Coleridge as the most fitting and articulate expression of his despair. He described the early months of his crisis by the lines from the 'Dejection Ode':

> A grief without a pang, void, dark and drear,
> A drowsy, stifled, unimpassioned grief,
> Which finds no natural outlet or relief
> In word, or sigh, or tear.

He found the true estimate of his own attempt to apply the Carlylean dogma of Work to his problem in Coleridge's

> Work without hope draws nectar in a sieve,
> And hope without an object cannot live.

His choice of Coleridge out of the abundant modern literature of despair available to him in 1854 confirmed the suspicion of his friends that Mill's early leavening of Benthamite doctrine with the thought of Coleridge had been the intellectual reflection of a profound spiritual change. Mill himself acknowledged, in a letter of 1834, that 'few persons have exercised more influence over my thoughts and character than Coleridge has.'[8] Perhaps Leslie Stephen had these pages of the *Autobiography* in mind when he concluded his biography of James Mill by instituting a remarkable comparison between him and Coleridge:

> S. T. Coleridge, born about six months before Mill, died two years before him. The two lives thus coincided for more than sixty years, and each man was the leader of a school. In all else the contrast could hardly be greater. If we were to apply the rules of ordinary morality, it would be entirely in Mill's favour. Mill discharged all his duties as strenuously as a man could, while Coleridge's life was a prolonged illustration of the remark that when an action presented itself to him as a duty he became physically incapable of doing it. Whatever Mill undertook he accomplished, often in the face of enormous difficulties. Coleridge never finished anything, and his works are a heap of fragments of the prolegomena to ambitious schemes. Mill worked his hardest from youth to age, never sparing labour or shirking difficulties or turning aside from his path. Coleridge dawdled through life, solacing himself with opium, and could only be coaxed into occasional activity by skilful diplomacy. Mill preserved his independence by rigid self-denial, temperance, and punctuality. Coleridge was always dependent upon the generosity of his friends. Mill brought up a large family, and in the midst of severe labours found time to educate them even to excess. Coleridge left his wife and children to be cared for by others. And Coleridge died in the odour of sanctity, revered by his disciples, and idolised by his children; while Mill went to the grave amidst the shrugs of respectable shoulders, and respected rather than beloved by the son who succeeded to his intellectual leadership.[9]

John Stuart Mill was obliged to resort to Coleridge rather than to his father or to Bentham because Coleridge had suffered and because the Utilitarians, most of whom had a strong admixture of stoicism in their moral constitution, had not. Jeremy Bentham was reproached by many people for many things, but it is doubtful that anyone but John Stuart Mill ever blamed him for his failure to have a nervous breakdown:

> He [Bentham] had neither internal experience nor external; the quiet, even tenor of his life, and his healthiness of mind, conspired to exclude him from both. He never knew prosperity and adversity, passion nor satiety: he never had even the experiences which

sickness gives; he lived from childhood to the age of eighty-five in boyish health. He knew no dejection, no heaviness of heart. He never felt life a sore and a weary burthen. He was a boy to the last. Self-consciousness, that daemon of the men of genius of our time, from Wordsworth to Byron, from Goethe to Chateaubriand, and to which this age owes so much both of its cheerful and its mournful wisdom, never was awakened in him.[10]

John Stuart Mill had come to believe, what his father doubted, that knowledge was often sorrow and that sorrow often gave knowledge.

Not only had Coleridge suffered, he had suffered in the same way as John Stuart Mill: from the tendency of analysis, or 'abstruse research'[11] to destroy his powers of feeling and acting, and his spirit of imagination. By a brilliant sympathetic identification (which has since grown into a commonplace), he discovered the prototype of his spiritual dilemma, and of what Mill rightly called the daemon of all the great men of the age, in the suffering of Hamlet. Coleridge saw Hamlet as a man with 'a great, an almost enormous intellectual activity, and a proportionate aversion to real action, consequent upon it': a man who 'vacillates from sensibility, and procrastinates from thought, and loses the power of action in the energy of resolve.' Indeed, added Coleridge with a mixture of pride and shame, 'I have a smack of Hamlet myself, if I may say so.'[12]

But the suffering Hamlet and the suffering Coleridge saw deeply into the secrets of the universe. Their suffering was the price they paid for their knowledge. Mill, conscious of this fact, was to make brooding self-consciousness a touchstone of value in modern life and art. In an early (1833) unpublished criticism of Browning's *Pauline*, Mill offered the sharpest kind of rebuke to the poet because he was 'possessed with a more intense and morbid self-consciousness than I ever knew in any sane human being.' He condemned the poem as mere confessional literature, a psychological history filled with beautiful passages but a dreadful failure as a whole. He blamed the poem for exhibiting faults which Arnold would later attribute to all Romantic poetry: overattention to expression (fine lines or passages), subjectivism, and a fondness for giving the auto-biography of the poet's mind.[13] Gradually, however, Mill came to see that the state of mind revealed in Browning's poem was the state in which he and most of his contemporaries were condemned to live; and he decided to make the best of it. He wrote to Carlyle in 1833 that he expected another relapse into one of those moods of spiritual dryness and depression which usually afflicted him for several months. But even they served some useful purpose, and therefore, he wrote:

> I will not if I can help it give way to gloom and morbid despondency, of which I have had a large share in my short life, and to which I have been indebted for all the most valuable of such insight as I have into the most important matters, neither will this return of it be without similar fruits, as I hope and almost believe.[14]

Now the two cardinal principles of Bentham's system were that there is no difference in the quality of pleasures, and that pleasure can be considered apart from the objects which give rise to it and from the persons who feel it. Mill denied both principles because experience had taught him that 'a being of higher faculties requires more to make him happy, is capable probably of more acute suffering, and certainly accessible to it at more points, than one of an inferior type.' He went still further—too far, in fact, any longer to be considered a believer in the pleasure-pain calculus—and maintained that the highly endowed person would never be completely satisfied with the happiness available to him: 'It is better to be . . . Socrates dissatisfied than a fool satisfied.'[15]

Mill's acceptance of an inevitable connection between self-consciousness, sorrow, and knowledge helped him to make a virtue out of necessity. Not only did he insist that a hero of Plutarchan stature might exist 'amidst all the pettinesses of modern civilization, and with all the cultivation and refinement, and the analyzing and questioning spirit of the modern European mind';[16] he maintained that modern poetry was superior to the poetry of the ancients in its substance (though not in its form) precisely because, like modern science, it plumbed nature more deeply:

> The modern mind is, what the ancient mind was not, brooding and self-conscious; and its meditative self-consciousness has discovered depths in the human soul which the Greeks and Romans did not dream of, and would not have understood.[17]

If wisdom could emerge from Hamlet-like gloom and despondency, could action arise from intellectual activity cut loose from its moorings in customary, inherited modes of life? Mill believed that it could, and tried to refute Burke's assertion that without blind submission to prejudice and custom the individual will be paralyzed by inaction. He was aware that Utilitarianism, like most 'new' standards of morality, stood accused of preventing its adherents from undertaking action of any kind until they had consulted the first principle of utility and painstakingly weighed and measured the effects of a particular action upon the general happiness. He presented two arguments to obviate this criticism. First, he asserted, there is no reason why utility cannot, like any other first principle, generate its own secondary principles, which might be inculcated by education and made to prevail through the influence of law and opinion. But, Mill conceded, perhaps the charge leveled by Burke and others is meant to apply only to the transitional or critical period when the old sanctions of action have been overthrown and new ones have not yet been established: in other words, to a period such as the middle of the nineteenth century. In that case, surely neither philosophers nor ordinary persons will ignore all the 'intermediate generalisations' which human experience has produced simply because those generalizations are known to fall far short of perfection: 'The beliefs which have . . . come down,' Mill concluded his rejoinder, 'are the rules of morality for the multitude, and for the philosopher until he has succeeded in finding better.'[18]

The modern obsession with action has led some critics to deal harshly with nineteenth-century Hamletism. Henry Adams, for example, wrote that

> the class of Englishmen who set out to be the intellectual opposites of Bright, seemed to an American by-stander the weakest and most eccentric of all. These were the trimmers, the political economists, the anti-slavery and doctrinaire class, the followers of de Tocqueville, and of John Stuart Mill. As a class, they were timid—with good reason—and timidity, which is high wisdom in philosophy, sicklies the whole cast of thought in action.[19]

But Morley, who perfectly characterized Mill's intellectual receptivity by calling it a kind of emotional sensibility, distinguished two kinds of Victorian Hamlet complex. Mill's intellectual sensibility, he maintained, was the sensibility which arose from strength and not from weakness. 'We may estimate the significance of such a difference,' he continued, 'when we think how little, after all, the singular gifts of a Newman or a Maurice have done for their contemporaries, simply because these two eminent men allowed consciousness of their own weakness to "sickly over" the spontaneous impulses of their strength.'[20] The Hamlet figure appears once more, but its usual application, in terms of nineteenth-century personalities, has been reversed.

Dr. Arnold, whose turn of mind, even in his most abstruse historical investigations, was, as we have seen, eminently practical, thought he understood why Coleridge, despite his great gifts, had failed of the highest achievement:

> I think, with all his faults, old Sam was more of a great man than anyone who has lived within the four seas in my memory. It is refreshing to see such a union of the highest philosophy and poetry, with so full a knowledge, on so many points at least, of particular facts. But yet there are marks enough that his mind was a little diseased by the want of a profession, and the consequent unsteadiness of his mind and purposes; it always seems to me that the very power of contemplation becomes impaired or perverted when it is made the main employment of life.[21]

Would that Arnold had seen how the moral and intellectual discipline which he instituted at Rugby was calculated to produce like effects in many of his scholars!

Arthur Hugh Clough is often singled out as the typical victim of Dr. Arnold's Rugby education. The interest in the relationship between Clough and Matthew Arnold centers upon the fact that Matthew, who felt the same influences as Clough, and felt them with greater frequency and at closer proximity, managed to escape without being overwhelmed by them. The editor of Arnold's letters to Clough sees the irony of the attempt of Dr. Arnold's son 'to remove from Clough an excessive habit of mind that Dr. Arnold had himself engendered, or at least fixed.'[22] The effects of the Rugby education provided by Thomas Arnold had, in Clough's case, to be undone by his son.

Clough had been the apple of Dr. Arnold's eye at Rugby. Intellectually astute, morally upright, he was eagerly awaited at Oxford as the ideal product of the new Rugby system. But he disappointed—the Rugby conscience and the Rugby spirit of independent inquiry proved to be not armour against the shafts of Dr. Arnold's enemies, but direct encouragements to their attacks.

Clough arrived at Oxford when it was in the midst of a turmoil caused by Newman and the Tractarians; and when it was, in the opinion of Goldwin Smith, less a place of learning than a battlefield for theological warfare.[23] Clough's faith was shaken and his mind unsettled (deeply and permanently, if we can believe the man who, by his own testimony, was primarily responsible for the damage—W. G. Ward)[24] by the intense theological controversies. He neglected his studies to such an extent that the special protégé of Dr. Arnold failed to take a first in the academic awards.

Dr. Arnold had imbued Clough with the conscientious spirit of inquiry and also with a religious temper. But when Clough's belief in religious doctrine was shaken, the Arnoldian assets turned into liabilities. Too religious by temperament to be satisfied by unbelief, Clough was also too intellectually conscientious to be satisfied by the conventional supports and traditional evidences of his religion. In 1848, finding himself unable to subscribe in good conscience to the Thirty-Nine Articles of the Anglican faith, he resigned his fellowship at Oriel College.

The fullest and most accurate account of the mental bugbears which beset Clough is that which he himself gave in his review of a volume of poems by Alexander Smith and of two volumes by a poet called 'A'—that is, by his friend Matthew Arnold. Only the bugbears were presented not as the obsession of the reviewer, but as the curse of the anonymous poet. Clough contrasted the impassioned mechanic-poet, Alexander Smith, full of righteous purpose, with the 'reflecting, pondering, hesitating, musing, complaining' 'A.' He discerned in the author of *Empedocles on Etna* all the evils of what Mill called the analyzing and questioning habit of the modern European mind; and he concluded that

> for the present age, the lessons of reflectiveness and the maxims of caution do not appear to be more needful or more appropriate than exhortations to steady courage and calls to action. There is something certainly of an overeducated weakness of purpose in Western Europe—not in Germany only, or France, but also in

more busy England. There is a disposition to press too far the finer and subtler intellectual and moral susceptibilities; to insist upon following out, as they say, to their logical consequences, the notices of some organ of spiritual nature; a proceeding which perhaps is hardly more sensible in the grown man than it would be in the infant to refuse to correct the sensations of sight by those of touch. Upon the whole, we are disposed to follow out, if we must follow out at all, the analogy of the bodily senses; we are inclined to accept rather than investigate; and to put our confidence less in arithmetic and antinomies than in

'A few strong instincts and a few plain rules.'[25]

The disposition to think rather than act, and to accept nothing as true that is not proved, nothing as good that is not true, which Clough claimed, justifiably enough, to detect in the author of *Empedocles on Etna* and *The Strayed Reveller*, was essentially his own disposition. His brash foot-stampings and bugle calls to action were affirmations of his will, and not of his conviction. Anyone who had read the correspondence which Clough carried on with Arnold in the years, and even the weeks, prior to the appearance of Clough's review, would at first have rubbed his eyes in disbelief upon reading Clough's loud assurances, but then probably have recognized that his criticism of Arnold was, in effect, a criticism of himself, a public *mea culpa*. For the burden of Arnold's letters to Clough was, as we shall see presently, the attempt to talk, coax, or jar his friend out of his earnest habit of moral and intellectual conscientiousness.

Matthew Arnold's own public confession of 1852—*Empedocles on Etna*—seemed to some of his friends and relatives as absolute a contradiction of his normal demeanor as Clough's public statement in the review of 1853 was of his private convictions. For Matthew, despite his Rugby training and his home discipline, seemed, to outward view, the very opposite of the earnest Rugbeian, and hardly at all the son of his father. Some hard shell of personality appeared to have protected his character from the forces which were trying to mould it.

The theological controversies of Oxford which ruined Clough left Arnold unruffled.[26] There is a mixture of envy and disapproval in Clough's description of Arnold at college:

Matt is full of Parisianism; Theatres in general, and Rachel in special: he enters the room with a chanson of Béranger's on his lips—for the sake of French words almost conscious of tune: his carriage shows him in fancy parading the Rue de Rivoli; and his hair is guiltless of English scissors: he breakfasts at 12, and never dines in Hall, and in the week or 8 days rather (for 2 Sundays must be included) he has been to Chapel once.

High seriousness indeed! Charlotte Brontë was so disturbed by Arnold's 'seeming foppery' that she imagined she saw 'the shade of Dr. Arnold frown on his young representative.'[27] Trilling holds that the young Arnold was almost everything of which his father disapproved: Dr. Arnold preached earnestness and conscientious work; but his son seemed carefree, easy-going, almost a dandy.[28] Yet, like the Hamlet to whom his critics would so often compare him, Arnold only seemed, for he had that within which escaped their vision. His outward gaiety and intellectual indifference served not only as a protection, but as a disguise.

Arnold's first two volumes of poetry, *The Strayed Reveller* (1849) and *Empedocles on Etna* (1852), revealed that he, too, was a victim of the *maladie du siècle*: an obsessive intellectual analysis and a morbid, Methodistical self-scrutiny. In 1849, he complained to Clough:

These are damned times—everything is against one—the height to which knowledge is come, the spread of luxury, our physical enervation, the absence of great *natures*, the unavoidable contact with millions of small ones, newspapers, cities, light profligate friends, moral desperadoes like Carlyle, our own selves, and the sickening consciousness of our difficulties.[29]

The first and the last items are the most important: too much knowledge and too much consciousness. In a poem of the same year, written in his copy of Bishop Butler's sermons, Arnold expressed a horror of philosophical analysis which by 'unravelling God's harmonious whole/Rend[s] in a thousand shreds this life of ours.'[30] As philosophical analysis loosened the universe into its component parts, the poet, instead of reassembling them, applied the destructive process of analysis to his own being, with the expected results:

Fret not yourself [Arnold wrote to his sister in 1853] to make my poems square in all their parts, but like what you can my darling. The true reason why parts suit you while others do not is that my poems are fragments—*i.e.* that I am fragments, while you are a whole.[31]

Like Coleridge before him, Arnold found that intense intellectual endeavour was incompatible with the genial or creative powers of poetry. 'I feel immensely,' he wrote to Clough, 'what I have (I believe) lost and choked by my treatment of myself and the studies to which I have addicted myself. But what ought I to have done in preference to what I have done? there is the question.' There was, indeed, the question. For Arnold anticipated Clough's unfavorable reaction to the 1852 volume of poetry, and apologized for it even before it appeared by saying that 'woe was upon me if I analysed not my situation: and Werter [,] Réné [,] and such like [,] none of them analyse the modern situation in its true *blankness* and *barrenness*, and *unpoetrylessness*.'[32] Some conscientious scruple—perhaps a legacy from his father—forced Arnold to try to see things as they were, whatever might be the poetical consequences.

What is the substance of the title poem of the 1852 volume which stirred Clough to such righteous indignation? Three characters appear in 'Empedocles on Etna': Empedocles, the philosopher; Pausanias, a physician; and Callicles, a young harp player. Most of Act I is taken up by a consideration of what should be our proper reaction to the recognition that we are strangers in a world that is not arranged to suit our needs and is indifferent to our highest aspirations.

Empedocles advises Pausanias not to be dismayed and preaches to him the Carlylean antihappiness doctrine:

> Couldst thou but once discern
> Thou hast no *right* to bliss,
> No title from the Gods to welfare and repose.[33]

Man must lessen his denominator if he would secure a reasonable and peaceful—albeit not a joyous—existence in a natural world that is indifferent, if not hostile, towards him. Empedocles, like Carlyle (but without the ranting), tells men they must forsake the search for happiness if they would find peace in *this* life:

> Fools! That so often here
> Happiness mock'd our prayer,

> I think, might make us fear
> A like event elsewhere;
> Make us, not fly to dreams, but moderate desire.[34]

> .   .   .   .

> I say: Fear not! Life still
> Leaves human effort scope.
> But, since life teems with ill,
> Nurse no extravagant hope;
> Because thou must not dream, thou need'st not then despair![35]

Thus Empedocles completes his reassurance of Pausanias.

We learn, however, at the beginning of Act II, that the Carlylean panacea which the philosopher has expounded so successfully cannot reassure Empedocles, however adequate it may be for the slightly obtuse and superstitious physician. Empedocles' only desire is to leave the world before it has been completely divested of its divinity and its humanity:

> Pausanias is far hence, and that is well,
> For I must henceforth speak no more with man.
> He hath his lesson too, and that debt's paid;
> And the good, learned, friendly, quiet man
> May bravelier front his life, and in himself
> Find henceforth energy and heart. But I—

> .   .   .   .

> What should I do with life and living more?[36]

The leitmotiv of 'Empedocles on Etna' is the hostility which exists between emotion and intellect, between the heart and the head. Empedocles laments that

> The brave, impetuous heart yields everywhere
> To the subtle, contriving head;[37]

and fondly recalls the happy time when

> We had not lost our balance . . . nor grown
> Thought's slaves, and dead to every natural joy.[38]

The equilibrium which is supposed to have existed between thought and feeling has been supplanted by what Mill called the tendency of intellectual analysis to wear away the emotions until thought reigns unchallenged in each human being:

> But no, this heart will glow no more; thou art
> A living man no more, Empedocles!
> Nothing but a devouring flame of thought—
> But a naked, eternally restless mind![39]

And once the intellect has gained sovereignty, it not only destroys the wholeness of the world but dissolves the union (also supposed to have existed once) between man and nature. Empedocles, dreading an existence in which mind and thought

> . . . will be our lords, as they are now;
> And keep us prisoners of our consciousness,
> And never let us clasp and feel the All
> But through their forms, and modes, and stifling veils,[40]

leaps into the crater of Etna in a desperate attempt to re-establish his bond with nature.

Arnold's letters about the fragmentation of the world and of his consciousness suggest a similarity between himself and the fictional Empedocles. Arnold, like John Stuart Mill, was sucked into the maelstrom of Hamletism. Hamletism has been defined by Bonnerot, who discerns its symptoms in Matthew Arnold, as 'cette maladie spécifiquement moderne qui résulte d'un abus de l'analyse et qui se traduit par un doute incurable.' Bonnerot, having diagnosed the illness, is much annoyed that Arnold should persist in suffering from it. He compares Arnold unfavorably with Goethe and Carlyle because, unlike them, he is more concerned with diagnosis than synthesis; with thought than action. He is impatient with Arnold for not having recognized the necessity for a working hypothesis, 'qui permette d'ordonner, au fur et à mesure, les données de l'observation, sans préjuger pour cela de leur interprétation. Cette hypothèse peut être mystique ou scientifique, il n'importe; mais elle est indispensable.'[41] But Bonnerot cannot be more impatient of the distractions and doubts of Hamletism than Arnold was himself. For Arnold refused to make the best of a bad situation with the good grace that Mill had shown. Less than a year after its publication, and just a few months after Clough's severe attack upon it, Arnold decided to withdraw 'Empedocles on Etna' from the 1853 edition of his poems.

To justify this act of self-censorship, Arnold wrote a long Preface to the new edition of his poems. Lest it should be thought that he was making too abject a surrender to the demands of Clough and the *Zeitgeist*, Arnold began by saying that he did not omit the poem because its subject was a Greek who lived two thousand years ago and whose experience could have no relevance to modern life. On the contrary, he withdrew the poem precisely because Empedocles and his problems were all too modern.

Arnold maintained that the fragments of Empedocles show that their author reflected in his work the decline of the early Greek genius and the gradual disappearance of 'the calm, the cheerfulness, the disinterested objectivity,' which it possessed. Once these disappear, we find that 'the dialogue of the mind with itself has commenced; modern problems have presented themselves; we hear already the doubts, we witness the discouragement, of Hamlet and of Faust.' Empedocles thus became the prototype—Arnold could find the prototype of nearly everything in ancient Greece—of the modern mind turning in upon itself. There are, Arnold proceeded (following Aristotle), certain kinds of human situation which can give no enjoyment when they are represented in poetry. These are situations in which

> suffering finds no vent in action; in which a continuous state of mental distress is prolonged, unrelieved by incident, hope, or resistance; in which there is everything to be endured, nothing to be done. In such situations there is inevitably something morbid, in the description of them something monotonous. When they occur in actual life, they are painful, not tragic; the representation of them in poetry is painful also.[42]

The phrase 'occur in actual life' is a telling one, for Arnold was in effect saying that the typical predicament of the greatest minds of the nineteenth century is exactly the predicament with which poetry can do nothing.

Mill, we must remember, discovered the superiority of modern poetry to ancient poetry in the very fact that it could take as its subject the brooding and self-conscious modern mind. Was not this, after all, the subject of most of Arnold's poetry, and not only of 'Empedocles on Etna'? Is it not thought rather than action, indecision rather than resolution, introspection rather than assertion, sadness rather than joy, which characterize such poems as 'To a Gipsy-Child by the Sea Shore,' 'In Utrumque Paratus,' 'Resignation,' the Switzerland poems, 'Self-Deception,' 'Dover Beach,' 'Growing Old,' 'The Buried Life,' and a number of others? The omission of 'Empedocles on Etna' from the 1853 volume could be no more than a symbolic gesture, and Arnold could not really be faithful to his critical doctrines unless he stopped writing poetry altogether—as he later did. The contradiction between Arnold's poetical impulse and his critical assumptions and precepts is absolute. Just those things which he condemned as a critic attracted him as a poet.

As a practicing poet, Arnold substantiated Mill's belief in the poetic value of modern intellectual suffering; as a critic, he vigorously denied it. It was therefore natural that, as Mill surrendered part of his philosophic allegiance in order to embrace poetry, Arnold deserted poetry for criticism. Arnold's ultimate desertion of poetry for criticism was, after all, a victory for the influence of the father whom he had bravely resisted. Dr. Arnold, we recall, had wanted to transform carefree young men into earnest, conscientious adults. And Matthew, as early as 1852, was dismayed by the way in which 'life rushes away, and youth. One has dawdled and scrupled and fiddle faddled— and it is all over.' In the next year, he wrote, 'I am past thirty, and three parts iced over—and my pen, it seems to me is even stiffer and more cramped than my feeling.'[43] Trilling states succinctly the essence of Dr. Arnold's triumph over his son: 'If we are to understand the relation of Arnold's poetry to his life we must understand the relation of the cockiness to his philosophy; for when the dandyism was at work, Arnold produced poetry, but when the dandyism failed, poetry failed too.'[44] Arnold, like Mill, was to regret that the 'fountains of vanity' had too quickly dried up within him. Sainte-Beuve was paying as much of a compliment to the power of Dr. Arnold as to the example of his own career when he said of his English disciple's 1852 poem on Obermann:

> Un jeune poète Anglais, fils d'un bien respectable père, et dont le talent réunit la pureté et la passion, M. Mathieu Arnold, voyageant en Suisse et y suivant la trace d'Obermann, lui a

dédié un poème où il a évoqué tout son esprit et où, lui-même, à la veille de rentrer par devoir dans la vie active, il fait ses adieux au grand méditatif rêveur.[45]

That dispute about moral and intellectual conscientiousness which I have asserted to be the chief interest of the correspondence between Clough and Arnold helps to explain Arnold's psychological objections to the liberalism of John Stuart Mill.

Mill often remarked of the Oxford Movement that, while he disagreed with and even abhorred nearly all of its premises, he thought its existence an excellent thing, as being a strong encouragement to controversy among the undergraduates of the university. Because it signified a revived interest in speculation and in the discussion of old assumptions, Tractarianism was, in his view, a healthy phenomenon destined to have a good effect: 'I always hailed Puseyism, and predicted that Thought would sympathise with Thought. . . .'[46] But Arthur Clough drew small benefit from the Oxford Movement turmoil. Some even said it had ruined him by plunging him into a condition 'in which,' as J. A. Symonds described it, 'aspiration mingles with a childlike desire for the tranquillity of reverence and belief —in which self-analysis has been pushed to the verge of monomania, and all springs of action are clogged and impeded by the cobwebs of specualtion.'[47]

Arnold warned Clough that emotional well-being, enthusiasm, and force of character were essential bases for the writing of poetry. Moping, misanthropy, melancholy would destroy the poetical talent and impulse.[48] But Clough could no more will himself into health at his friend's request than the author of *Empedocles on Etna* could do so when urged by Arthur Hugh Clough, reviewer.

In the course of his correspondence with Clough, Arnold became the foe of intellectual conscientiousness in all its forms. Clough, as I have indicated, refused to violate his conscience by continuing to subscribe to the Thirty-Nine Articles and, in consequence, at last resigned his Oriel fellowship. But Arnold (who had, if anything, less belief than Clough in the Anglican articles) signed with no qualms of conscience. He later urged it upon Clough that habitual conformity in matters religious and political was highly commendable, not because of any high-sounding conservative principle, but because conformity 'frees us from the unnatural and unhealthy attitude of contradiction and opposition.' Nonconformity was for Arnold not so much wrong as psychologically damaging; and conformity was useful as a psychological anodyne, an antidote to negativism.[49]

Psychological justification took precedence over logical or rational justification in other matters as well. Although in 1851 Arnold spoke guiltily to his sister of his failure to befriend the people most unlike himself,[50] in 1853 he began to think that what seemed weakness from a moral point of view was strength from the point of view of mental health. Clough suspected that Arnold was drawing away from him; Arnold denied the allegation, yet admitted that at one time he considered severing relations with Clough because he hoped to bar out 'all influences that I felt troubled without advancing me.'[51] Psychological well-being had become a sufficient excuse for sheltering his convictions from adverse criticism.

Arnold tried to explain to Clough the reasons for their growing lack of sympathy:

> You ask me in what I think or have thought you going wrong: in this: that you would never take your assiette as something determined final unchangeable for you and proceed to work away on the basis of that: but were always poking and patching and cobbling at the assiette itself—could never finally, as it seemed— 'resolve to be thyself'—but were looking for this and that experience, and doubting [wondering] whether you ought not to adopt this or that mode of being of persons qui ne vous valaient pas because it might possibly be nearer the truth than your own: you had no reason for thinking it *was*, but it *might* be—and so you would try to adapt yourself to it. You have I am convinced lost infinite time in this way: it is what I call your morbid conscientiousness—you are the most conscientious man I ever knew: but on some lines morbidly so, and it spoils your action.[52]

With a marvelous precision Arnold put his finger on the emotional illness that was the almost inevitable outcome of the intellectual dilemma of the nineteenth century. The individual who doubted the sanctions of customary, generally accepted rules of behavior was reluctant to trust his impulses. Lacking the assurance of any certainties, he became a fragmented being whose emotional impulses were resisted by a skeptical intellect. He was paralyzed by indecision.

When Arnold told Clough to be himself, he was, in effect, asking his friend to reread a poem from the 1852 volume called 'Self-Dependence.' The speaker in this poem is weary of the search after self-knowledge, weary of asking 'what I am, and what I ought to be.'[53] He looks up at the stars and it occurs to him that his salvation lies in following unhesitatingly an ordered course like theirs:

> Unaffrighted by the silence round them,
> Undistracted by the sights they see,
> These demand not that things without them
> Yield them love, amusement, sympathy.[54]

What is wanted is not to know oneself but to be oneself:

> Resolve to be thyself; and know that he,
> Who finds himself, loses his misery.[55]

Arnold's criticism of Clough for his refusal to be himself is the basis of his psychological objection to Mill's kind of liberalism. Arnold's theory of mental health, like his theory of history, is impatient of endless analysis, anxious to approach synthesis, harmony, and wholeness. In Clough's refusal to place the burden of proof for an opinion upon his antagonist rather than himself, in his conscientious devotion to following the argument whither it may lead, Arnold recognized the psychological price which individuals had to pay for their commitment to Millite liberalism; and he said it was too high. The differences between Arnold's social and political philosophy and that of Mill are rooted in the opposition of their psychologies.[56]

The particular Utilitarian doctrine which, according to Halévy, was destined to transform almost every existing political institution was a psychological doctrine. It held that a truth accepted under constraint, or inherited as customary, without being openly and freely discussed, is really an error.[57] This doctrine was the modern and secular version of the nonconformist principle of conscience which had been expressed by Milton in *Areopagitica*:

> Truth is compared in scripture to a streaming fountain; if her waters flow not in a perpetual progression, they sicken into a muddy pool of conformity and tradition. A man may be a heretic in the truth; and if he believe things only because his pastor says

so, or the assembly so determines, without knowing other reason, though his belief be true, yet the very truth he holds becomes his heresy.[58]

Arnold was right to see in Clough's conscientious refusal to subscribe to the Thirty-Nine Articles a dual enemy: religious nonconformity and secular liberalism.

James Mill held religiously conscientious views about the way in which opinions should be formed and beliefs concurred in. He would inveigh against what he called the sin of believing without evidence. He insisted upon the specifically moral obligation to collect all available evidence and to evaluate it disinterestedly before making up one's mind:

> This habit of forming opinions, and acting upon them without evidence, is one of the most immoral habits of the mind. . . . As our opinions are the fathers of our actions, to be indifferent about the evidence of our opinions is to be indifferent about the consequences of our actions. But the consequences of our actions are the good and evil of our fellow-creatures. The habit of the neglect of evidence, therefore, is the habit of disregarding the good and evil of our fellow-creatures.

Following out a remorseless logic, James Mill represented a lack of concern with the evidence of opinions as the cause of all the evil which existed in the world. For how could institutions whose interest differed from that of the community at large, and which were positively maleficent in their operation, have continued to exist 'if the human mind was not ruined by the habit of adopting opinions, without evidence?' Intellectual scrupulosity became the cardinal virtue; blind acceptance of customary opinions the primal sin. Not surprisingly, Mill concluded his article 'Formation of Opinions' with a statement of the arch-Protestant belief that the real heretic is one who believes without reason shown, while the true believer always seeks for proof. 'It is not belief,' asserted the former Presbyterian clergyman, 'which is called, in the scripture, faith, but the proper mode of dealing with evidence.'[59]

John Stuart Mill inherited his father's habit of applying the language and the method of religious conscientiousness to the intellectual life. It was one legacy from his father which Mill retained, nourished, and developed until it became the guiding principle of his life, a life of secular spirituality. The conscientious principle of John Stuart Mill was not unknown in the Victorian period, especially among scientists. Huxley wrote that 'the improver of natural knowledge absolutely refuses to acknowledge authority, as such. For him skepticism is the highest of duties; blind faith the one unpardonable sin.'[60] But Mill alone gave the principle its full application and carried it out to its logical conclusion—so single-mindedly that he frightened even those who thought themselves its most rigorous adherents.

Mill believed that truth could only emerge from the conflict and collision of ideas. In *On Liberty*, he gave as the second justification of liberty of thought and discussion (the first was that a suppressed opinion may be the true one) 'the clearer perception and livelier impression of truth, produced by its collision with error.' No individual, he argued, is entitled to think his opinion true unless he has defended it against those who hold the opposite opinion or opinions. Only by constant submission to criticism and collision with intellectual adversaries is wisdom attainable. 'The steady habit of correcting and completing his own opinions by collating it [*sic*] with those of others,' asserted Mill, 'so far from causing doubt and hesitation in carrying it into practice, is the only stable foundation for a just reliance on it. . . .'[61]

Arnold found Clough's unwillingness to assume a firm conviction upon which he could rest once and for all with immovable certainty his friend's great weakness and a hindrance to his action. Mill would have proclaimed it Clough's great strength and his only justification for action—assuming he retained the power and the will to act. Far from wanting an 'assiette' for assurance, Mill said that certainty about a belief is most nearly approached when the ground of the belief is left open to criticism: 'The beliefs which we have most warrant for have no safeguard to rest on, but a standing invitation to the whole world to prove them unfounded. . . . This is the amount of certainty attainable by a fallible being, and this is the sole way of attaining it.'[62]

But what if that blessed state, which all of Arnold's work anticipated, should arrive when all people are united and of one mind? In such a state, Mill implied, truth would suffer because 'if opponents of all important truths did not exist, it is indispensable to imagine them.' The ordinary mortal, lacking Mill's mental agility and spiritual firmness (which even he had not always possessed), cannot but be frightened by the strenuous demands he makes upon the human mind for a kind of disinterestedness which makes the disinterestedness Arnold asked for seem, by contrast, unworthy of any but *l'homme moyen sensuel*. Mill refused to allow the mind to rest in a fixed position, and insisted that it continually cut the ground out from under itself by putting its most cherished beliefs ever more strictly to the test of hostile criticism and open controversy:

> Nor is it enough that he should hear the arguments of adversaries from his own teachers, presented as they state them, and accompanied by what they offer as refutation. . . . He must be able to hear them from persons who actually believe them. . . . He must feel the whole force of the difficulty which the true view of the subject has to encounter and dispose of.[63]

It was the vision of just such a restless intellectual existence as Mill depicted here that horrified Matthew Arnold when he saw it in Arthur Hugh Clough; for Clough adopted Mill's principles without acquiring Mill's confidence.

Even the avowed free spirits among Mill's contemporaries found the conscientious intellectual discipline which he recommended too demanding. Caroline Fox, in a letter of December, 1859, expressed not so much her disagreement with as her terror at the uncompromising secular spirituality of *On Liberty*:

> I am reading that terrible book of John Mill's on Liberty, so clear, and calm, and cold: he lays it on one as a tremendous duty to get one's self well contradicted, and admit always a devil's advocate into the presence of your dearest, most sacred truths, as they are apt to grow windy and worthless without such tests, if indeed they can stand the shock of argument at all. He looks through you like a basilisk, relentless as Fate. We knew him well at one time, and owe him very much: I fear his remorseless logic has led him far since then.[64]

Harriet Martineau, epitome of the emancipated woman and of the radical, confessed a desire, in intellectual matters, 'in the midst of confusion, to hold tight where she had got footing.'[65]
The disagreement between Arnold and Mill over how far, if

at all, mental health ought to be made to wait upon intellectual conscientiousness is a fundamental one. Where Mill clung to Sterling and Carlyle just because they were so unlike him, and so much at odds with him, Arnold kept Clough at a distance because he was sharply conscious of the things separating them intellectually and spiritually. Where Arnold, in 'Self-Dependence,' desired a course of existence as ordered as that of the stars, Mill rebuked Auguste Comte for boasting that, in Mill's paraphrase, 'under the reign of sentiment, human life may be made equally [sic], and even more, regular than the courses of the stars.'[66] Where Mill thought the controversy aroused by the Oxford Movement would benefit Oxford undergraduates, Arnold thought it had nearly ruined Clough. Whereas Mill believed that liberty of thought and discussion was almost the greatest good of life, Arnold, while reluctantly admitting its necessity, pointed to those, like the editors of the Daily Telegraph, who were sacrificed to it.[67] Whereas Mill found the spirit of controversy and collision encouraged by Protestantism (though not by the Church of England variety) the great advantage which that faction of Christianity had over Catholicism,[68] Arnold asked the nonconformist manufacturer who believed in the Millite doctrine that collision keeps beliefs alive and minds resilient to 'only think of all the nonsense which you now hold quite firmly, which you would never have held if you had not been contradicting your adversary in it all these years!' For Arnold, the claims of psychology counted for more than the claims of logic and philosophy; mental health for more than the rightness or wrongness of what he would often contemptuously refer to as speculative opinions.[69]

Mill did not ignore the claims of mental health; his confidence was not the result of callous insensitivity. If he was sometimes led by the pressure of controversy to maintain that the unending submission of a person's beliefs to analysis and to hostile criticism kept his faculties not only alive but healthy, he also recognized the injurious effects of the ideological conscientiousness which he insisted upon. He sympathized with a friend who seemed to him 'full of a morbid conscientiousness.'[70] He expressed his gratitude to Harriet for having served as an anchor to keep him firm against the constant temptation to question his own position and to put the burden of proof and defense upon himself rather than his adversary.[71] In *On Liberty* he admitted that collision of opinion has its salutary effect not upon any of the parties directly involved, but upon 'the calmer and more disinterested bystander.'[72] In the posthumously published 'Utility of Religion,' he dulled the edge of his logical scalpel so far as to allow that in matters of religion, where the need for belief is so great, people may sustain themselves on hypotheses of which the best that can be said is that they are not certainly false.[73]

Mill could understand the emotional dilemma of Arnold and Clough because he had himself confronted it. He did not fail to notice the individual casualties strewn along the path of intellectual advance; and in an article on Alfred de Vigny, he even paid tribute to them. He defined the conservative and the radical types of poet, and then attempted to define the position of a 'poet of conservative sympathies' who, like Vigny, has fallen upon an age of revolution; an age which destroys all symbols of what was once great and gives birth—but in painful travail—to a new order. How, Mill asked, would such a combination of circumstances affect the imagination and feelings of the poet? Mill's answer had Vigny in mind, but we may justifiably think of Matthew Arnold:

> He [the poet] will lose that blind faith in the Past, which previously might have tempted him to fight for it with a mistaken ardour, against what is generous and worthy in the new doctrines. The fall of the objects of his reverence, will naturally . . . open his mind to the perception of that in them whereby they deserved to fall. But while he is thus disenchanted of the old things, he will not have acquired that faith in the new, which animated the Radical poet. . . . The destiny of mankind, therefore, will naturally appear to him in rather sombre colours; gloomy he may not be, but he will everywhere tend to the elegiac, to the contemplative and melancholy rather than to the epic and active; his song will be a subdued and plaintive symphony, more or less melodious according to the measure of his genius, on the theme of blasted hopes and defeated aspirations.[74]

Mill was emotionally capable of comprehending the gravity of Arnold's quarrel with intellectual analysis, but he steadfastly refused to admit that mental health could take precedence in importance over the search for truth.

Arnold admitted the necessity of intellectual analysis; his historical theory obliged him to do so. But he never succeeded, as Mill did, in transforming this necessity into a virtue. The situation of the poet in 'Stanzas from the Grande Chartreuse' is very like that of the poet described in Mill's essay, and still more like that of Arnold himself. Wandering about a Carthusian monastery, he suddenly remembers who were his spiritual fathers, the bearers of what Arnold in his prose works called the modern spirit of disinterested scientific pursuit of truth:

> Rigorous teachers seized my youth
> And purged its faith, and trimm'd its fire,
> Show'd me the high, white star of Truth,
> There bade me gaze, and there aspire.
> Even now their whispers pierce the gloom:
> What dost thou in this living tomb?[75]

Mill, however belatedly, patched up his feud with Jeremy Bentham, but Arnold could never quite forgive the Enlightenment. Intellectually, Arnold had committed himself to the modern spirit; emotionally, he lingered between the old world and the new.

I have shown how Matthew Arnold and John Stuart Mill responded in different ways to the mental crises which they underwent as a result of the peculiar educations they received from their fathers. When the two men are viewed in isolation from their contemporaries, their differences of response to the malady of Hamletism inevitably stand out more clearly than their similarities. But they were not the only Victorians troubled by the problem of a conflict between thought and action. In the *Autobiography* Mill voiced his belief that others had gone through a crisis similar to his, though he added that 'the idiosyncrasies of my education had given to the general phenomenon a special character.'[76] The same could be said of Arnold. When we place Arnold and Mill against the wider background of their age, the similarities of their response to the thought-action dilemma stand out far more clearly.

J. H. Buckley, reacting against the tendency to Hamletize all intellectual problems of the nineteenth century, argues that the cultural setting of the Victorian era was so different from that of the Elizabethan age that 'the paralysis of doubt that is said to have gripped Arnold's generation is far removed from the divided aims of a disillusioned Hamlet.'[77] This may be so, but what is more important, surely, is the simple recognition that many Victorians did believe themselves to be in Hamlet's situation, if not, in fact, to be modern Hamlets. W. H. Mallock, looking at the typical man living in the nineteenth century, wrote:

> Much of his old spontaneity of action has gone from him. He has become a creature looking before and after; and his native hue of resolution has been sicklied over by thought. We admit nothing now without question; we have learnt to take to pieces all motives to actions. We not only know more than we have done before, but we are perpetually chewing the cud of our knowledge.[78]

Arnold and Mill encountered the typical dilemma of their age, though special circumstances aggravated their situation. But theirs was not the typical solution, for they were isolated from their contemporaries in their response to this as to so many other problems. The atypicality of Arnold and Mill may be illustrated by comparing their attempts to untie the knot into which action had been tied by speculation with those of two of their contemporaries, Thomas Carlyle and John Newman; the more readily because Carlyle exercised over both Arnold and Mill, and Newman over Arnold, a considerable attraction for a number of years.

Sartor Resartus, which appeared in 1833 and 1834, told the tale of Carlyle's passage from suicidal doubt and despair to robust affirmation. Herr Professor Teufelsdröckh, Carlyle's German *alter ego*, has been driven near to suicide (from which he is restrained only by a certain detritus of Christianity) by his recognition that the universe, especially after the mechanistic philosophers of the Enlightenment have done with it, is 'all void of Life, of Purpose, of Volition, even of Hostility: [is] one huge, dead, immeasurable Steam-engine, rolling on, in its dead indifference, to grind me limb from limb.' The Professor, as if he knows that subsequent events will undermine the credibility of such a claim, professes unswerving devotion to Truth, even though the heavens fall and 'a whole celestial Lubberland were the price of Apostasy.' But no sooner has he said this than he proudly announces his unbridled contempt 'for the folly of that impossible Precept, *Know thyself*; till it be translated into this partially possible one, *Know what thou canst work at.*'[79] The writer of 'Self-Dependence' knew his Carlyle.

Teufelsdröckh decides that he will not live in the mechanistic universe which the eighteenth century has left him; he simply wills (no conviction is involved) indignation and defiance against it, and independence from it. After vacillating in a 'Centre of Indifference,' Teufelsdröckh succeeds in subduing what is essentially a spiritual and intellectual problem by the main force of will. He decides that much of his difficulty has arisen from his excessive demands upon life and upon the universe. Man, he now knows, has no right whatever to be happy: 'Foolish soul! What Act of Legislature was there that *thou* shouldst be Happy? A little while ago thou hadst no right to *be* at all.' Man's desires, increased as they have been by Byron's exaltation of the ego, outrun his and the universe's capacity to fulfill them. Better that man surrender the wish for happiness altogether; for life may be *'increased in value not so much by increasing your Numerator as by lessening your Denominator.'*[80]

It was here that Carlyle issued his famous injunction, which had its effects upon both Arnold and Mill: 'Close thy *Byron*; open thy *Goethe*.' Instead of aspiring, complaining, speculating, choose the work (never mind what it may be) which lies nearest to hand. Blessedness, Carlyle asserted, is the substitute for happiness, and doubt can be resolved only by action. The 'Everlasting Yea' ends with a call to arms, or to tools:

> Produce! Produce! Were it but the pitifullest infinitesimal fraction of a Product, produce it, in God's name! 'Tis the utmost thou hast in thee: out with it, then. Up, up! Whatsoever thy hand findeth to do, do it with thy whole might. Work while it is called Today, for the Night cometh, wherein no man can work.[81]

Fearful, perhaps, that his message might be lost amidst the sound and fury of *Sartor Resartus*, Carlyle also stated it in the much quieter and calmer work, the essay called 'Characteristics.' Here the full implications of the Carlylean doctrine were unashamedly drawn out for the edification and guidance of the perplexed. If the world or any part of it seems a mystery to us, we ought not, Carlyle argued, to trouble ourselves about solving it. On the contrary, we should not merely accept mystery, we should embrace it, for nothing is great that is not mysterious and incomprehensible. We ought especially to glorify and celebrate that in the mind which is dark and unconscious, for unconsciousness is the sign of health, self-consciousness the sign of disease: 'The healthy Understanding, we should say, is not the Logical, argumentative, but the Intuitive; for the end of Understanding is not to prove and find reasons, but to know and believe.'[82]

Carlyle's exaltation of mystery and of the unconscious led him to equate action with health and contemplation with sickness. Goodness and virtue, he said, are constituted by actions or works; contemplation, as it hinders action, is the negation of virtue even if it is not positively vicious. '*Bad*,' as Carlyle said in another essay, 'is by its nature negative, and can do *nothing*; whatsoever enabled us to *do* anything is by its very nature *good*.' Action thus becomes 'natural' and contemplation 'unnatural'; whatever is conscious is artificial, whatever is unconscious is natural.[83]

Carlyle believed that action is impossible without certainty. Since thought leads to doubt and destroys certainty, it is necessary to destroy doubt—how?—by action. The chief doctrine upheld by Carlyle in 'Characteristics' is that 'in Action alone can we have certainty.' Doubt is not to be resolved by speculation, but exorcised by Action. The only useful speculation is that which answers the question, 'What is to be done; and How is it to be done?'[84]

Having decided that the certainty given by action was the one thing needful, Carlyle went on a frantic search for it in the societies of the past. He had tried the eighteenth century in his youth, but that had proved a bitter disappointment to him. For even in Samuel Johnson's age, 'Opinion and Action, which should live together as wedded pair, "one flesh," more properly as Soul and Body [had] commenced their open quarrel, and [were] suing for a separate maintenance—as if they could exist separately.'[85] No, he decided, it would be better and safer to return to that happy refuge of Victorian lost causes: twelfth-century Catholicism.

Carlyle's conception of this particular society, as depicted in 1843 in *Past and Present*, was as fantastical as Ruskin's notion of the motives which impelled medieval architects to build in the

Gothic style, but it was a myth which served his purposes. The ordered hierarchy of the paternalistic feudal system he used as a measuring stick with which to beat down the confused anarchy of the laissez-faire society of the nineteenth century; the bustling industriousness of Abbot Samson he opposed to the morbid self-contemplation of the religion of the hour in nineteenth-century England:

> Methodism with its eye forever turned on its own navel; asking itself with torturing anxiety of Hope and Fear, 'Am I right, am I wrong? Shall I be saved, shall I not be damned?'—what is this, at bottom, but a new phasis of *Egoism*, stretched out into the Infinite; not always the heavenlier for its infinitude![86]

In Carlyle's view, Methodism was the religious counterpart of the introspective affliction torturing unbelieving intellectuals.[87]

Even in *Past and Present*, however, Carlyle indicated a desire to find an object of worship nearer to home and more congenial to a Protestant and industrial country. This object he found in 'the English' themselves. In what others thought the most beastly characteristics of the typical Englishman, Carlyle claimed to discern the most beautiful revelations of divinity. Everything which was to Arnold and Mill the shame of the English—their hatred of art, of theory, of novelty, and of other nations—was to Carlyle their glory. What does it matter, asked Carlyle, that the English are stupid and inarticulate if 'they can do great acts, but not describe them'? What does it matter that England has no artists and no composers if she can create cotton mills? Carlyle especially admired English silence because he knew that dumbness often grows from stupidity, and inarticulate stupidity always seemed to him tinged with the divine. Besides, he asked, is it not the quiet and stupid man who works least hesitatingly, and most efficiently?

> How one loves to see the burly figure of him, this thick-skinned, seemingly opaque, perhaps sulky, almost stupid Man of Practice, pitted against some light adroit Man of Theory, all equipped with clear logic, and able anywhere to give you Why for Wherefore!
> . . . The cloudy-browed, thick-soled, opaque Practicality, with no logic utterance, in silence mainly, with here and there a low grunt or growl, has in him what transcends all logic-utterance; a Congruity with the Unuttered.[88]

Thus did Carlyle 'solve' the problem of the relation between thought and action by discovering in John Bull a substitute for Hamlet as the Platonic ideal of the Victorian man.

The essential truth of Carlyle's diagnosis of the sickness of his age was attested by the widespread Victorian infatuation with him. That the remedy he prescribed for the Victorian ailment was far less acceptable than his diagnosis of it had been is suggested by the widespread defection of early admirers from his ranks. Clough complained to Emerson in 1848 that 'Carlyle has led us all out into the desert, and he has left us there.'[89] Mill, the story of whose close friendship and subsequent falling-out with Carlyle has often been told, wrote in 1869 that Carlyle was of use only at a certain stage in one's mental development, even though he could still be read with pleasure 'after one has ceased to learn anything from him.'[90] Arnold came to look upon Carlyle as one of those friends of his youth about whom 'it is not always pleasant to ask oneself questions.'[91] He saw Carlyle 'preaching earnestness to a nation which had plenty of it by nature' and thus simply carrying coals to Newcastle.[92] Finally, Arnold, like the lapsed Utilitarian Mill, never ceased to believe that 'the desire for happiness is the root and ground of man's being' and consequently found Carlyle's contempt for the desire of happiness the fatal flaw in his philosophy.[93]

John Henry Newman did not, like Carlyle, deprecate contemplation and call it wicked, unnatural, and un-English. He merely said that it had nothing to do with life.

The letter in *The Tamworth Reading Room* entitled 'Secular Knowledge not a Principle of Action' ought to be, by virtue of it insistence upon the primacy of action in human life, a *locus classicus* of Victorian anti-intellectualism.[94] It was Newman's intention in this letter to deny the autonomy of secular knowledge and to show that only faith can serve as the basis for action (not necessarily good action, but action of any kind). Poetry, science, above all logic, become harmful rather than beneficial when they are not employed in the cause, and under the direction, of religion. 'Many a man,' Newman declared, 'will live and die upon a dogma; no one will be a martyr for a conclusion.'[95]

The test of action is the foundation of Newman's argument. Unlike Aquinas, he set little store by logic; he was one of those devotees who believe, as Voltaire scornfully put it, that religion departs as soon as reason appears. Newman's case for faith rested upon psychology rather than logic. 'After all,' he assured his readers of a sad and discomforting truth, 'man is not a reasoning animal; he is a seeing, feeling, contemplating, acting animal.'[96] Above all, acting—for, as with Carlyle, action presented itself to Newman as natural and contemplation as unnatural; action is human and contemplation is not so much inhuman as it is the eminently artificial pastime of an idle hour. If thought and knowledge have nothing to do with determining conduct and belief, which Newman held to be matters of intuition or instinct, they can be little more than forms of dilettantism.

There is no more lucid exposition of the powerful Victorian impulse to elevate psychology above logic and to escape from the labyrinth of thought into the seemingly straightforward certainties of action than Newman's:

> Life is not long enough for a religion of inferences; we shall never have done beginning if we determine to begin with proof. We shall ever be laying our foundations; we shall turn theology into evidences, and divines into textuaries. We shall never get at our first principles. Resolve to believe nothing, and you must prove your proof and analyze your elements, sinking further and further, and finding 'in the lowest deep a lower deep,' till you come to the broad bosom of scepticism. I would rather be bound to defend the assumption that Christianity is true than to prove a moral governance from the physical world. *Life is for action.* If we insist on proof for everything, we shall never come to action; to act you must assume, and that assumption is faith.[97] (*Italics mine.*)

Newman wrote as a man who had experienced the horrors of skepticism, and could therefore testify to the differences between the state of doubt and the state of certainty. It was a commonplace of his contemporaries, who shared Dr. Arnold's suspicions, that Newman's temper, like that of Montaigne or of Bayle, was essentially skeptical. Leslie Stephen, as we have seen, found a parallel between Newman's skepticism of mind and Mill's. Huxley claimed that a 'primer of infidelity' might be collected from Newman's writings. Newman was aware of this view of himself; and he wrote, of a friend who had fallen away from him:

My surmise is, that he thinks me a profoundly sceptical thinker, who, determined on not building on an abyss, have, by mere strength of will, bridged it over, and built upon [it] my bridge— but that my bridge, like Mahomet's coffin, is self-suspended, by the action of the will.[98]

Though the psychological sophistication is greater, and the place of refuge chosen is different, Newman's solution of the Hamlet problem is not basically different from Carlyle's. For, like Carlyle's, it is really an escape from the problem and not a legitimate solution of it. A doubtful premise does not become an ascertained truth by virtue of the fact that one is able to act upon it. After becoming a Catholic, Newman wrote in *Apologia Pro Vita Sua*, he never again had any changes in his religious opinions, nor any 'anxiety of heart whatever. I have been in perfect peace and contentment. I never have had one doubt.' The conversion was not marked for him by any change in the opinions he held or in the doctrines he believed, 'but it was like coming into port after a rough sea.'[99] Newman's description of the aftermath of his conversion to Roman Catholicism must have appealed strongly to pragmatists for whom mental health was more important than belief, the claims of psychology vastly superior to those of logic.

Carlyle and Newman are examples among many of the Victorian habit of soothing intellectual doubts by action. Tennyson, who said he had conceived 'Maud' as 'a little *Hamlet* . . . the history of a morbid poetic soul, under the blighting influence of a recklessly speculative age,'[100] could only rescue the hero of that poem from reckless speculation by transforming him from a Hamlet into a Fortinbras. Ruskin showed himself the faithful disciple of Carlyle when he said that perplexed men could very easily find out the work appointed for them to do as soon as they had made up their minds to do it; or when he laid the blame for the religious agonies of Victorian young women on their inability to do useful work, since 'no syllable [of the Bible] was ever yet to be understood but through a deed.'[101] All the world's troubles were due, he thought, to metaphysicians and philosophers who, too lazy to work themselves, were 'always entangling *good* and *active* people, and weaving cobwebs among the finest wheels of the world's business.' The highest kind of human being, in Ruskin's view, is the one who 'loses sight in resolution, and feeling in work.'[102] Browning, the disciple of Ruskin, showed in 'Bishop Blougram's Apology' his understanding of and even—some thought—his sympathy with the devious psychological process which led a man from extreme skepticism into total resignation to authority. Blougram was presented as that rarest type of man in 1850, 'the able to think yet act.'[103] Kingsley (and he was a Cambridge professor of modern history) attacked book-learning because it encourages men to know *about* all kinds of things without learning how to *do* them.[104] Fitzjames Stephen, the vigilant critic of Arnold and of Mill, preached the gospel of working at whatever lies ready to hand in order to escape from intellectual doubts and difficulties.[105]

Carlyle and Newman are thus only the best-known and most articulate spokesmen of a deep-seated yearning felt by the great majority of Victorians. As G. M. Young puts it: 'The age was learning, but it had not mastered, the lesson that truth lies not in the statement but in the process: it had a childlike craving for certitude, as if the natural end of every refuted dogma was to be replaced by another dogma.'[106] But Arnold and Mill were exceptions. The claims of mental health weighed more heavily upon Arnold than upon Mill, but they could never, as with Carlyle and Newman, outweigh all other considerations. Even in the midst of a touching tribute which he paid to Newman before an American audience, Arnold warned that the cardinal had 'adopted, for the doubts and difficulties which beset men's minds to-day, a solution which, to speak frankly, is impossible.'[107]

After due allowance has been made for the differences between them, it turns out that the solutions offered by Arnold and Mill to the intellectual dilemma of their age resembled each other far more than they resembled the solution adopted by so many of their contemporaries. To them the question was how we may continue to act and to live without certainty; and by different paths they arrived at a single answer. Both men were fond of Pericles and liked to quote that part of his funeral oration which holds that full discussion and deliberation of a question are not incompatible with boldness of action upon it. Pericles had said: 'We do not esteem discussion a hurt to action; what we consider mischievous is rather the setting oneself to work without first getting the guidance of reason.'[108] It would be fair to say that both Arnold and Mill adopted this principle and, though with different degrees of reluctance, adhered to it.

Arnold preached, even if he did not always practice, the principle that sound theory is the only foundation for sound practice. He was suspicious of the unconscious element in man, and insisted that 'the right thing is, while conscious of this element, and of all that there is inexplicable round one, to keep pushing on one's posts into the darkness, *and to establish no post that is not perfectly in light and firm.*'[109] He was the first to admit that 'men have . . . need of joy' but it had to be 'joy whose grounds are true.'[110] He liked to intone Goethe's dictum: 'To act is easy, to think is hard.' He wrote, in *Culture and Anarchy*, one of the longest and most comprehensive attacks ever made upon action taken with insufficient knowledge; for he presented Hellenism, 'the force which encourages us to . . . try the very ground on which we appear to stand,'[111] as the most effective and persistent kind of deterrent to premature action.

Frederic Harrison showed the same irritation with Arnold that an anxious Caroline Fox had shown with the Mill of *On Liberty*. Harrison could not abide what he called Arnold's 'opening of all questions, and answering of none.' His irritation and impatience are apparent even through the good humor of this famous portrait of the disbeliever in action:

> Here are we, in this generation, face to face with the passions of fierce men; parties, sects, races glare in each other's eyes before they spring; death, sin, cruelty stalk amongst us, filling their maws with innocence and youth; humanity passes onwards shuddering through the raging crowd of foul and hungry monsters, bearing the destiny of the race like a close-veiled babe in her arms, and over all sits Culture high aloft with a pouncet-box to spare her senses aught unpleasant, holding no form of creed, but contemplating all with infinite serenity, sweetly chanting snatches from graceful sages and ecstatic monks, crying out the most pretty shame upon the vulgarity, the provinciality, the impropriety of it all. Most improper, quotha, most terrible, most maddening.[112]

Arnold calmly replied to Harrison, in *Culture and Anarchy*, that the light or intelligence which would enable a man to see the flimsiness of the rationale given for the hectic action going on about him would also lead him to refrain from such action and

141

to show his active fellow men the mischief—even in practical terms—which they caused.[113] When he was writing *Culture and Anarchy*, Arnold found moral support in the figure of Plato, who 'could not in his day have been a man of action,' and would have been a less perfect man if he had.[114]

Mill, too, argued that action ought to be dependent upon thought. He showed how action could be consonant with 'new' moral philosophies, and made certainty depend not upon closing questions but upon keeping them open. Absolute certainty Mill thought an impossibility, yet he believed that individuals may legitimately act without having what they suppose to be infallible knowledge. He maintained in the *Logic* that neither the conduct of society nor that of private life requires 'that we should be able to foresee infallibly the results of what we do.' The wise man would recognize that all rules of conduct must be provisional, and that the nature of the world and the nature of thought often condemn us to 'seek our objects by means which may perhaps be defeated, and take precautions against dangers which possibly may never be realised.'[115] Mill thought that action or certainty could be realized only by fair means. The course of his career proved the truth of Bacon's maxim that 'if a man will begin with certainties, he shall end in doubts; but if he will be content to begin with doubts, he shall end in certainties.'[116]

Arnold and Mill recognized that one consequence of their conscientious refusal to acquiesce in custom or to act at all except in accordance with what they believed to be true was a terrible spiritual loneliness. In *The Spirit of the Age*, Mill had complained that the lack of any recognized authorities unsettled the mind of the average individual, who was suddenly forced to weigh his every action instead of unconsciously obeying custom.[117] Mill believed that such an individual would be not only paralyzed by inaction but isolated from the social bonds of common desire.

In 1829, Mill expressed to Sterling his fear of future loneliness. He foresaw the loss of 'that feeling which has accompanied me through the greater part of my life, that which one fellow traveller, or one fellow soldier has towards another—the feeling of being engaged in the pursuit of a common object.'[118] Mill's peculiar education combined with the spirit of the age to aggravate his loneliness,[119] yet he could not blame his loneliness entirely on environmental conditions. For it became a matter of principle with him that no individual was truly alive who acted simply in conformity with custom:

> Where, not the person's own character, but the traditions or customs of other people are the whole of conduct, there is wanting one of the principal ingredients of human happiness, and quite the chief ingredient of individual and social progress.[120]

The belief that a person's way of life should be an exact reflection of his character placed a terrible new burden of responsibility upon the individual. Although he admitted that customs and traditions had their use as the collective result of the human experience of the past transmitted to the present, Mill said that it was the privilege and responsibility of each human being to interpret experience for himself. 'Customs are made,' he argued, 'for customary circumstances and customary characters; and [the individual's] circumstances or his character may be uncustomary.' Even if customs were both good and suitable, mere conformity to them would prevent a man from developing his properly human qualities.[121] But, as the absolute duty of obeying the intellect was likely to thwart action, so the related absolute duty of living in strict accordance with one's own character and beliefs was well suited to isolate the individual from his fellows. After reading *On Liberty*, Caroline Fox commented that Mill was 'in many senses isolated, and must sometimes shiver with the cold.'[122]

Upon Arnold as upon Mill education and environment inculcated the twin duties of conscientious intellection and individuality: and the like causes produced like effects. Arnold pictured Empedocles as being rewarded for his vision of things as they really are with spiritual despair and physical and mental isolation. Arnold's poems are pervaded by a generalized sense of loneliness and isolation, of which the outcry in the fifth of the 'Switzerland' poems is typical:

> Yes! in the sea of life enisled,
> With echoing straits between us thrown,
> Dotting the shoreless watery wild,
> We mortal millions live *alone*.[123]

Arnold knew that the devotees of his ideal of culture would be sorely tried not only by their obligation to eschew action but also by their desertion of the customary ways of thinking and acting peculiar to their class. Those who went in search of their best self would leave their respective classes and be counted not as Barbarians, Philistines, or Populace, but as men:

> Natures with this bent emerge in all classes,—among the Barbarians, among the Philistines, among the Populace. And this bent always tends to take them out of their class, and to make their distinguishing characteristics not their Barbarianism or their Philistinism, but their *humanity*. They have, in general, a rough time of it in their lives.[124]

Arnold, committed like Mill to seeing things as they are without regard to ulterior considerations of any kind, also suffered from doubt and spiritual isolation.

But we have seen how Arnold and Mill, though their attitudes may be contrasted in several respects, both endured the doubt and isolation general in their age much more patiently than did their contemporaries. Both attributed their ability to do so to the influence of the poetry of Wordsworth, which taught them that the essence of life was not action but contemplation, not doing but being.

According to Mill's account of his mental crisis in the *Autobiography*, it was the *Mémoires* of Marmontel which made him feel capable of recovering his spiritual health, and the poetry of Wordsworth which made his recovery possible. During the worst period of his depression, Mill, hungry for 'feeling,' read Byron in order to see whether the vaunted master of the passions could awake any feeling in him. To no avail, for Byron's heroes 'had the same burthen on them which I had; and I was not in a frame of mind to derive any comfort from the vehement sensual passion of his Giaours, or the sullenness of his Laras.' But where Byron failed, Wordsworth succeeded. For Wordsworth's poems revived Mill's susceptibility to the love of natural objects and his ability to contemplate the pleasures inherent in the natural world. Still more important,

> what made Wordsworth's poems a medicine for my state of mind, was that they expressed, not mere outward beauty, but states of

feeling, and of thought coloured by feeling, under the excitement of beauty. They seemed to be the very culture of the feelings, which I was in quest of.

Wordsworth had awakened in Mill the feeling of 'real, permanent happiness in tranquil contemplation.' He had also lightened Mill's sense of isolation because he was able to communicate the happiness of tranquility and contemplation in connection with 'the common feelings and common destiny of human beings.' Mill concluded his account of Wordsworth's healing power by pointing out the similarity between Wordsworth's youth and his own: 'He too had had similar experience to mine; . . . had felt that the first freshness of youthful enjoyment was not lasting.'[125]

Mill was not the only Victorian who found a parallel between his plight and Wordsworth's. Arnold's 'Memorial Verses,' a poem of 1850, exhibits a similar pattern of rejection of Byron and acceptance of Wordsworth. This poem, if not for the fact that it was written twenty-three years before the appearance of Mill's *Autobiography*, might be taken as a factual account of Mill's encounter with the two Romantic poets; much as Mill's description of the would-be conservative poet in the Vigny essay might be taken, if not for the chronological impossibility of doing so, as a description of Arnold. The spiritual kinship between Arnold and Mill that is revealed by a comparison of the two documents is striking.

Arnold's poem was written to honor Wordsworth, who had recently died; and Arnold could think of no greater honor to accord the poet than a recognition that his poetry restored a considerable number of men of the age from an unfeeling aridity to spiritual health. The poem begins by considering what Goethe and Byron have done for the age. Arnold, like Mill, talks of Byron's supposed power to arouse feeling:

> He taught us little; but our soul
> Had *felt* him like the thunder's roll.[126]

But, after fifty lines of due consideration, Arnold—thrusting consistency aside—declares that a power other than Byron's is wanted to make us feel.

Wordsworth, the argument continues, like men of the present

day, suffered from the inability to feel, but Wordsworth succeeded in discovering the secret of health:

> He too upon a wintry clime
> Had fallen—on this iron time
> Of doubts, disputes, distractions, fears.
> He found us when the age had bound
> Our soul in its benumbing round;
> He spoke, and loos'd our heart in tears.
> He laid us as we lay at birth
> On the cool flowery lap of earth,
> Smiles broke from us and we had ease;
> The hills were round us, and the breeze
> Went o'er the sun-lit fields again;
> Our foreheads felt the wind and rain.
> Our youth return'd; for there was shed
> On spirits that had long been dead,
> Spirits dried up and closely furl'd,
> The freshness of the early world.

Arnold's description of Wordsworth's effect upon him corresponds closely to Mill's expression of gratitude to the poet who
enabled him once again to feel the pleasures of the natural
world; and Mill's contrast between Byron, as the poet of active
temperaments, and Wordsworth, as the poet of contemplative
spirits, is paralleled by Arnold's summary celebration of
Wordsworth's powers:

> Time may restore us in his course
> Goethe's sage mind and Byron's force;
> But where will Europe's latter hour
> Again find Wordsworth's healing power?
> Others will teach us how to dare,
> And against fear our breast to steel:
> Others will strengthen us to bear—
> But who, ah who, will make us feel?[127]

In 1879 Arnold reiterated his appreciation of Wordsworth's
healing power. Mill's fear that his appreciation of Wordsworth,
although generous and enthusiastic, was impure because wholly
personal would have been allayed by Arnold's essay on the poet,
had Mill lived to read it. For Arnold attributed the greatness of
Wordsworth's poetry to 'the extraordinary power with which
Wordsworth feels the joy offered to us in the simple primary

affections and duties, and because of the extraordinary power with which, in case after case, he shows us this joy, and renders it so as to make us share it.' At the same time that Wordsworth reveals that inner joy which everyone seeks, Arnold pointed out, he discovers it in a source from which everyone can draw.[128]

In an essay on Byron which appeared two years later, Arnold insisted upon the superiority which Wordsworth, the poet of passive natures, would always have over Byron, the poet of action and power. As if to apologize for a passionate tribute which he had offered Byron (upon whose power he always looked with mixed feelings of guilt and admiration), Arnold said that Wordsworth must be placed above Byron because of his greater spiritual value. The sympathy one may have with Byron's power is, after all, but an ephemeral elevation of the soul; Wordsworth, on the other hand, 'has an insight into permanent sources of joy and consolation for mankind,' and can give us 'more which we can rest upon now, and which men may rest upon always.'[129]

The poet whom Arnold called 'one of the best and deepest spiritual influences of our century' and the greatest English poet after Shakespeare and Milton[130] was to become for Mill the symbol of all which is valuable in life and yet unconnected with action. Mill's addiction to Wordsworth signaled his separation from the Utilitarian school as it had usually been conceived. Shortly after his conversion to Wordsworth, Mill engaged in a debate, first privately and then before the Debating Society, with J. A. Roebuck, later to become Matthew Arnold's helpless adversary in *Culture and Anarchy*. Roebuck, 'all whose instincts were those of action and struggle,' frowned contemptuously upon Wordsworth's poetry as frivolous and ineffectual and exalted Byron's 'as the poetry of human life.'[131] Mill tried unsuccessfully to persuade Roebuck that in the cultivation of the feelings and imagination there lay great value; and this dispute about poetry, the first significant disagreement between the two friends, proved to be at bottom the dispute between two opposed conceptions of human life and helped to alienate Mill and Roebuck from one another.

In 1831, Mill, who had met Wordsworth several times at Henry Taylor's London breakfasts, made a special pilgrimage to the poet 'in his own kingdom' of the lake country, and was granted an audience. He thought Wordsworth the best talker he had ever heard. Having assumed that the contemplative quality of Wordsworth's poetry was an adequate reflection of the whole character of the man, Mill was surprised to find Wordsworth a man of large and expansive feelings, possessed of knowledge of and interest in not only those active pursuits of men so notably absent from his poetry but in questions of political and social importance.[132]

Wordsworth's poetry, once Mill had come to appreciate it, largely determined his view of poetry in general. Thus, in the review which he wrote of Tennyson's poetry in 1835, he condemned the fashion which exalted a poet only if he delineated 'the more violent passions; . . . states of excitement approaching to monomania, and characters predisposed to such states.'[133] In a letter of 1841 he remarked that the England of his day was too committed to earnest practicality and external effort to admit that poetry has a serious intention (Mill discounted Victorian demands for morality as simply an insistence by the reigning proprieties that they receive due respect) or that the inner life has its appropriate form of expression. Yet, predicted Mill,

> the time will come again when its due rank will be assigned to Contemplation, & the calm culture of reverence and love. Then Poetry will resume her equality with prose, an equality like every healthy equality, resolvable into reciprocal superiority. But that time is not yet, & the crowning glory of Wordsworth is that he has borne witness to it & kept alive its traditions in an age which but for him would have lost sight of it entirely & even poetical minds would with us have gone off into the heresy of the poetical critics of the present day in France who hold that poetry is above all & preeminently a *social* thing.[134]

Mill saw that poetry would have to play the same role in the life of modern society that Wordsworth's poetry had played in his own life.

Thus it was that Wordsworth rescued Arnold and Mill from the nearly moribund state in which they found themselves as a result of their commitment to incessant thought and analysis. Both men testified that, when all else failed, Wordsworth's poetry enabled them to feel fully alive even when they might also feel hesitant in action.

Arnold and Mill, as Trilling has pointed out,[135] learned more from Wordsworth than how to feel; they learned how to be. Both protested against the worship of 'machinery,' by which they meant the confusion of various kinds of action, which can be no more than means, with the end, which is a state of being: the perfection of the spirit. Throughout *Culture and Anarchy*, Arnold inveighed against the elevation of various kinds of 'machinery,' including commerce, health, population, liberty, even religion and morality, into self-justifying ends. In criticizing the false estimate given to the last-mentioned piece of machinery, Arnold accused the English of confusing the 'relative moral perfection' of right conduct with the inward spiritual perfection that culture seeks.[136] His distinction between moral and spiritual perfection is the distinction between perfect acting and perfect being. In *On Liberty* Mill countered what he thought the authoritarian and conventionally religious obsession with the right conduct of man by asking whether the guarantee, by external compulsion, of a man's right action is worth the sacrifice of the possibility of his spiritual perfection. His argument here (as elsewhere) resembles that in *Areopagitica*, where Milton asserted that God 'esteems the growth and completing of one virtuous person, more than the restraint of ten vicious.'[137] For being, Mill contended, is at least as important as doing:

> It really is of importance, not only what men do, but also what manner of men they are that do it. Among the works of man, which human life is rightly employed in perfecting and beautifying, the first in importance surely is man himself. Supposing it were possible to get houses built, corn grown, battles fought, causes tried, and even churches erected and prayers said, by machinery—by automatons in human form—it would be a considerable loss to exchange for these automatons even the men and women who at present inhabit the more civilised parts of the world, and who assuredly are but starved specimens of what nature can and will produce.[138]

The emphasis which Arnold and Mill came to place upon being rather than doing was evident in the way they chafed at the idea of religious commandment. In *On Liberty* (and again in *Utilitarianism*) Mill maintained that the Christian gospel expressed itself 'in terms most general, often impossible to be interpreted literally, and possessing rather the impressiveness of poetry or eloquence than the precision of legislation.'[139] Arnold was severely critical of Tolstoy for attempting to turn Christianity into a set of commandments (and only five at that!). He was discomforted by the possibility of having Jesus' teachings (especially the more radical or, as Goethe would have it, fanatical ones) interpreted as commands to action. Was Jesus no better than one of the liberal practitioners? Of course he was, said Arnold, because he did not intend his 'hard sayings' as literal commands to action but as spiritual utterances which 'sink down into our soul, work there, set up an influence, form habits of conduct, and prepare the future.'[140]

What Carlyle took to be Goethe's chief lesson—the need to build dikes in order to prevent the erosion of the spirit by intellectual doubts—Arnold rejected. His poem called 'Resignation: To Fausta' said that the poet, in particular, must not be what Fausta (a female version of Goethe's Faust) is: filled with the impulse to action and to positive achievement. But Arnold knew how widespread the Faustian habit of trying to solve spiritual problems by means of action taken for its own sake had become, and he warned all his contemporaries against the doctrine that life is for action:

> Not milder is the general lot
> Because our spirits have forgot,
> In action's dizzying eddy whirl'd,
> The something that infects the world.[141]

It was once the fashion to contrast the spiritual uncertainty and anarchy of the twentieth century with the safe refuge of Victorian certainty and order. Against such wistful naïveté there was bound to be a reaction; and it would be fair to say that most of those who resort to the Victorians at all now seek in them, a few of them, not certainty but the faculty which makes the endurance of uncertainty possible. Bertrand Russell, in 1945, wrote:

Uncertainty, in the presence of vivid hopes and fears, is painful, but must be endured if we wish to live without the support of comforting fairy tales. It is not good either to forget the questions that philosophy asks, or to persuade ourselves that we have found indubitable answers to them. To teach how to live without certainty, and yet without being paralyzed by hesitation, is perhaps the chief thing that philosophy, in our age, can still do for those who study it.[142]

Ten years later, in a speech before the British Academy, Russell found Mill's characteristic distinction not in his intellect but in his intellectual virtues: 'His intellectual integrity was impeccable.'[143] Lionel Trilling apologized for thrusting Arnold upon a public preoccupied with more urgent matters when he wrote in 1939 that

> in a day when intellectual men are often called upon to question their intellect and to believe that thought is inferior to action and opposed to it, that blind partisanship is fidelity to an idea, Arnold has still a word to say—not against the taking of sides but against the belief that taking a side settles things or requires the suspension of reason.[144]

It is precisely Arnold's and Mill's capacity for living with uncertainty which makes them, on the one hand, favorite targets for devout believers in infallible churches or infallible philosophies, and, on the other, the support of those who subscribe to neither.[145] Thus W. J. Bate has championed Arnold's 'disinterestedness' against contemporary political and religious dogmatists who censure him for eclecticism and lack of commitment;[146] and the late Richard Chase has argued that 'among the Victorians, it is Mill who tests the modern mind' because he always brings to the fore the 'morose desire for dogmatic certainty' of his modern critics.[147]

It would have pleased Arnold and Mill to know that their stubborn refusal to relieve the paralysis of action into which the age had thrown them by the illegitimate anodynes used by their contemporaries had been vindicated, even partially, by posterity. For it was their concern with the plight of future generations living without religious belief that led Arnold and Mill to formulate theories of poetry which would show others where they might find a source of consolation for anxiety, doubt, and hesitation as effective as that which Arnold and Mill had discovered in Wordsworth.

V

THE UTILITY OF POETRY

We know how easily the uselessness of almost every branch of knowledge may be proved, to the complete satisfaction of those who do not possess it. How many, not altogether stupid men, think the scientific study of languages useless, think ancient languages useless, all erudition useless, logic and metaphysics useless, poetry and the fine arts idle and frivolous?

JOHN STUART MILL

As to useful knowledge, a single line of poetry, working in the mind, may produce more thoughts and lead to more light, which is what man wants, than the fullest acquaintance . . . with the processes of digestion. MATTHEW ARNOLD

ARNOLD AND MILL inherited the Romantic reverence for poetry —which had, perhaps, never before seemed so important as it did to Wordsworth and Coleridge—and yet they found themselves in an environment hostile even to poetry's most modest claims. Victorian hostility to poetry drew from many sources. Benthamites doubted the utility of poetry; Puritans in modern dress suspected its moral intentions or its lack of them; scientists and logicians thought poetry incompatible with knowledge and truth; religionists deplored what they thought poetry's schismatic desire for an autonomous existence. To meet all these criticisms Arnold and Mill attempted to refurbish the inadequate theoretical machinery left to them by eighteenth-century criticism with the tougher materials afforded by certain strands of both the Classical and the Romantic traditions.

In discussing the poetic theory of Arnold and Mill, I shall, as in the previous chapter, dwell on their differences before stressing the similarities which appear when they are contrasted with their contemporaries. In the first part of my chapter, where I deal with the attempts of Arnold and Mill to reconcile such pairs of opposites as thought and feeling, culture and nature, the ancient and the modern, their differences will be more apparent than in the second and third parts, which show how they upheld the moral function and the truthfulness of poetry against its detractors.

Arnold's and Mill's writings on poetry may be looked at as attempts to arrive at a *via media* between the precepts of Classicism and Romanticism. They are most often concerned with the proper relation between thought and feeling, matter and style, the poet and his society.

The question of the proper relation between thought and feeling in poetry was always near the center of Mill's speculation on the subject. In the second half of a two-part essay of 1833, Mill attempted to answer the question of whether there are poetic *natures*. He recognized a certain kind of 'mental and physical constitution or temperament' which is specially fitted for poetry but does not necessarily produce it, and made the conventional English distinction, familiar to Dryden and Addison, between the poetry of nature and the poetry of 'mere culture.' But he argued that only those persons may be called poets whose ideas are linked by emotions. For everyone else poetry is something artificially induced, and not ingrained in habit and character:

> Whatever be the thing which [natural poets] are contemplating, if it be capable of connecting itself with their emotions, the aspect under which it first and most naturally points itself to them, is its poetic aspect. The poet of culture sees his object in prose, and describes it in poetry; the poet of nature actually sees it in poetry.[1]

Mill proposed Wordsworth and Shelley as examples of the two kinds of poet. In comparing these two poets Mill must have been disturbed by conflicting personal loyalties, for he owed his mental health to Wordsworth, whom he had called the only living English poet of the first rank,[2] but he respected Shelley because he was the favorite poet of Harriet Taylor.[3] In Wordsworth, Mill argued, the thought rather than the emotion is of primary importance. Wordsworth's poetry consists of thoughts which are colored by emotions; it uses emotions to convey thoughts: 'He lets the thought dwell in his mind, till it excites, as is the nature of thought, other thoughts, and also such feelings as the measure of his sensibility is adequate to supply.'[4]

Mill held that the absence of intense and abundant feeling from Wordsworth's poetry made it essentially unlyrical; and, since Mill believed that lyric poetry is 'more eminently and peculiarly poetry than any other,'[5] he designated Shelley the chief representative of the 'natural' poets. Lacking the consecutiveness of thought necessary for a long poem, Shelley best succeeded in the short lyric. His poetry, Mill asserted, was inspired and nourished by emotions, and was 'little else than a pouring forth of the thoughts and images that pass across the mind while some permanent state of feeling is occupying it.'[6] Such poetry can be written only by those capable of both greater happiness and greater unhappiness than mankind in general; its production is contingent not upon the acquisition of knowledge and the technical skills of a craft but solely upon the poet's ability to preserve his peculiar powers of mind and sensibility from the destructive pressures of ordinary life and education.

Mill saw both the value and the dangers of uneducated sensibility. He saw that the powerful emotions which often disturb the poet's equilibrium of judgment and undermine his respect for truth also supply the stuff from which all motives, including the motive which leads men to seek truth, spring. He maintained that the poetic sensibility is a great amoral force that, for the good of society, must be educated, not thwarted. The most impassioned natures have the greatest desire for truth; if their emotional natures are complemented by an adequate intellectual culture, they usually become the most powerful intellects. But the corruption of the best, Mill warned, is still the worst: 'Strong feelings require a strong intellect to carry them, as more sail requires more ballast: and when, from neglect, or bad education, that strength is wanting, no wonder if the grandest and swiftest vessels make the most utter wreck.'[7]

By the time of his 1835 essay on Tennyson, Mill had become still more wary of undisciplined poetic emotion. Instead of positing two different kinds of poet, as he had done earlier, Mill now saw 'in the character of every true poet two elements, for one of which he is indebted to nature, for the other to cultivation,'[8] and spoke of the ideal poet as a harmonious blending of the two elements. Writing at a time when Tennyson had received no acclaim as a poet,[9] Mill predicted a high place for him in English poetic literature—but on one condition. Mill thought him generously endowed with that special gift of the natural poet: 'a nervous organization . . . so constituted, as to be, more easily than common organizations, thrown . . . into *states* of enjoyment or suffering.' But Mill warned that, although Tennyson had shown an advance in 'intellectual culture' from the 1830 to the 1833 volume, his intellect still lagged behind his great natural gifts for poetry. He urged Tennyson to bring his 'powers of thought' abreast of his enormous 'powers of execution' if he wished to become a great poet.[10]

His remarks on Tennyson show that Mill was losing his sympathy for the Shelleyan type of poet. The 1835 essay, unlike its predecessor, makes emotion subservient to thought. Poetry, Mill argued, seeks to transmute thoughts into equivalent poetical feelings in order to communicate them; for feelings are the only things which poetry can deal with and communicate directly. But the task of perfecting the 'desires and character' of men by purifying their emotions is 'the work of cultivated reason' and the poet's success in it will depend upon the value of his thoughts and his ability to impress them on the feelings of mankind. For the mastery of all that part of poetry which is not simply the result of poetic temperament, Mill asserted, the poet must rely on the cultivation of his mental powers. Nor is it enough that he refrain from the endemic anti-intellectualism of the pretenders to poetry; he must consciously involve himself in philosophic studies, for

> every great poet, every poet who has extensively or permanently influenced mankind, has been a great thinker;—has had a philosophy though perhaps he did not call it by that name;—has had his mind full of thoughts derived not merely from passive sensibility, but from trains of reflection, from observation, analysis, and generalization.[11]

The high praise which Mill accorded to Shelley in the earlier essay was the kind of praise which, in philosophy, he generously accorded to half-thinkers. For a poet without intellectual powers who remained content with his natural gift was an incomplete and unsatisfactory poet. Shelley, Mill decided in 1835, was just such a half-poet; because he relied upon the stuff of his own mind and temper, upon subjective, private, perhaps eccentric material, he produced 'vivid representations of states of passive and dreamy emotion fitted to give extreme pleasure to persons of similar organization to the poet, but not likely to be sympathized in, because not understood, by any other persons.'[12] Mill discerned a causal relation between intellectual failure and inability to deal with a tangible and generally available subject. He had come to see that the spontaneous overflow of powerful feeling could not by itself suffice to produce great poetry.

In his 1865 essay, 'The Function of Criticism at the Present Time,' Matthew Arnold condemned the English Romantic movement because, 'with plenty of energy, plenty of creative force, [it] did not know enough.' A poet, he argued, cannot deal adequately with life and the world in poetry unless he knows them as they really are. But modern life and the modern world are so complex that they cannot be understood without a supreme effort of the critical intelligence; and such an effort the English Romantic poets either would not or could not make. The only modern poet who did make the effort was Goethe, and it is Goethe's greater power of critical intelligence, in a word, his greater knowledge, which makes him the superior of, say, Byron:

> Both Byron and Goethe had a great productive power, but Goethe's was nourished by a great critical effort providing the true materials for it, and Byron's was not; Goethe knew life and the world . . . much more comprehensively and thoroughly than Byron.[13]

Arnold concurred in Mill's 1835 judgment of Shelley, and, had he known of it, would have called Mill's warning of the disaster which might befall Tennyson prophetic. Arnold said that Shelley was unable to master the poetic medium because he had 'neither intellectual force enough nor sanity enough.'[14] Like Mill, Arnold found that Shelley's great weakness as a poet, the absence of the tangible from his work, resulted from his lack of 'a sound subject-matter.'[15] Arnold's judgment of Tennyson was that 'with all his temperament and artistic skill, [he] is deficient in intellectual power; and no modern poet can make very much of his business unless he is pre-eminently strong in this.'[16]

For Arnold as for Mill the problem of attaining an equilibrium between thought and feeling was the central problem of the modern poet. Arnold remarked, in a letter of 1863 about the poetry of Jean Ingelow, that 'it is a great deal to give one true feeling in poetry, and I think she seemed to be able to do that; but I do not at present very much care for poetry unless it can give me true *thought* as well. It is the alliance of these two that makes great poetry, the only poetry really worth very much.'[17] Much of Arnold's poetic criticism was an attempt to mediate between the excesses of emotional poets on the one hand and intellectualizing poets on the other. He was as much irritated by Clough's attempt 'to *solve* the Universe' as he was fatigued by Tennyson's 'dawdling with its painted shell.'[18] He thought poetry superior to what is included under the generic term 'art,' for it is 'thought and art in one.'[19]

As Mill had distinguished between the natural and the cultured poet, Arnold, in his essay on Maurice de Guérin, distinguished between the poet who interprets the natural world and the poet who interprets the moral world. Corresponding to what, in Mill's theory, is the gift of the natural poet, we find Arnold's description of the natural endowment of the poet who interprets the natural world, who gives his readers a sense of harmony with the lives of objects outside them, as a 'peculiar temperament, an extraordinary delicacy of organisation and susceptibility to impressions.' That invaluable but amoral force which Mill discerned in the poet of nature reappears in Arnold's first type of poet, who is 'a sort of human Aeolian harp, catching and rendering every rustle of Nature.' Such a poet 'goes into religion and out of religion, into society and out of society, not from the motives which impel men in general, but to feel what it is all like; he is thus hardly a moral agent. . . .'[20]

But for Arnold, as for Mill, there was a kind of poet other than the interpreter of nature. Poetry interprets the world not only through '*natural magic*' but through '*moral profundity*'; and neither faculty can by itself give rise to great poetry. In Lucretius and in Wordsworth, as Mill, too, had noticed, 'expression tends to become too little sensuous and simple, too much intellectualised.' In the greatest works of the greatest poets, such as

Aeschylus and Shakespeare, however, the two faculties are united and balanced.[21]

Thus Arnold and Mill agreed not only upon the need for a poetical alliance between feeling and thought, but even upon which poets suffered from a lack of knowledge, or from under-developed intellect. Yet they disagreed in their recommendations for making good the deficiency. Mill had urged Tennyson to acquire intellectual culture as fast as he could, but Arnold did not think that the individual was capable of improving his situation by his own efforts. In 'The Function of Criticism at the Present Time,' he blamed Wordsworth for not having read enough books, and then added:

> To speak of books and reading may easily lead to a misunderstanding here. It was not really books and reading that lacked to our poetry at this epoch; Shelley had plenty of reading, Coleridge had immense reading. Pindar and Sophocles . . . had not many books; Shakespeare was no deep reader. True, but in the Greece of Pindar and Sophocles, in the England of Shakespeare, the poet lived in a current of ideas in the highest degree animating and nourishing to the creative power; society was, in the fullest measure, permeated by fresh thought, intelligent and alive. And this state of things is the true basis for the creative power's exercise, in this it finds its data, its materials, truly ready for its hand; all the books and reading in the world are only valuable as they are helps to this.

It is not the poet's task but the philosopher's to analyze data and discover material; these must lie ready to the poet's hand for synthesis and exposition.[22] As Arnold pointed out elsewhere, what a man has to say in poetry is provided by his age; he is responsible for the way in which he says it.[23] Arnold believed that poets contemporary with him, try as they would, read as many books as they might, could not produce a literary masterpiece, because 'for the creation of a master-work of literature two powers must concur, the power of the man and the power of the moment, and the man is not enough without the moment.'[24]

What, then, was to be done? Arnold believed that a great critical effort must precede any new era of poetic creativity. The poet must stand aside while the critical intellect performs its duty, which is 'to establish an order of ideas, if not absolutely true, yet true by comparison with that which it displaces; to make the best ideas prevail.' When these ideas reach society, 'there is a stir and growth everywhere; out of this stir and growth come the creative epochs of literature.' Such, at least, was Arnold's hope, and to show the courage of his convictions, he resigned himself to the secondary role of being a forerunner— albeit an indispensable one—of a great literary epoch to come:

> That promised land it will not be ours to enter, and we shall die in the wilderness: but to have desired to enter it, to have saluted it from afar, is already, perhaps, the best distinction among contemporaries; it will certainly be the best title to esteem with posterity.[25]

But Arnold also offered a less drastic solution for those poets sufficiently gifted to adopt it. In ages such as the Athenian or the Elizabethan, the poet was absolved from the duty to acquire intellectual culture by the arduous reading of many books; but in less fortunate ages and nations, the reading of many books and the keeping abreast of the thought and achievement of the country's intellectual elite did help the poet to make up for much, though never all, of what society failed to give him.[26]

Goethe was, in Arnold's view, the best example of the success which may come to such a poet. Goethe himself had said to Eckermann that 'if a great talent is to be speedily and happily developed, the great point is that a great deal of intellect and sound culture should be current in a nation.'[27] And Arnold thought Goethe had done more than any other modern poet to recreate the cultural atmosphere favorable to poetic creation. As early as 1853, he proclaimed that Goethe was 'the greatest poet of modern times, the greatest critic of all times.'[28] In one of his lectures on the study of Celtic literature he announced his opinion that the 'only first-rate body of contemporary poetry' was the poetry of Goethe himself. Despite his frequent flatness of speech, Goethe had to be considered the most important of modern poets. It is useless, Arnold maintained, to object that, as a poet, Goethe hardly deserves comparison with men who possessed the poetic style and the infinite power that Dante and Shakespeare did. For the special task which was Goethe's could not have been accomplished only by 'style, eloquence, charm, poetry.' Goethe was obliged, as Dante and Shakespeare (who had materials available for exposition) were not, to create his world anew:

> When Goethe came, Europe had lost her basis of spiritual life; she had to find it again; Goethe's task was,—the inevitable task for the modern poet henceforth is,—as it was for the Greek poet in the days of Pericles, not to preach a sublime sermon on a given text like Dante, not to exhibit all the kingdoms of human life and the glory of them like Shakspeare, but to interpret human life afresh, and to supply a new spiritual basis to it.

For the fulfillment of this task, Arnold argued, a German was peculiarly suited, since it was as much a task for science as for poetry; and here Goethe's prosaic, serious, patient—in a word, scientific—German nature stood him in good stead.[29]

The Goethe whom Arnold esteemed is the thinker and critic rather than the poet. 'It is by no means as the greatest of poets,' Arnold later wrote, 'that Goethe deserves the pride and praise of his countrymen. It is as the clearest, the largest, the most helpful thinker of modern times.'[30] Even in the 1853 Preface, where he proclaimed Goethe the greatest of modern poets and critics, Arnold called *Faust* defective when 'judged strictly as a poetical work.'[31] It is, after all, like so much English Romantic poetry, subjective, autobiographical, overly concerned with expression and with parts at the expense of the whole. In a letter of 1853, Arnold noted that Goethe 'had all the negative recommendations for a perfect artist'—that is, good taste and intellectual control—'but wanted the positive'—that is, creative energy.[32] What Goethe represented in the 1853 Preface was the importance of architectonic—the structural as opposed to the spiritual or inspirational element in literature. The Classical ideals of balance and symmetry had come, as early as 1853, to assume the greatest importance in Arnold's conception of poetry.

But Arnold did not adopt his classicism without a prior struggle against contrary impulses in himself. In a letter written late in 1847 or early in 1848, he described to Clough the peculiar difficulties confronting the modern poet in the subject matter presented to him. Modern literature, he said, cannot afford the luxury of close attention to matters of style and form because modern poets are overwhelmed by the multitude of new thoughts and feelings demanding to be treated in poetry. A poet's primary duty, Arnold wrote, is to his subject matter rather than to his style. But subject matter depends upon the age in which the poet lives:

> The *what you have to say* depends on your age. In the 17th century it was *a smaller harvest than now*, and sooner to be reaped: and therefore to its reaper was left time to stow it more finely and curiously. Still more was this the case in the ancient world. The poet's matter being *the hitherto experience of the world, and his own*, increases with every century.[33]

Eventually, Arnold decided that the subject matter imposed upon the modern poet by his age was not only more immense but more chaotic than poetic subject matter ever had been; and he decided that it was too large and confused to be safely contained within the symmetrical framework of Classical poetry. His desire to escape from a confused, multitudinous subject matter which would hardly yield to philosophical analysis, much less to poetic synthesis, grew steadily. In 1848, he explained the poetic weakness of Keats and Browning by saying: 'They will not be patient neither understand that they must begin with an Idea of the world in order not to be prevailed over by the world's multitudinousness. . . .' In 1849 he wrote to Clough that the age was 'not unprofound, not ungrand, not unmoving:—but *unpoetical.*' In the same letter, he told his friend that a mastery of form is 'the sole *necessary* of Poetry as such: whereas the greatest wealth and depth of matter is merely a superfluity in the Poet *as such.*'[34] Unable to master the enormous mass of material which his age thrust upon him, Arnold said that he would preserve the poetic framework at the expense of the matter which threatened to destroy its traditional shape.

The emotionalism and subjectivism of the Romantic poets seemed to Arnold an assault by the chaos of modern life upon the Classical ideal of order. In his 1853 Preface he suggested that 'it is impossible for us, under the circumstances amidst which we live, to think clearly, to feel nobly, and to delineate firmly.' If it has become necessary to choose,[35] in poetry, between mechanical proficiency without spirituality or feeling, and spirituality without mechanical proficiency, let us, said Arnold, unhesitatingly choose the first alternative because it does less harm to art.[36] Art becomes, in Arnold's definition, essentially rules, framework, boundaries, a map without colors or a stage without actors.

Twelve years later, in 'The Function of Criticism,' Arnold proposed the substitution of critical for creative activity. But he insisted that criticism had to obey the rule of disinterestedness to be effective. Carlyle and Ruskin, artists who had already deserted creation for criticism, had invalidated much of their criticism by transgressing against the rule of disinterestedness and entering the sphere of political and social practice.[37]

The collocation of Goethe, Carlyle, and the idea of disinterestedness occurs in another Victorian document besides 'The Function of Criticism at the Present Time.' In 1840, John Stuart Mill wrote to his friend John Sterling:

> What you say about the absence of a disinterested & heroic pursuit of Art as the greatest want of England at present, has often struck me, but I suspect it will not be otherwise until our social struggles are over. Art needs earnest but quiet times—in ours I am afraid Art itself to be powerful must be polemical—Carlylean not Goethian.[38]

Mill, as I have shown, was still more chary than Arnold of syntheses undertaken before analyses were complete. He did not ask of art any more than he did of philosophy that it be disinterested, in Arnold's sense, so long as society is in a state of growth and imperfection, for he considered art one of the tools of analysis and discovery. That is why, unlike Arnold, he could think of Carlyle as an artist.[39] Arnold's—or Goethe's—insistence on Classical symmetry and perfection of form in poetry was for Mill the equivalent of Comte's premature synthesis of available data in philosophy; for it sacrificed fullness to harmony.

Mill shared with Arnold certain premises about the peculiar dilemma with which modern life confronted the poet. Like Arnold, he believed that most literary men 'take their colour from the age in which they live,'[40] and that literature must be viewed 'as an emanation of the civilization of the period.'[41] The period, as a subject for poetry, impressed him much as it did Arnold:

> Every modern thinker has so much wider a horizon, & there is so much deeper a soil accumulated on the surface of human nature by the ploughings it has undergone & the growths it has produced

of which soil every writer or artist of any talent turns up more or less even in spite of himself—in short the moderns have vastly more material to reduce to order than the ancients dreamt of & the secret of harmonizing it all has not yet been discovered.

But Mill's reaction to the modern age and to the material with which it threatened to deluge the poet was almost opposite to Arnold's. Mill was not ready to sacrifice matter to form. He did not believe that the time for synthesis, and for Classicism, had yet arrived:

> It is too soon by a century or two to attempt either symmetrical productions in art or symmetrical characters. We all need to be blacksmiths or ballet dancers with good stout arms or legs, useful to do what we have got to do, and useful to fight with at times— we cannot be Apollos and Venuses just yet.[42]

Yet sometime in the future. For Mill's ideal was, like Arnold's, the Classical ideal. But he feared losing the way in haste to arrive at the goal.

Mill was interested in what he called Goethe's lifelong effort 'to make himself a Greek.' Goethe seemed to him obsessed with symmetry: not only was he irritated by the wildness and irregularity of Gothic architecture, but even Greek architecture, when it was 'too gigantic,' disturbed him. In judging human character as in judging art, Mill noted, Goethe always sought balance and symmetry. Despite all his critical precepts, Goethe 'never could succeed in putting symmetry into any of his own writings, except very short ones.' Goethe's failure to practice what he preached was for Mill a proof of 'the utter impossibility for a modern with all the good will in the world, to tight-lace himself into the dimensions of an ancient.'[43]

Arnold, on the other hand, attempted to uphold, with Goethe's help, the Classical ideal against the heresies of the Romantics, and Classical subjects against those offered him by modern life and prescribed by modern critics. Goethe had advised Eckermann that 'one should not study contemporaries and competitors, but the great men of antiquity, whose works have, for centuries, received equal homage and consideration. . . . Let us study Molière, let us study Shakespeare, but above all things, the old Greeks, and always the Greeks.'[44] Arnold, as a faithful disciple of Goethe, told Clough in 1853 that he 'read Homer and toujours Homer.'[45] To the 'intelligent critic' who had urged poets to leave 'the exhausted past' in order to fasten upon subjects which were modern and therefore interesting, Arnold replied, in his 1853 Preface, that subjects are interesting not by virtue of their modernity or antiquity, but by virtue of their ability to appeal 'to the great primary human affections: to those elementary feelings which subsist permanently in the race, and which are independent of time.' An inherently great human action a thousand years old, he argued, is a fitter subject for poetic representation than a trivial action of his own time. Not content with correcting the moderns for their predilection for contemporary subject matter, Arnold fell by reaction into the opposite error of praising the ancients because they usually eschewed present actions as subjects for tragedy and preferred those of the past. The Greeks avoided subjects drawn from contemporary life, Arnold maintained, because they appreciated the value of mythic subjects which were familiar to their audience, and understood the difficulty of seeing things close at hand in true perspective—since only time enables the poet to disentangle what is transient and accidental from what is eternal and universal.[46]

Arnold thought modern poets had other lessons to learn from the Greeks. Where the moderns were primarily concerned with the quality of expression, the Greeks subordinated expression to the action; where the moderns' first concern was with 'single lines and passages,' the Greeks were primarily concerned with the effect of the whole, the total impression made by a poem. Perhaps the most disastrous delusion of the Romantic poets was their belief that 'a true allegory of the state of one's own mind in a representative history' is a suitable subject for poetry. The ancients, who understood 'the all-importance of the choice of a subject,' would not have degraded an art intended to convey general and universal truth into a medium for autobiography.

Mill, too, was alive to the defects of modern or Romantic style. In 1826 he contrasted English writers, preoccupied with expression, with those of France who, though endowed with stylistic gifts, 'never seem desirous of showing off their own eloquence; [and] seem to write because they have something to say, and not because they desire to say something.'[47] In 1828, he accused modern writers of eschewing nature and simplicity because they recognized that popular taste was attracted by 'gaudy, affected, and meretricious ornament, contributing nothing either to the clearness of the idea or the vividness of the leading image; the effusions of a mind not in earnest; the play of an imagination occupied with everything in the world except the subject.'[48] In his article on Tennyson he attributed great importance to the central thought or harmonizing principle of a poem and to the general impression the poem makes; individual expressions in a poem are 'nothing in themselves, but everything as they conduce to the general result.'[49]

Like Arnold, Mill looked to the ancients to provide a corrective example to modern faults of style. He attributed to the literature of the ancients a perfection of form or composition which should serve as a standard for modern writers. He held that the superiority of the ancient literature lay in its 'perfect adaptation of means to ends.' The Greek and Roman authors never lost sight of their end in preoccupation with the means to its attainment:

> They always . . . had a meaning; they knew what they wanted to say; and their whole purpose was to say it with the highest degree of exactness and completeness, and bring it home to the mind with the greatest possible clearness and vividness. It never entered into their thoughts to conceive of a piece of writing as beautiful in itself, abstractedly from what it had to express: its beauty must all be subservient to the most perfect expression of the sense.[50]

Thus Mill agreed with Arnold that the moderns had much to learn from the ancients in matters of style and construction. But he would not allow the ancients to prescribe substance as well as form to the moderns. In a notable exception to his general preference for ancient over modern literature, Mill said that

> as regards substance, I consider modern poetry to be superior to ancient, in the same manner, though in a less degree, as modern science: it enters deeper into nature. The feelings of the modern mind are more various, more complex and manifold, than those of the ancients ever were.[51]

Like Arnold, Mill recognized that such variety, complexity, and multiplicity could not be contained within the ancient mould. But he would not sacrifice substance to form, and he would have condemned Arnold's desire to flee to a realm where form is everything as futile escapism. Though he shared Arnold's belief in the immense superiority of both the form and the style of the ancients, he insisted that modern life had to be dealt with in poetry; not simply because it was modern, but because it presented an immensely rich, albeit troublesome, subject matter. Like Arnold, he attributed the slovenliness and prolixity of modern literary composition to the peculiar demands of modern life, which were such that

> the work to be done, the mass to be worked upon, are so vast, that those who have anything particular to say—who have, as the phrase goes, any message to deliver—cannot afford to devote their time to the production of masterpieces.[52]

But he did not think that art ought to raise itself to a pure region where its only concern is beauty, and whence it may gaze with Olympian detachment upon human affairs. Rather, he sympathized with the French apologists for an art deeply engaged in the real world. Such an art, Mill argued, when possessed by an idea about human life or about society, will follow it through to its consequences regardless of offenses committed against abstract beauty, and even at the cost of descending to hideousness.[53]

I have shown how, for Arnold and Mill, the question of whether modern life can be dealt with in poetry turned, to a considerable extent, upon the thought and the poetry of Goethe. For Goethe himself, as Pater pointed out, the overwhelming question had been: 'Can the blitheness and universality of the antique ideal be communicated to artistic productions, which shall contain the fulness of the experience of the modern world?'[54] Both Arnold and Mill answered the question negatively, and illustrated their answers by reference to the disparity between Goethe's Classical tenets and his Romantic poetry. But whereas Arnold used the Classical tenets to measure the inadequacy of the poetry, Mill used the poetry as a proof of the inadequacy of the Classical tenets.[55]

Arnold and Mill were so far products of their age as to respect its demand that poetry, like all other human activities, serve a moral purpose. But they had also inherited from the Romantic movement the conviction that rhetorical didacticism was incompatible with poetry. Therefore, they sought to provide a moral justification for poetry that did not rely upon rhetoric and didacticism.

For the average eighteenth-century poet or critic, full of reverence for the *Ars Poetica* of Horace, poetry was still a branch of rhetoric. Poetry had a moral purpose and was expected to achieve its end by means of didacticism. Dr. Johnson, for example, saw no contradiction between hortatory and poetic statement. He scolded Shakespeare for being 'so much more careful to please than to instruct, that he seems to write without any moral purpose.'[56] Most eighteenth-century poets were incapable of imagining any means less artificial and mechanical than didacticism by which poetry might achieve its moral end. Jeremy Bentham was only taking the eighteenth-century poet at his own word when he charged that the poet's business 'consists in stimulating our passions, and exciting our prejudices. . . . The poet must see everything through colored media, and strive to make every one else to do the same.'[57]

Mill replied to Bentham's charges by asserting that poetry has nothing whatever to do with swaying the passions of an audience in the attempt to influence its beliefs or move it to action. Poetry, he said, must be without any taint of eloquence or rhetoric. Poetry is essentially soliloquy, which may be overheard by, but is not addressed to, an audience:

> When the act of utterance is not itself the end, but a means to an end,—viz. by the feelings he himself expresses, to work upon the feelings, or upon the belief, or the will, of another,—when the expression of his emotions, or of his thoughts tinged by his emotions, is tinged also by that purpose . . . of making an impression upon another mind, then it ceases to be poetry, and becomes eloquence.[58]

Arnold discerned the weakness of eighteenth-century didacticism in its artificial conception of language. No one has judged eighteenth-century poetry more harshly than Matthew Arnold. His backhanded compliment paid to Dryden (who died in 1700) and Pope as, respectively, the 'glorious founder' and 'the splendid high priest' of England's 'age of prose and reason,' and his refusal to allow to them the title of poet are by now famous. But why did such a judgment seem true to Arnold? The primary reason for Arnold's rejection of Dryden and Pope was their inability to think of language as something organic:

> True Wit is Nature to Advantage drest,
> What oft was Thought, but ne'er so well Exprest.

Pope's conception of language was for Arnold the inevitable consequence of didacticism, the conscious and purposeful attempt to inculcate doctrine through poetry. When another eighteenth-century poet, Burns, fell into the didactic mood, Arnold had this to say of his poetry:

> Surely, if our sense is quick, we must perceive that we have not in those passages a voice from the very inmost soul of the genuine Burns; he is not speaking to us from these depths, he is more or less preaching.

Arnold's theory of poetry demanded an organic conception of substance and manner as inseparable elements. Didactic work violated what should be poetry's organic, natural quality and destroyed 'the high seriousness which comes from absolute sincerity.'[59] In his essay on Gray, Arnold, who illustrates the paradox of the Classicist *par excellence* discarding all the Neoclassical poetry of the century preceding his own, condemned the poetry of the eighteenth century, in a manner that Mill would thoroughly have approved, for not being unconscious enough:

> The difference between genuine poetry and the poetry of Dryden, Pope, and all their school, is briefly this: their poetry is conceived and composed in their wits, genuine poetry is conceived and composed in the soul.[60]

The eighteenth-century aestheticians who thought it possible to unite men on the basis of moral doctrines generally concurred in were not quixotic. The poet of the eighteenth century addressed a fairly homogeneous society which had a substantial stock of common beliefs, and it was not unreasonable for him to adopt an aesthetic ideal the purpose of which was the general inculcation of intellectual and moral doctrines. The Victorian writer was confronted with a pluralistic society rent by ideological discord and characterized by variety and diversity. George Eliot drew the inevitable conclusion in such a situation for an artist with a high moral intention. She wrote, in a letter of 1859, that

> if Art does not enlarge men's sympathies, it does nothing morally. I have had heart-cutting experience that opinions are a poor cement between human souls; and the only effect I ardently long to produce by my writings, is that those who read them should be better able to *imagine* and to *feel* the pains and the joys of those who differ from themselves in everything but the broad fact of being struggling erring human creatures.[61]

Tocqueville went further than George Eliot and maintained that the democratic societies of the nineteenth century encouraged the ideal of unity through imaginative sympathy. Democracy, he argued, softens manners and widens sympathies more effectively than any other form of polity. Feudal bonds did not create any real sympathies between men, 'for real sympathies can exist only between those who are alike, and in aristocratic ages men acknowledge none but the members of their own caste to be like themselves.' Even in the seventeenth century, Tocqueville argued, sympathy extended so little beyond class boundaries that a humane and civilized person like Mme de Sévigné could descend to jocularity about the fate of galley slaves. But in democratic society imaginative sympathy had been immeasurably extended by a social revolution. The democratic man, feeling himself equal to all his fellow men, and in some sense actually being so, could, with his imagination, enter into sympathy with the most wretched of his fellow men.[62]

Arnold and Mill, aware of the inherent weakness of the didactic theory of poetry, and close observers of the failures of sympathy in earlier literature, sought to provide a moral justification for poetry which did not rest upon eighteenth-century notions of rhetoric and exhortation.

Mill's definition of poetry as soliloquy did not preclude a view of poetry as moral inspiration. For so long as the poet remains unaffected by consciousness of an audience when he is writing his poetry, nothing ought to prevent him from showing the finished product to others: 'What we have said or done in solitude, we may voluntarily reproduce when we know that other eyes are upon us.'[63]

Though he insisted that between poetry and rhetoric there is an absolute contradiction, Mill maintained that the end of poetry is entirely moral; for poetry seeks to act 'upon the desires and characters of mankind through their emotions, to raise them towards the perfection of their nature.' Poetry has a purpose primarily moral; and it aims to bring about nothing less than human perfection. Mill said in the essay on Tennyson that poetry transmutes ideas into their equivalent emotions in order to communicate them effectively.[64] He assumed that there is little use swaying men's minds without touching their emotions, for men are feeling as well as thinking beings.

Two years after Mill offered this definition of the purpose of poetry, he published a review of Carlyle's *The French Revolution* which tried to show how poetry could be carefully dissociated from rhetoric and yet act as a moral agent. The French Revolution, which for Mill and Arnold was the greatest event of modern times, had, according to the review, found in Carlyle both its historian and its poet. Carlyle had combined, in his work, the critical intelligence and accuracy of such historians as Hume and Gibbon with the imaginative and sympathetic sensibility of such a dramatist as Schiller; he had achieved the highest form of literature by applying the genius of the poet to the factual material of history.[65]

Mill especially admired Carlyle's objectivity. Carlyle, Mill noted, fully acquaints his reader with men and events before he ventures to express his opinion of them, whereas other historians allow their prejudices and opinions to determine the character of their descriptions and presentations. The reader of Carlyle is as free to draw his own conclusions from the evidence presented as he would be if he actually saw the events passing before his eyes.[66]

Mill's distinction between the author who keeps his opinions distinct from his representation and the author who wilfully confuses them is analogous to his distinction between the poet and the rhetorician. The integrity of Carlyle's 'evidence' is preserved by the fact that it is not tainted by rhetorical intentions. Its real value lies in its perfectly accurate emotional reflection of a reality. Carlyle's capacity for completely rendering what he sees and feels, without distorting the object by what he thinks, makes him a poet:

> Not falsification of the reality is wanted, not the representation of it as being anything which it is not; only a deeper understanding of what it is; the power to conceive, and to represent, not the mere

outside surface and costume of the thing, nor yet the mere logical definition, and *caput mortuum* of it—but an image of the thing itself in the concrete, with all that is lovable or hateable or admirable or pitiable or sad or solemn or pathetic, in it, and in the things which are implied in it.[67]

The power of poetry, Mill thought, lies in its capacity for arousing imaginative sympathy. Carlyle is able to give his readers not only the ability to see through the eyes of the men who are the actors of history, but the ability to see the same world which they saw. In his condemnation of historians who, unlike Carlyle, provide 'little but a canvas, which, if we ourselves can paint, we may fill with almost any picture,'[68] Mill used the very metaphor with which William Hazlitt had criticized James Mill's *History of India* for an aesthetic deficiency which was also a moral shortcoming.

The stress on sympathetic imagination and identification becomes the moral component of Mill's aesthetic theory. In his essay on Bentham,[69] published in 1838, the year after his review of Carlyle, Mill defined imagination as 'that which enables us, by a voluntary effort, to conceive the absent as if it were real, and to clothe it in the feelings which, if it were indeed real, it would bring along with it.' He had come to the heart of the nineteenth century's quarrel with the eighteenth over the manner in which poetry properly performs its moral function when he said that without imagination and the sympathy it creates, 'nobody knows . . . the nature of his fellow-creatures, beyond such generalizations as he may have been enabled to make from his observation of their outward conduct.'[70]

Poetry, then, is the indispensable source of knowledge of humanity. But is knowledge the equivalent of virtue? Mill had tried to answer this question in his 1834 series of articles on Plato's more popular dialogues. He noted that Plato was firmly convinced of the 'absolute identity, of knowledge and virtue.' Plato tried to show that evil actions were never committed voluntarily but always from insufficient knowledge; for he believed that 'scientific instruction is the source of all that is most desirable for man; [and] that whoever had knowledge to *see* what was good, would certainly *do* it; that morals are but a branch of intelligence.'[71]

Mill was not prepared to endorse Plato's doctrine except in a

THE UTILITY OF POETRY

very limited sense. He doubted the efficacy of arguments for virtue, and did not think them capable of providing the motive power which is needed to *be* virtuous. To this end, he said, men require 'inspiration or sympathy from those who already have [virtue],' from artists who can communicate the love of virtue through the imagination and the feelings, and from the example of great men.[72] Knowledge is equal to virtue, Mill argued, only when the knowledge is of the kind which is impressed upon the feelings rather than urged upon the reason; when, in other words, it is poetic as opposed to scientific knowledge.

Mill believed that poetry performs its moral function directly, by making men different from what they are, rather than by urging them to act differently from the way they usually do. The ordinary stage actor, Mill remarked, 'observes and imitates what men of particular characters, and in particular situations, *do*'; the actor of genius 'can, by an act of imagination, actually *be* what they *are*.'[73] Poetry, though it does not, like rhetoric, urge men to act in a certain way, puts men in the state of being which prepares them for virtuous action; for poetry

> brings home to us all those aspects of life which take hold of our nature on its unselfish side, and lead us to identify our joy and grief with the good or ill of the system of which we form a part; and all those solemn or pensive feelings, which, without having any direct application to conduct, incline us to take life seriously, and predispose us to the reception of anything which comes before us in the shape of duty.[74]

Mill thought of poetry as performing its moral function in two different ways. By extending sympathies outward, it acted democratically, in the way that Tocqueville and George Eliot desired; by extending sympathies upwards, poetry acted aristocratically. Its dual function is implicit in Mill's assertion that upon the existence of the capacity for sympathy 'rests the possibility of any cultivation of *goodness* and *nobleness* and the hope of their ultimate entire ascendancy.'[75] (Italics mine.)

Because he was aware of the peculiar shortcomings of democratic society, Mill took great pains to emphasize the aristocratic moral function of poetry. He blamed modern literature for its intolerance of the virtues which had given to the ancient literatures their unique value. In the past, he held, literature had, while remaining within the bounds of probability, tried to present characters 'whose actions and sentiments were of a more generous and loftier cast than are ordinarily to be met with by everybody in everyday life.' But the dogmatic realism of modern literature ruled out of fictional existence all characters on a scale larger than those the reader 'is accustomed to meet at a dinner or a quadrille party.' Yet the justification of a literary education had been, and still was, that from the heroic characters of the ancient literatures 'not only the noblest minds in modern Europe derived much of what made them noble, but even the commoner spirits what made them understand and respond to nobleness.' In place of this genuine and valuable education, Mill argued, modern pedagogues had put either scientific information or theological dogmas, 'as if science and religion were to be taught, not by imbuing the mind with their spirit, but by cramming the memory with summaries of their conclusions.'[76]

Mill always returned to the argument that knowledge is inert without poetry, and that morality is impossible without the kind of knowledge that poetry alone can give. Style, which for the eighteenth century was essentially ornamental, became in Mill's theory the moral agent of the writer. The reader was now asked to measure his own style of life—its very rhythm and texture—against the style of life that was embodied in a particular poem or story which conveyed to him an element of goodness or of nobility which his own existence lacked. If style was something moral, it became of the greatest importance that the character reflected in the style, the character of the writer, be good and noble: 'There are no great writers,' said Mill, 'but those whose qualities as writers are built upon their qualities as human beings—are the mere manifestations and expression of those qualities: all besides is hollow and meretricious. . . . '[77] Consequently, Mill called that book most valuable which incorporated 'any rare kind of moral qualities in its author' in such a way as to convey them to the reader.[78] Dr. Johnson himself could not have asked for a higher moral tone than Mill adopted in dealing with literature.[79]

Arnold's definitions of poetry have led overzealous critics to accuse him of wanting to reduce poetry to amateur philosophizing or to versified sermonizing. Yet Arnold's critical effort was largely directed towards preserving the moral office of poetry while discarding poetic didacticism. He, too, sought to give poetry a moral justification once didacticism had been ruled out as impure and bathetic.

In a series of three lectures delivered from the Oxford chair of poetry late in 1860 and early in 1861 Arnold maintained that no one could adequately translate Homer who did not realize in his translation 'the grand style.' The grand style arises in poetry, Arnold asserted, *'when a noble nature, poetically gifted, treats with simplicity or with severity a serious subject.'* But to describe the circumstances in which the grand style may arise and to give—as Arnold did—examples of the grand style is still not to define it; and this Arnold knew full well. He was even too ready to acknowledge the highhanded dogmatism of his inner light: 'I may say,' he said in the second lecture, 'that the presence or absence of the grand style can only be spiritually discerned; and this is true, but to plead this looks like evading the difficulty.' Yet, when in the last lecture he chided unbelieving critics, Arnold was still evading the difficulty:

> 'The grand style,—but what *is* the grand style?'—they cry; some with an inclination to believe in it, but puzzled; others mockingly and with incredulity. Alas! the grand style is the last matter in the world for verbal definition to deal with adequately. One may say of it as it is said of faith: 'One must feel it in order to know what it is.' But, as of faith, so too one may say of nobleness, of the grand style: 'Woe to those who know it not!'[80]

The grand style evoked a mystical reverence from Arnold because it does what, in his view, all works of literature, philosophy, and religion should: it edifies. But it edifies neither by preaching nor by didacticism, but by working, in the manner proper to poetry, on the emotions. It is essential to 'know' the grand style, but poetic knowledge can be gained only through feeling. Poetry does not fulfill its moral function by trying to inculcate doctrines in the ordinary man. Rather, it attempts to transform him directly:

> The grand style, which is Homer's, is something more than touching and stirring; it can form the character, it is edifying.

The old English balladist may stir Sir Philip Sidney's heart like a trumpet, and this is much: but Homer, but the few artists in the grand style, can do more; they can refine the raw natural man, they can transmute him.[81]

Arnold specifically denied that his moral theory of poetry was an apology for poetic didacticism. In his essay on Wordsworth, he supported his definition of poetic genius as 'the noble and profound application of ideas to life' by noting that Voltaire, a critic of 'signal acuteness,' had attributed the greatness of English poetry to the fact that it treated moral ideas more energetically and profoundly than did the poetry of any other nation. Voltaire, Arnold pointed out, did not mean by the treatment of moral ideas in poetry 'the composing moral and didactic poems,' for these belong to 'a lower kind' than even ballad poetry. The expression *moral idea*, Arnold argued, includes everything which attempts to answer the question, '*how to live.*' An overtly didactic passage by Milton, a line by Keats consoling the lover who never will get to kiss his beloved, and Shakespeare's

> We are such stuff
> As dreams are made on, and our little life
> Is rounded with a sleep,

are all, according to Arnold, examples of poetry dealing with moral ideas.[82] Arnold believed that poetry's moral power is constituted by style as well as ideas; one is not enough without the other. The poet obsessed, like Gautier, with style and expression at the expense of ideas is a poet indifferent to life. But poets like Chaucer or Burns, who exhibited a powerful application of ideas to life, nevertheless, in Arnold's view, fell short of greatness because they did not achieve a powerful *poetic* application of ideas to life.

The idea of the moral influence of poetic style appeared in Arnold's early thoughts on the purpose of poetry. In 1849 he told Clough that Sophocles is less important for what he teaches us about psychology and emotions than for what he directly *does* for us by means of 'the grand moral effects produced by *style*.' In 1853 he minimized the value of 'The Scholar Gipsy' by reminding Clough that what men want from poetry is 'something to animate and ennoble them'; and he added that such a feeling was the basis of his poetics.[83] Style, for Arnold, was as inevitably the expression of the poet's character as the poet's matter was the expression of his mind. Consequently, a poet's character and personality were matters of the greatest importance in Arnold's poetics—for he did not dwell on the private lives of Shelley, Keats, and Byron merely out of a biographical inquisitiveness. One of the few prose passages of Milton which Arnold admired is the one in which Milton discourses upon the theme that he who would be a good poet 'ought himself to be a true poem.'[84]

Milton played a key role in Arnold's thoughts about the morality of poetic style. In spite of his frequent strictures upon the bad Puritan temper of the great Puritan poet, Arnold said that the unique elevation of Milton's poetic style came from the elevation and purity of Milton's life.[85] Milton was for Arnold the sole English representative of the grand style. Although he did not go so far as to say that Milton was England's greatest poet, Arnold called him 'of all our gifted men the best lesson, the most salutary influence.' Since, Arnold argued, the greatest power of poetry is its ability to refine and elevate character by means of the great style, Milton should be especially recommended to the hordes of Anglo-Saxons on both sides of the Atlantic who are hostile to distinction and eloquence, which they look upon as relics of aristocracy.[86] For Arnold, as for Tocqueville and Mill, the grand style was an antidote to the democratic tendency towards coarseness and mediocrity.

The personality of Byron represented for Arnold another aspect of the aristocratic grandeur which he thought poetry might communicate to the men of democratic societies. Nowhere does Arnold's respect for the power of personality, as it is conveyed through literature, emerge more clearly than in some of his remarks on the man whom he considered 'the greatest natural force, the greatest elementary power ... which has appeared in our literature since Shakespeare.'[87] It is the 'daring, dash, and grandiosity' (in Goethe's words) of Byron's personality which are the salutary things in his work. Arnold believed that the poetical personality of Byron—whatever qualifications and reservations we may have about it—'does us good' because it elevates human nature and enlarges men's sense of possibility.[88] For Arnold poetry's moral function was more aristocratic than democratic; he thought more of extending sympathy upward than outward.

In 'The Study of Poetry,' published in 1880, Arnold tried to show that really great poetry arises from the union of a style whose diction and movement are in the grand manner and a matter and substance which have high truth and high seriousness. The powerful application of ideas to life, he argued, is not an effective criticism of life unless it is made 'under the conditions fixed for such a criticism by the laws of poetic truth and poetic beauty.'[89] Ideally, he said, there exists an indissoluble connection between manner and matter, language and thought, style and idea; even though in practice it is possible to point out the shortcomings of a poet in terms of his inability to fulfill one or the other requirement for an effective criticism of life.

In this essay Arnold prescribed his method of judging poetry by means of touchstones. These are lines and passages which embody poetic excellence: high truth and high seriousness in the substance, and unmistakable superiority of diction and movement in the style. The touchstone theory rests upon Arnold's belief in the extreme usefulness of having always fixed in our minds, as sturdy fortifications against the lure which mediocrity in literature or life constantly holds out to us, 'lines and expressions of the great masters' which, if we have tact in applying them, serve as 'infallible' touchstones 'for detecting the presence or absence of high poetic quality, and also the degree of this quality, in all other poetry which we may place beside them.'[90]

Arnold thought that these touchstones might be applied to life as effectively as to literature. The direct application of a line of poetry to a situation in life was the most literal realization of Arnold's 'criticism of life.' Poetry, governed by its own laws of truth and beauty, is by virtue of its autonomy the fittest vehicle for criticizing life. It can ask us to suspend our own rhythm of existence and to try whether the rhythm of a Homer, a Shakespeare, or a Milton does not have a greater dignity or energy or nobility.

Poetry's criticism of life could be effective on even the most mundane level. In the lecture called 'Literature and Science,' when he argued the cause of humane letters against the advocates of a predominantly scientific education, Arnold used a single line of poetry to criticize life as it appeared in an English schoolroom:

> I once mentioned in a school-report, how a young man in one of our English training colleges having to paraphrase the passage in *Macbeth* beginning,
>
> > 'Can'st thou not minister to a mind diseased?'
>
> turned this line into, 'Can you not wait upon the lunatic?' And I remarked what a curious state of things it would be, if every pupil of our national schools knew, let us say, that the moon is two thousand one hundred and sixty miles in diameter, and thought at the same time that a good paraphrase for
>
> > 'Can'st thou not minister to a mind diseased?'
>
> was, 'Can you not wait upon the lunatic?' If one is driven to choose, I think I would rather have a young person ignorant about the moon's diameter, but aware that 'Can you not wait upon the lunatic?' is bad, than a young person whose education had been such as to manage things the other way.[91]

The young man's failure in poetry is at once recognizable as a failure in sympathy and knowledge as well. For Arnold, like Mill, wished to show that scientific knowledge, unlike poetic, did not develop the moral sense.

Thus Arnold and Mill responded to the pressures of their age by developing a moral theory of poetry which refused to countenance the degradation of poetry into didacticism. But the defense of poetry's integrity as a moral agent entailed, as I have shown, the insistence that vital knowledge had to do more with emotion than with intellect. And such a claim met as fervent opposition from Victorian scientists and philosophers as did poetry's claim to moral inspiration from the religionists of the age.

Jeremy Bentham had charged that 'all poetry is misrepresentation' and that 'truth, exactitude of every kind, is fatal to poetry.'[92] Mill, conscious of the Benthamite suspicion of poetry, answered Bentham by saying that the standard of truth must indeed be applied to poetry though only in a very specialized sense. Mill said that he followed Wordsworth in distinguishing science from poetry according to the different ways in which they work: 'The one addresses itself to the belief, the other to the feelings. The one does its work by convincing or persuading, the other by moving. The one acts by presenting a proposition to the understanding, the other by offering interesting objects of contemplation to the sensibilities.'[93] In this early (1833) attempt at definition, Mill tried to prevent science and poetry from trespassing on each other's territory by asserting that they appeal to different human faculties.

In order to minimize poetry's dependence upon the external world, Mill inverted the meaning of the traditional aesthetics of imitation. He defined faithfulness of imitation as truth not to the external object but to the internal emotion under the influence of which that object is viewed. He tried to show how poetry must pass the test of truth, but of truth to the inner world rather than the outer:

> Descriptive poetry consists, no doubt, in description, but in description of things as they appear, not as they *are;* and it paints them not in their bare and natural lineaments, but arranged in the colours and seen through the medium of the imagination set in action by the feelings. If a poet is to describe a lion, he will not set about describing him as a naturalist would, nor even as a traveller would, who was intent upon stating the truth, the whole truth, and nothing but the truth. He describes him by *imagery,* that is, by suggesting the most striking likenesses and contrasts which might occur to a mind contemplating the lion, in the state of awe, wonder, or terror, which the spectacle naturally excites, or is, on the occasion, supposed to excite. Now this is describing the lion professedly, but the state of excitement of the spectator really. The lion may be described falsely or in exaggerated colours, and the poetry be all the better; but if the human emotion be not painted with the most scrupulous truth, the poetry is bad poetry, *i.e.* is not poetry at all, but a failure.[94]

The poet's first obligation is not to that external, more or less objective world which is common property, but to that internal, subjective world which is his alone and about the true condition of which he is the final authority.

M. H. Abrams has pointed out that Mill, at the same time that he clung to the standard terminology of imitation and description, was adumbrating an expressive theory of poetry. But if the poet's primary aim is the description of his own feelings, why, asks Abrams, does he even need to mention external objects?[95] The answer is, that, even when he came closest to complete subjectivism, Mill continued to believe that poetic feelings must be anchored in actuality, and that truth is unitary and harmonious, even though it may have several different aspects.

Mill's letters to Carlyle during the years 1832–34 show him approaching a more sophisticated view of the relations between poetry and science or philosophy than that which looks upon them as representatives of two different kinds of truth. In 1832, Mill told Carlyle how he, as an artist, was more important than a 'logical expounder' like Mill:

> You I look upon as an artist, and perhaps the only genuine one now living in this country: the highest destiny of all, lies in that direction; for it is the artist alone in whose hands Truth becomes impressive, and a living principle of action.

Nevertheless, the 'logical expounder' must demonstrate a truth before the artist can bring it to life. Few people can grasp truth unless they first perceive its 'logical side'; and 'then it must be quite turned round before them, that they may see it to be the same Truth in its poetic that it is in its metaphysical aspect.'[96] Truth, Mill said, is one but it has several aspects.

Mill decided that the poet needed a 'Logician in Ordinary, to supply a logical commentary on his intuitive truths.' The logician's task, he said, is to persuade the reader who cannot, either directly or through poetry, receive intuitive truths that such truths are 'not inconsistent with anything he *does* know; that they are even very *probable*, and that he may have faith in them when higher natures than his own affirm that they are truths.' Mill must have thought of himself, for a time, as the Logician in Ordinary to Carlyle. He championed Carlyle's early works when nearly everyone else was either offended or puzzled by the apoplectic wildness and pseudo-Germanic style of the Scot. He knew that he himself was 'not in the least a poet, in any sense,' but believed himself capable of feeling, understanding, and revering poetry sufficiently to be able to help his 'inferiors' to understand it. He even began to suspect that men who could move easily and capably between the realms of poetry and philosophy were more wanted in his age than the poets themselves.[97]

180

In 1834, Mill wrote that his vocation might well turn out to be 'the [translation of] the mysticism of others into the language of Argument.' Logic, Mill said, is the means of pointing out whether things are proved and how they are proved; and mystical 'truths' must be subjected to the test of logic before they can be accepted. But Mill was more concerned with translating the truths of poetry than with testing them:

> Have not all things two aspects, an Artistic and a Scientific; to the former of which the language of mysticism is the most appropriate, to the latter that of Logic? The mechanical people, whether theorists or men of the world, find the former unintelligible, & despise it. Through the latter one has a chance of forcing them to respect even what they cannot understand—and that once done, they may be made to *believe* what to many of them must always be in the utmost extent of the term 'things unseen.' This is the service I should not despair of assisting to render, & I think it is even more needed now than works of art, because it is their most useful precursor, & one might, almost say, in these days their necessary condition.[98]

Mill's desire to reconcile poetry with science, and emotion with fact, led him, for a time, to believe that Carlyle had found the ideal solution in a kind of historical writing at once highly emotional and completely objective. He said, in his review of *The French Revolution*, that in the ordinary poetic fiction poetry is not inherent in the facts of the story 'but [in] the *feelings* . . . which the story, or the manner of relating it, awaken in our minds.' Admitting this to be so, Mill asked, 'would not all these thoughts and feelings be far more vividly aroused if the facts were *believed*; if the men, and all that is ascribed to them, had actually *been*; if the whole were no play of imagination, but a truth?'[99]

But Mill came eventually to recognize that the supposed facts of history were neither certain nor permanent enough to serve as the sources of poetic emotion. Poetry would have to attach its emotion to ideas, which are less at the mercy of scientific processes of verification than are supposed historical facts. In 1854, he wrote:

> Those who think themselves called upon, in the name of truth, to make war against illusions, do not perceive the distinction between an illusion and a delusion. A delusion is an erroneous

opinion—it is believing a thing which is not. An illusion, on the contrary, is an affair solely of feeling, and may exist completely severed from delusion. It consists in extracting from a conception known not to be true, but which is better than the truth, the same benefit to the feelings which would be derived from it if it were a reality.[100]

Here we see Mill reverting to his earlier, more cautious defense of poetry's truthfulness as consisting primarily in faithfulness to the inner world rather than to the indispensable emotional half of the whole truth. He could never be wholly satisfied with this justification of poetry; but he always kept it in reserve as a rationale for poetry's independence from fact. The reply which he made to Roebuck's charge that poetry is the denial of fact and the cultivation of illusion was significantly different. He said that

the imaginative emotion which an idea, when vividly conceived, excites in us, is not an illusion but a fact, as real as any of the other qualities of objects; and far from implying anything erroneous and delusive in our mental apprehension of the object, is quite consistent with the most accurate knowledge and most perfect practical recognition of all its physical and intellectual laws and relations. The intensest feeling of the beauty of a cloud lighted by the setting sun, is no hindrance to my knowing that the cloud is vapour of water, subject to all the laws of vapours in a state of suspension; and I am just as likely to allow for, and act on these physical laws . . . as if I had been incapable of perceiving any distinction between beauty and ugliness.[101]

In Mill's conception of poetry, emotions which are aroused by ideas become facts of supreme importance. Mill, still following Wordsworth, denied that there is any necessary conflict between the conclusions of science and those of the poetic imagination; and he insisted that the several aspects of a unified truth cannot be inconsistent with each other.

In affirming the compatibility of poetry with science, Mill was setting himself not only against his scientific and Baconian friends like Bentham and Roebuck but also against those in the literary camp who wanted to preserve a truth of poetry distinct from, and generally superior to, the truth of science. Ruskin, for example, called scientific pursuits hostile to the 'higher contemplation,' and thought they had 'a tendency to chill and subdue the feelings, and to resolve all things into atoms and numbers.' The thought of science unweaving the rainbow launched Ruskin upon a eulogy of ignorance:

> For most men an ignorant enjoyment is better than an informed one; it is better to conceive the sky as a blue dome than a dark cavity, and the cloud as a golden throne than a sleety mist. I much question whether any one who knows optics, however religious he may be, can feel in equal degree the pleasure or reverence which an unlettered peasant may feel at the sight of a rainbow.[102]

The desire to leave a man in ignorance so that he might better feel the glory of the rainbow betrayed, in Mill's view, not merely a misunderstanding of the relations between science and poetry but a failure to conceive of human perfection as the development of all the human faculties, rational as well as emotional. The question of the relation between science and literature was always bound up for Mill with the question of the relative importance of science and literature in education; and he thought the dispute as to whether science or literature should form the basis of the curriculum a sterile one because he did not think literature and science were incompatible, theoretically or practically.[103] For him the strongest argument in favor of a curriculum incorporating both literature and science was that they represented complementary human endeavors after the truth; and whoever was deficient in one or the other lacked a vital element of human perfection:

> Can anything deserve the name of a good education which does not include literature and science too? If there were no more to be said than that scientific education teaches us to think, and literary education to express our thoughts, do we not require both? and is not any one a poor, maimed, lopsided fragment of humanity who is deficient in either?[104]

For Arnold, as for Mill, Wordsworth was the starting point for considerations of the proper relation between poetry and science. 'Finely and truly,' Arnold wrote in 'The Study of Poetry,' 'does Wordsworth call poetry "the impassioned expression which is in the countenance of all science." '[105] In the

1800 Preface to the *Lyrical Ballads*, Wordsworth had uttered a prophecy:

> If the labours of Men of science should ever create any material revolution, direct or indirect, in our condition, and in the impressions which we habitually receive, the Poet will sleep then no more than at present; he will be ready to follow the steps of the Man of science, not only in those general indirect effects, but he will be at his side, carrying sensation into the midst of the objects of the science itself. The remotest discoveries of the Chemist, the Botanist, or Mineralogist, will be as proper objects of the Poet's art as any upon which it can be employed. . . . If the time should ever come when what is now called science, thus familiarised to men, shall be ready to put on, as it were, a form of flesh and blood, the Poet will lend his divine spirit to aid the transfiguration, and will welcome the Being thus produced, as a dear and genuine inmate of the household of man.[106]

Wordsworth's suggestion of a Poet in Ordinary to attend the man of science was to become the pivot of Arnold's speculations upon the relation between poetry and science.

Arnold recognized that the scientific revolution which Wordsworth foresaw had come to pass. He wrote early in 1865 that 'as *Science*, in the widest sense of the word, . . . becomes, as it does become, more of a power in the world, the weight of the nations and men who have carried the intellectual life farthest will be more and more felt.' Later in the same year, he asserted: 'Through all Europe the movement is now towards science.' In 1866, Arnold replied to his sister's query about the best way to cultivate mental perception and discipline in her daughter by strongly recommending the study of science above that of Latin grammar and mathematics, and predicting that, in the future, science would play a much greater part in the education of youth.[107]

Although Arnold had no desire to suppress the scientific revolution before it had done its work of destruction and dissolution, he thought that the work of reconstruction and reunification might proceed concurrently. Wordsworth had asserted that whereas the poet 'binds together by passion and knowledge the vast empire of human society' the scientist's knowledge fails to connect human beings with one another by a 'habitual and direct sympathy.'[108] Arnold saw that it was still necessary for science to analyze in order that poetry might eventually synthesize. But he denied the existence of any conflict between the ultimate aims of science and poetry:

> Science has and will long have to be a divider and a separatist, breaking arbitrary and fanciful connections, and dissipating dreams of a premature and impossible unity. Still, science,—true science,—recognises in the bottom of her soul a law of ultimate fusion, of conciliation. To reach this, but to reach it legitimately, she tends. She draws, for instance, towards the same idea which fills her elder and diviner sister, poetry,—the idea of the substantial unity of man; though she draws towards it by roads of her own.[109]

Like Mill, Arnold proposed two different means by which poetry might collaborate with science in the pursuit of truth and unity. Arnold was willing to entertain the idea that poetry presents illusions which, neither true nor false, are nevertheless useful. In his essay on Maurice de Guérin, Arnold said that poetry treats the objects of the external world in such a way that 'we feel ourselves to be in contact with the essential nature of those objects, to be no longer bewildered and oppressed by them, but to have their secret, and to be in harmony with them.' Arnold refused to argue the question of whether this sense of harmony is 'illusive.' He maintained that the undoubted existence of the created illusion is the genuinely important and valuable fact.[110]

But if Arnold sometimes fastened upon the defense of poetry which establishes its value independently of its truthfulness, he more often argued that truth is the product of a partnership between science and poetry; and he was unwilling to surrender the privilege of speaking about poetry as a road to the truth. Just after defending poetry as useful illusion in the essay on Maurice de Guérin, he asserted that the sense of harmony and unity provided by poetry cannot be provided by science:

> The interpretations of science do not give us this intimate sense of objects as the interpretations of poetry give it; they appeal to a limited faculty, and not to the whole man. It is not Linnaeus or Cavendish or Cuvier who gives us the true sense of animals, or water, or plants, who seizes their secret for us, who makes us participate in their life; it is Shakespeare with his
>
> 'daffodils
> That come before the swallow dares, and take
> The winds of March with beauty;'

it is Wordsworth, with his

> 'voice . . . heard
> In spring-time from the cuckoo-bird,
> Breaking the silence of the seas
> Among the farthest Hebrides;'

it is Keats, with his

> 'moving waters at their priestlike task
> Of cold ablution round Earth's human shores.'[111]

From speaking of poetry as neither true nor false, Arnold could pass quickly to speaking of poetry as, in fact, giving us the truth. The ambivalence in Arnold's defense of poetry arose from the same cause that brought it about in Mill: the desire to exonerate poetry from accusations of misrepresentation of things as they are, and at the same time assert that poetry is a means of approaching truth. Both men wanted poetry to be, on the one hand, a medium beyond the realm of factual assertions, and, on the other, the only medium in which factual assertions can become truths. For they hoped not only to defend poetry from science, but to substitute it for religion.

Arnold concluded 'The Study of Poetry' by predicting that literature would never lose currency and supremacy in the world as long as humanity retained 'the instinct of self-preservation.'[112] To understand what Arnold meant by this portentous albeit commonplace expression, it is necessary to refer to a lecture delivered two years later (1882) in which he again mentioned the instinct for self-preservation: 'Literature and Science.' Here we find that the instinct of self-preservation in humanity is essentially the impulse which men have for relating their knowledge to their sense for conduct and to their sense for beauty, two of the four 'powers' of human nature which Arnold never tired of enumerating.[113] The 'modern' age being what it is, scientific knowledge being what it is, through literature alone, said Arnold, can men continue to satisfy this impulse.

No single doctrine or incantatory phrase of Arnold's has aroused more controversy than his pronouncement of 1880 about poetry and religion:

> The future of poetry is immense, because in poetry, where it is worthy of its high destinies, our race, as time goes on, will find an

ever surer and surer stay. There is not a creed which is not shaken, not an accredited dogma which is not shown to be questionable, not a received tradition which does not threaten to dissolve. Our religion has materialized itself in the fact, in the supposed fact; it has attached its emotion to the fact, and now the fact is failing it. But for poetry the idea is everything; the rest is a world of illusion, of divine illusion. Poetry attaches its emotion to the idea; the idea *is* the fact. The strongest part of our religion to-day is its unconscious poetry.[114]

Arnold was repeating what had been affirmed seven years earlier in Mill's *Autobiography*: that poetry's power derives from its independence of fact, and from its ability to attach its emotion to ideas. Religion, Arnold argued, can no longer console and sustain us because it is in bondage to a set of facts which can no longer be accepted by anyone who has acquired the habit of intellectual seriousness. Arnold's intellectual integrity would allow of no illegitimate solutions, countenance no brash assertions that theological explanations of phenomena are every bit as valid as scientific explanations, and that one chooses between them according to one's taste.

Yet Arnold could not believe that science was the alternative to religion, either for interpreting life or for giving it value. The mode of perceiving and verifying facts and organizing them into knowledge which science provides has greater intellectual integrity than that of religion, and therefore, by its very nature, less concern than religion for the emotional consolation and sustenance which humanity demands. The modern task, in Arnold's view, is to discover a way of attaching emotion to knowledge without, as Bacon said, 'accommodating the shows of things to the desires of the mind.'[115]

In proposing poetry as the means of closing the breach between new knowledge and emotion, Arnold confronted the problem of what the critical jargon of our day calls the 'dissociation of sensibility.' But Arnold, unlike later critics, recognized it as the problem not just of the modern poet but of modern man, and he understood that its solution involves not merely the unification of feeling with some system of thought or belief but with a scientifically acceptable system of thought or belief.

Arnold rested his case for literary education in the debate

with Huxley over the relative importance of science and literature in the curriculum upon the Wordsworthian argument that
knowledge remains inert unless it is conveyed to the heart by
poetic passion:

> Now, says Professor Huxley, conceptions of the universe fatal to
> the notions held by our forefathers have been forced upon us by
> physical science. Grant to him that they are thus fatal, that the
> new conceptions must and will soon become current everywhere,
> and that everyone will finally perceive them to be fatal to the
> beliefs of our forefathers. The need of humane letters, as they are
> truly called, because they serve the paramount desire in men that
> good should be forever present to them,—the need of humane
> letters, to establish a relation between the new conceptions, and
> our instinct for beauty, our instinct for conduct, is only the more
> visible. The Middle Age could do without humane letters, as it
> could do without the study of nature, because its supposed know-
> ledge was made to engage its emotions so powerfully. Grant that
> the supposed knowledge disappears, its power of being made to
> engage the emotions will of course disappear along with it,—but
> the emotions themselves, and their claim to be engaged and
> satisfied, will remain. Now if we find by experience that humane
> letters have an undeniable power of engaging the emotions, the
> importance of humane letters in a man's training becomes not
> less, but greater, in proportion to the success of modern science
> in extirpating what it calls 'mediaeval thinking.'[116]

To establish a relation between the new facts and conceptions
of science, and the human instinct for beauty and harmony was
the immense task of poetry.

Arnold thus combined two different justifications of poetry.
Poetry's power, he said, is independent of any particular system
of facts because it is emotional rather than intellectual. Poetry
does not fix itself immovably upon a set of dogmas or facts.
But if poetry does not commit itself to saying that such and such
things are true, it is nevertheless certain that knowledge which
is gained scientifically, i.e., with regard only to seeing things
as they are and not as we would like them to be, does not
become impressive and vital truth until it has been 'humanized'
by poetry. Arnold claimed that poetry transforms facts into
truths without misrepresenting things as they really are.

Arnold did not consider the religious and scientific parties so
different from each other as their absolute opposition in contro-

versy often suggested. He was even inclined to suspect that their hostility to each other arose, in part, from the fact that each party recognized its own imperial ambitions in the other. If the strongest part of religion seemed to Arnold its unconscious poetry, then the weakest part seemed its science, or rather its pretension to science. He remarked upon the extent to which the claims of the physical and biological sciences, their pretension to certainty and their contempt for letters, had invaded the pronouncements of theologians contending for dogma, or 'a scientific and exact presentment of religious things, instead of a literary presentment of them.'[117]

The unity of Arnold's work in literature and religion is suggested by his statement, in the Preface to *God and the Bible*, that the criticism of religion which he undertook in *Literature and Dogma* was motivated by his desire 'to re-unite man's imagination with his virtue and conduct, when the tie between them has been . . . broken.'[118] Arnold hoped that poetry could infuse life into religious doctrines and scientific facts. His fears of a future in which poetry did not play its proper role alongside religion and science were expressed in a letter to his mother about James Bryce, whom Arnold thought a dangerous man because he lacked

> any true sense and experience of literature and its beneficent function. Religion he knows, and physical science he knows, but the immense work between the two, which is for literature to accomplish, he knows nothing of, and all his speeches at Oxford pointed this way. On the one hand, he was full of the great future for physical science, and begging the University to make up her mind to it, and to resign much of her literary studies; on the other hand, he was full, almost defiantly full, of counsels and resolves for retaining and upholding the old ecclesiastical and dogmatic form of religion. From a juxtaposition of this kind nothing but shocks and collisions can come.[119]

Mill, as I have shown, was preoccupied with poetry's role in vivifying philosophical and completing scientific truth. But he had learned from personal experience of the way in which poetry might fill the gap in human life left by the decay of religion.

In February of 1854, Harriet Taylor proposed to Mill that he write an essay on the utility of religion, in which he could 'show how religion and poetry fill the same want, the craving after higher objects, the consolation of suffering, the hope of heaven for the selfish, love of God for the tender and grateful.'[120] Never slack in taking up Harriet's suggestions, Mill responded handsomely to this one in the posthumously published essay 'Utility of Religion.' 'Religion and poetry,' he wrote there, 'address themselves, at least in one of their aspects, to the same part of the human constitution; they both supply the same want, that of ideal conceptions grander and more beautiful than we see realized in the prose of human life.' Religion, Mill argued, differs from poetry insofar as it arises from the human desire to discover literal realizations of these ideal conceptions in another, a future world. Because religion has been able to provide concrete forms for these idealized conceptions, it has won the adherence of the great majority of people. It has, moreover, given to human life those hopes and consolations which are necessary to mitigate the inadequacies and disappointments inherent in it.[121]

But Mill thought poetry could transform the otherworldly ideals of religion into the possibilities of human life. Religion, he admitted, had been of undoubted value to the individual 'as a source of personal satisfaction and of elevated feelings.' But why, he asked, is it necessary, in order to receive the benefit which the idealized conceptions of religion confer, to transcend earthly life in the fond expectation that the imaginings of this world correspond to facts in the next? Mill posed what became for many in the nineteenth century the crucial question of

> whether the idealization of our earthly life, the cultivation of a high conception of what *it* may be made, is not capable of supplying a poetry and, in the best sense of the word, a religion equally fitted to exalt the feelings and (with the same aid from education) still better calculated to ennoble the conduct than any belief respecting the unseen powers.[122]

Mill looked to poetry as the means—once provided by religion —for gaining admission to the world of infinite possibility. It is in the realm of poetry that the successive approximations to an ideal of human perfectibility are made. Poetry enables men to conceive of life as it may be, and thus consoles them for the inadequacies of life as it still is.

Mill, like Arnold, came to look upon poetry not merely as a mediator between science or philosophy and religion, but as the incorporation of the permanently valuable—and valid—elements of both. As early as 1838, Mill had called the study of heroic literature true education, and had said that 'it would be well if the more narrow-minded portion, both of the religious and of the scientific education-mongers, would consider whether the books which they are banishing from the hands of youth, were not instruments of national education to the full as powerful as the catalogues of physical facts and theological dogmas which they have substituted. . . .'[123]

Many people thought Arnold had frivolously imperiled his reputation for foresight when he predicted in 1879 that men would one day assent to the general proposition that 'poetry is the reality, philosophy the illusion.'[124] Yet three years later Alexander Bain, the friend and biographer of the man generally acknowledged to be the foremost English philosopher of the age, remarked that John Stuart Mill 'seemed to look upon Poetry as a Religion, or rather as Religion and Philosophy in one.'[125]

VI

THE BEST THAT IS KNOWN
AND THOUGHT IN THE WORLD

———————◦∞◦———————

English freedom, being rooted in insular peculiarities, required,
if it was ever to reach its full growth, a period of isolation from
European influences and dangers. Elizabeth and Drake had
rendered that isolation possible.   G. M. TREVELYAN

> But we, brave *Britons, Foreign Laws* despis'd,
> And kept *unconquer'd*, and *unciviliz'd*.
>   ALEXANDER POPE

IN proposing the substitution of poetry for religion, Arnold and
Mill believed that they were substituting the cultural ideal of a
human nature fully developed on all sides for the religious ideal
of a human nature perfect on its moral side. They attributed
the narrowness of the religious ideal of their own country to
the alliance between the spirit of religion and the spirit of
business, and to English parochialism. They associated the
narrowness of English sensibility with English ignorance of the
life and thought of other countries, and they sought to broaden
the English ideal of human nature by making foreign experience
and ideas available to their countrymen; in order to recommend
culture they had to recommend cosmopolitanism.

Poetry, Arnold said, calls forth 'the most energetic and harmonious activity of all the powers of the human mind.'[1] The
ideal of poetry, he thought, is embodied in culture, which goes
beyond (and thus includes) religion because it conceives of
perfection as 'a harmonious expansion of *all* the powers which

make the beauty and worth of human nature, and is not consistent with the overdevelopment of any one power at the expense of the rest.'[2] Religion, Arnold charged, stresses the power of conduct at the expense of the other powers of human nature.

Arnold opposed culture not only to religion in general but to Puritanism in particular. He held that perfection must be a harmonious expansion of the human powers of beauty, manners, intelligence, and conduct, but English Puritanism equated perfection with right conduct, and was obsessed with doing the work it found lying closest to hand.[3] The work consisted in the development of commerce and industrial civilization:

> Your middle-class man thinks it the highest pitch of development and civilisation when his letters are carried twelve times a day from Islington to Camberwell, and from Camberwell to Islington, and if railway-trains run to and fro between them every quarter of an hour. He thinks it nothing that the trains only carry him from an illiberal, dismal life at Islington to an illiberal, dismal life at Camberwell; and the letters only tell him that such is the life there.[4]

Culture tentatively recommended poetry as a cure for the shortcomings of modern life, but the English middle class believed that, as Cobden asserted,

> commerce is the grand panacea, which, like a beneficent medical discovery, will serve to inoculate with the healthy and saving taste for civilization all the nations of the world. Not a bale of merchandise leaves our shores, but it bears the seeds of intelligence and fruitful thought to the members of some less enlightened community; not a merchant visits our seats of manufacturing industry, but he returns to his own country the missionary of freedom, peace, and good government—while our steam boats, that now visit every port of Europe, and our miraculous railroads, that are the talk of all nations, are the advertisements and vouchers for the value of our enlightened institutions.[5]

But the 'less enlightened' communities of the world did not fall down and worship England as Cobden had hoped; and Arnold thought he knew why. The rest of the world, although it emulated England's standards of freedom, industry, and bodily health, neither loved nor admired her because it saw how England lost sight of the ultimate goal of human perfection in her pursuit of freedom, industry, and health as ends in themselves.[6]

Arnold saw the alliance between the spirit of religion and the spirit of business as the most formidable obstacle to the realization of the ideal of human nature represented by poetry. The panacea of the middle-class businessman had been prescribed to him by Puritan nonconformity, which was, more often than not, his religion. Arnold, foreshadowing the conclusions of R. H. Tawney and Max Weber, thought the mechanical middle-class passion for making money was a direct outgrowth of the mechanical Puritan conception of religion and soul-saving. He cited the case of the devout Puritan who killed himself because he thought his commercial failure signified spiritual abandonment to support his contention that the Puritan obsession with conduct was not merely narrow but potentially destructive.[7] 'Culture without character,' Arnold wrote, 'is, no doubt, something frivolous, vain, and weak; but character without culture is . . . something raw, blind, and dangerous.'[8]

The conflict between Puritan religion and the ideal of culture was, for Arnold, the modern version of the conflict between Hebraism and Hellenism. The English Puritan, Arnold admitted, 'whenever and wherever called upon to do his duty, does it almost invariably with the old energy, courage, virtue.'[9] The modern Hellenists, the 'men of culture and poetry,' Arnold admitted, retained their old weaknesses: they failed in conduct and could not, like the Puritans, subdue their animality. Yet the devotees of culture and poetry, like their Greek prototypes, did pursue the true ideal of 'a human nature complete on all its sides,' while the Hebraizing Puritans went astray in pursuit of the narrow ideal of a human nature perfect on its moral side:

> Notwithstanding the mighty results of the Pilgrim Fathers' voyage, they and their standard of perfection are rightly judged when we figure to ourselves Shakespeare or Virgil,—souls in whom sweetness and light, and all that in human nature is most humane, were eminent,—accompanying them on their voyage, and think what intolerable company Shakespeare and Virgil would have found them![10]

Puritanism, Arnold believed, left England with 'a religion not true, the claims of intellect and knowledge not satisfied, the claim of beauty not satisfied, the claim of manners not satisfied.'[11] He recommended, in its stead, culture, which he defined, in *Culture and Anarchy*, as 'a pursuit of our total perfection by means of getting to know, on all the matters which most concern us, the best which has been thought and said in the world. . . .'[12] And he asserted that it was foreign rather than English thought and literature which constituted the best that was thought and known in the world at the time he wrote.[13] Arnold's recommendation of culture to England as a way out of her difficulties entailed a recommendation that she extend intellectual recognition to the continent of Europe.

The belief that culture is cosmopolitanism lies behind and unifies an immense portion of Arnold's work. The tendency of the English to violate the rule of culture by emphasizing one side of their nature at the expense of other sides corresponded to their tendency to violate the rule of cosmopolitanism by being concerned only with things English and ignoring the thought and experience of other countries. English contempt for the power of manners corresponded to English contempt for France, English contempt for the power of beauty to English contempt for Italy, English contempt for the power of intelligence to English contempt for Germany.[14] Arnold's desire to exhibit a necessary link between culture and knowledge of foreign countries appeared in his insistence upon *curiosity* as the motive for culture. Although to a foreigner like Sainte-Beuve the word connoted 'a liberal and intelligent eagerness about the things of the mind,' to the typical Englishman it suggested merely 'frivolous and unedifying activity.'[15]

Mill, who also proposed to his countrymen the substitution of poetry for religion, recognized the same obstacles to the acceptance of his proposition that Arnold did:

> Worldly advancement, or religion, are an Englishman's real interests: for Politics, except in connection with one of those two objects, and for Art, he keeps only bye-corners of his mind, which naturally are far apart from each other: and it is but a small minority among Englishmen who can comprehend, that there are nations among whom Politics, or the pursuit of social well-being, and Poetry, or the love of beauty and of imaginative emotion, are passions as intense, as absorbing—influencing as much the whole tendencies of the character, and constituting as large a part of the

objects in life of a considerable portion of the cultivated classes, as either the religious feelings, or those of worldly interest.[16]

Mill attributed the English inability to take art seriously to 'the two influences which have chiefly shaped the British character since the days of the Stuarts: commercial money-getting business, and religious Puritanism.' He noticed how middle-class business maxims and Puritan ethics alike looked upon the cultivation of beauty as, at best, a nonproductive activity, and, at worst, an indulgence in sin. Certainly, England had been rewarded for her stern devotion to duty with a moral advantage over other countries in the form of a 'greater tenderness of conscience.' But her superiority, said Mill, like the virtue from which it sprang, was essentially negative. It had fostered a type of Englishman who, though conscientiously aware of what was thought wrong, and scrupulous in refraining from the use of 'any very illegitimate means' to attain his ends, was essentially selfish and incapable of conceiving any higher object in life than the enrichment of himself and his family.[17]

Mill believed that education might convince conscientious, Puritanical Englishmen of 'the poorness and insignificance of human life if it is to be all spent in making things comfortable for ourselves and our kind, and raising ourselves and them a step or two on the social ladder.' But the essential element in such an education, he asserted, would have to be poetry, which is the indispensable means of elevating the mind.[18] Mill, like Arnold, thought poetry the agent of the ideal of culture, which is broader than, and includes, the ideal of religion. In *On Liberty*, as I noted earlier, Mill sought an embodiment of the virtuous mean between the extreme of the love of beauty and intelligence without conduct that is represented by Alcibiades and the extreme of good conduct lacking in light and in sweetness that is represented by John Knox.

Mill criticized not only Puritans but positivist philosophers for their narrow moralism. He belabored Bentham for not recognizing man as 'a being capable of pursuing spiritual perfection as an end,' and for overlooking—along with most other moralists—the fact that human actions have, in addition to a moral aspect, an aesthetic aspect and a 'sympathetic' aspect.[19] He charged Comte with forgetting that 'our more eminent, and peculiarly human, faculties are of various orders, moral, intellectual, and aesthetic.'[20] He chided the Utilitarians because they 'look on the morality of actions . . . with too exclusive a regard, and do not lay sufficient stress upon the other beauties of character which go towards making a human being lovable or admirable'; and he noted that Utilitarians who had developed the moral part of their being without regard to, or at the expense of, their 'sympathies' or 'artistic perceptions' would be limited both as moralists and as human beings.[21]

Like Arnold, Mill believed that the English had sacrificed their powers of intelligence, of beauty, and of manners to their obsession with conduct and all it involved. The lack of respect for intelligence which Tocqueville noticed in the Americans was not, Mill argued, a peculiarity of American democracy; for the very same characteristic abounded in England, where it resulted not from democracy but from 'the [English] habit of energetic action, without a proportional development of the taste for speculation.'[22] The power of social feeling was sacrificed, in England, to a kind of selfishness which, in league with English reticence, caused the feelings 'to remain undeveloped, or to develop themselves only in some single and very limited direction.'[23] When he noticed, in *The Times*, the compliment which Emerson, in a Boston lecture, had paid to the English as a people whose great characteristic is 'the steady balance of the qualities of their nature,' a people who 'surpass all others in general culture—none are so harmoniously developed,' Mill thought the American had lost his reason. 'It is hardly possible,' he wrote to Harriet, 'to be more stupidly wrong.'[24]

Mill believed the English were forsaking the ideal of a human nature perfect on all its sides in favor of their obsession with action and work without regard to the ends which action and work are to serve. He told d'Eichthal in 1829 that the disproportionate importance which the English gave to the idol of 'production' was the root of their worst national vices. It corrupted the action of statesmen and the doctrines of philosophers; and it hardened the spirit of the people against any enthusiasm of mind or heart.[25] In 1850, after his friendship with Carlyle had virtually ended, Mill attempted to expose the insanity of Carlyle's 'gospel of work':

Work, I imagine, is not a good in itself. There is nothing laudable in work for work's sake. To work voluntarily for a worthy object is laudable; but what constitutes a worthy object? On this matter, the oracle of which your [*Fraser's*] contributor is the prophet has never yet been prevailed on to declare itself. He revolves in an eternal circle round the idea of work, as if turning up the earth, or driving a shuttle or a quill, were ends in themselves, and the ends of human existence.[26]

Mill maintained that the only way for England to develop those sides of human nature which her Puritanism had led her to ignore was to study other nations and civilizations unlike her own. He supported the retention of Greek and Roman literature in their favored positions in the curriculum because he believed the study and mastery of a foreign language and literature indispensable to the development of the intellect. The cure for English narrowness was also the cure for English parochialism:

What the notions and habit of a single family are to a boy who has had no intercourse beyond it, the notions and habits of his own country are to him who is ignorant of every other. Those notions and habits are to him human nature itself; whatever varies from them is an unaccountable aberration which he cannot mentally realize: the idea that any other ways can be right, or as near an approach to right as some of his own, is inconceivable to him. . . . We are not likely to correct any of our opinions or mend any of our ways, unless we begin by conceiving that they are capable of amendment.

National improvement, Mill held, waits upon the ability of a people to bring their inherited, customary opinions into conformity with facts; and people cannot achieve this congruity except 'by frequently using the differently coloured glasses of other people: and those of other nations, as the most different, are best.'[27]

Mill spelled out the correspondence between the 'main ingredients of human culture' which are 'needful to the completeness of the human being' and the civilizations of ancient Greece and Rome and of modern Europe. He said of the aesthetic ingredient, for example, that it was 'only of late, and chiefly by a superficial imitation of foreigners,' that Britons had begun to recognize art as an entity, 'holding an equally important place [with philosophy, learning, and science] among the elements of the worth of humanity.' He established a connection between English neglect of certain human powers and English estrangement from the Continent in which it was nearly impossible to disentangle cause from effect:

> On these subjects the mode of thinking and feeling of other countries was not only not intelligible, but not credible, to an average Englishman. . . . To find even painting and sculpture treated as great social powers, and the art of a country as a feature in its character and condition, little inferior in importance to either its religion or its government; all this only did not amaze and puzzle Englishmen, because it was too strange for them to be able to realize it, or, in truth, to believe it possible: and the radical difference between the British people and those of France, Germany and the Continent generally, is one among the causes of that extraordinary inability to understand one another, which exists between England and the rest of Europe.[28]

Like Arnold, Mill found that the curiosity which was so favored in France was lacking in 'our stupid incurious people.' He attributed to English lack of curiosity the fact that England was 'the ballast of Europe, France its sail.'[29]

Nothing more clearly and decisively set Arnold and Mill apart from their contemporaries than their serious concern with the life and thought of Continental countries. They lived in a country whose habitual insularity had been increased by revolutions abroad and prosperity at home. The official organ of British Philistinism, *The Times*, was maintaining that the domestic affairs of France had no relevance or interest for the British public. When the French, in the interests of mutual understanding, proposed arrangements whereby the newspapers of both countries might easily be exchanged, the English, on grounds of economy, refused.[30] John Henry Newman, traveling from Italy back to England, turned his eyes away at the sight of the tricolor on a ship in Algiers and kept to his room during a one-day stopover in Paris.[31] For Tennyson, the French Revolution was but the manifestation of 'the schoolboy heat, the blind hysterics of the Celt.'[32] When Charles Kingsley's daughter asked him who Heine was, he answered: 'A wicked man, my dear.'[33] Cobbett gave as the reason for his unswerving attachment to the Church of England the fact that it bore the name of his country.[34]

Arnold and Mill saw insularity as the underlying weakness in many areas of English life, but they were especially conscious of its unfortunate effect upon English intellect and English politics.

Mill observed the intimate connection between English insularity and English intellectual shortcomings in the work of English historians. In a review of Sir Walter Scott's *Life of Napoleon*, Mill singled out two of the worst of Scott's many deficiencies: his belief that English institutions were best not only for England, but for all other countries (whose institutions were considered bad in proportion to their difference from England's), and his belief that all systems not English were merely '*untried theories*.'[35] Why was it, Mill asked in a later article on Guizot, that the scientific movement in historiography which was taking place on the Continent was almost unheard of in England? Probably, he answered, an Englishman can with difficulty be interested in any intellectual effort that does not carry the promise of practical reward. The national addiction to practicality and the accompanying suspicion of intellectual efforts whose validity is not immediately verifiable by application to practice resulted, Mill said, in an indifference to large-scale attempts to explain history. The English isolated themselves from the Continental nations because they had 'no faith in, and no curiosity about, the kind of speculations to which the most philosophic minds of those nations have lately devoted themselves.'[36]

Arnold discerned similar failures in English thought and literature. In a letter of 1848, he remarked:

How plain it is now, though an attention to the comparative literatures for the last fifty years might have instructed any one of it, that England is in a certain sense *far behind* the Continent. In conversation, in the newspapers, one is so struck with the fact of the utter insensibility, one may say, of people to the number of ideas and schemes now ventilated on the Continent—not because they have judged them or seen beyond them, but from sheer habitual want of wide reading and thinking: like a child's intellectual attitude *vis-à-vis* of the proposition that Saturn's apparent diameter subtends an angle of about 18°. Our practical virtues never certainly revealed more clearly their isolation. I am not sure but I agree in Lamartine's prophecy that 100 years hence the Continent will be a great united Federal Republic and England, all her colonies gone, in a dull and steady decay.[37]

The decay which was taking place in English intellect as a result of insularity was also infecting English literature. Arnold found Tennyson's 1855 volume of poetry (*Maud, and other Poems*) 'a lamentable production' partly because it was 'like so much of our literature thoroughly and intensely *provincial*, not European.'[38] Arnold also associated the stylistic and intellectual eccentricities of English writers like Taylor, Burke, and Ruskin with English provincialism.[39]

In the world of politics as in the world of ideas, Mill and Arnold saw how much England lost by her insularity. Knowledge of countries other than England became for Mill the *sine qua non* of a successful English politician. In a letter of 1858, he insisted that Lord John Russell, though a mediocre man, was worth more than the majority of his fellow statesmen, Liberal and Conservative, who knew nothing beyond the traditions of British politics and accentuated their ignorance of politics in general with an ignorance of the ideas and history of other countries.[40] Mill repeatedly blamed the disasters of English politics and the failures of English Liberalism upon ignorance of foreign thought and institutions. When he recalled how his proposals for turning land over to the Irish peasants had fallen on deaf English ears, Mill remarked bitterly that 'the profound ignorance of English politicians and the English public concerning all social phenomena not generally met with in England (however common elsewhere) made my endeavours an entire failure.' At a loss to explain the zeal with which most of his countrymen, unlike Continental Liberals, embraced the Southern cause in the American Civil War, Mill could only attribute it to 'the inattention habitual with Englishmen to whatever is going on in the world outside their own island.'[41]

Arnold and Mill were particularly hard upon the insularity of Liberals and of the Liberal party, which ought to have known better. When Arnold decided to travesty the platform of the Liberal party, he made the spokesman of the party express, among other indelicacies of intellect, his hostility (or indifference) to foreign thought: 'Don't let us trouble ourselves,' the Liberal said, 'about foreign thought; we shall invent the whole thing for ourselves as we go along.'[42] Arnold was peeved by Macaulay's estimate of English literature as 'of far greater value than all the literature which three hundred years ago was extant in all the languages of the world together'; and he called it an illustration of characteristically English conceit and self-satisfaction.[43] Mill, similarly, could not resist a conviction that Macaulay, for all his accomplishments, was intellectually a mere cockney because 'in politics, ethics, philosophy, even history, of which he knows superficially very much—he has not a single thought of either German or French origin, & that is saying enough.'[44] For his freedom from the insularity and parochialism of other British Liberals, as for so many other blessings, Mill had his education to thank. The extended visit to France prescribed by his father when Mill was fourteen had happy consequences, as he pointed out in the *Autobiography*:

> The chief fruit which I carried away from the society I saw was a strong and permanent interest in Continental Liberalism, of which I ever afterwards kept myself *au courant*, as much as of English politics: a thing not at all usual in those days with Englishmen, and which had a very salutary influence on my development, keeping me free from the error always prevalent in England, and from which even my father with all his superiority to prejudice was not exempt, of judging universal questions by a merely English standard.[45]

Arnold and Mill were aware of the force of the prejudice which they undertook to dissolve. In order to ensure themselves against charges of treason and in order to work effectively, they devised a strategy which would assure England that she had an important contribution to make to the cosmopolitan ideal of culture, and that she would not lose her identity by adopting foreign qualities or by joining a European confederation of nations.

First of all, Arnold and Mill conscientiously celebrated England's superiority over other nations in at least one line— and that a very important one. Just as they were always ready to grant the individual Englishman's superiority in conduct, so Arnold and Mill were ready to declare the English nation's moral superiority over her neighbors. In his pamphlet called *England and the Italian Question*, which was generally sympathetic to Louis Napoleon, Arnold nevertheless expressed his relief that the Frenchman had failed to liberate Italy. For success might have given the Emperor and France the moral predominance in

Europe—and 'England may not concern herself with material predominance in Europe; but a share in moral predominance may and must be dear to her.'[46] Mill often praised England as 'incomparably the most conscientious of all nations in her national acts,' and in 1859 he called upon England to assert her moral superiority by heading an alliance of free peoples pledged to the principle that no European power should intervene to aid established governments in the suppression of their revolted subjects.[47] Arnold and Mill would have been loath to see England surrender any of her national sovereignty.

Arnold, to be sure, was in principle an internationalist. His ultimate goal was not merely mutual understanding between nations, but the transcendence of nationality itself. At a time in history when nationalism was becoming the dominant passion of European nations (and sub-nations) Arnold became the advocate of internationalism. In 1865 he began to put forward the ideal of a cultural federation of man and parliament of the world. He wanted Europe to be regarded as

> for intellectual and spiritual purposes, one great confederation, bound to a joint action and working to a common result; and whose members have, for their proper outfit, a knowledge of Greek, Roman, and Eastern antiquity, and of one another.[48]

Sometimes, indeed, he seemed to think that his ideal of the good European above nationalism and even nationality was already in process of being realized—as when he proclaimed in the lectures on Celtic literature that 'Europe tends constantly to become more and more one community, and we tend to become Europeans instead of merely Englishmen, Frenchmen, Germans, Italians. . . .'[49]

But in his day-to-day encounters with English insularity, Arnold had to recognize the existence of separate nations and to content himself with combating nationalism by a skillful manipulation of the various qualities of distinct national cultures. In those same lectures on Celtic literature, therefore, he claimed to be a friend of variety, which he wanted 'to exist and to show itself to me'; for he was not, after all, like his fellow Saxons, who had 'a terrible way with them of wanting to improve everything but themselves off the face of the earth.'[50]

For Mill, who considered the diversity of the paths which

they had followed the greatest advantage which the European nations had over other groups of nations, the ideal of internationalism could not have held much attraction. Even if it had, Mill recognized that for the English, obsessed with narrow sectarian passions, the idea of nationality was something which, in a certain sense, they had to rise to rather than transcend:

> The world, to each individual, means the part of it with which he comes in contact; his party, his sect, his church, his class of society; the man may be called, by comparison, almost liberal and large-minded to whom it means anything so comprehensive as his own country or his own age.[51]

Thus Arnold and Mill retained the idea of separate and distinct national cultures in devising a practical method by which their general recommendation of cosmopolitanism might be implemented. They wanted to assure Englishmen that they could adopt ever so many foreign customs and ideas without destroying the English national character. National character was to be the one absolute in an otherwise relativistic system. It was not enough for Arnold and Mill to urge their countrymen to imbibe from other nations certain qualities which were wanting to their own; Englishmen needed to be persuaded that they could adopt these qualities without all the defects which seemed in other countries to be their necessary accompaniments. To achieve their ends, Arnold and Mill transferred the flexible, relativistic method which served them so well in manipulating the constituents of history to the realm of national cultures.

Once Arnold began to identify certain qualities needed in England with certain European nations, his ideal of a supernational European confederation receded into the background. In *Literature and Dogma*, after identifying Israel with the belief that happiness arises from righteousness, Arnold said that 'unless a sense or endowment of human nature, however in itself real and beneficent, has some signal representative among mankind, it tends to be pressed upon by other senses and endowments, and to be more and more pushed out of sight.'[52]

Arnold believed that each of the desirable powers of human nature found its special representative in some particular nation. England, he asserted, felt the power of conduct more strongly than any other nation; Italy was the first among nations in feeling the power of beauty; Germany was pre-eminent in knowledge; and France was supreme in her appreciation of the power of social life and of manners.[53]

Arnold tried to show how the benefits which one country received from the power with which it was identified might be transferred to another country. He admired the alliance of democracy with a strong state that had taken place in France and recommended it to England; and he knew that the most vehement objectors to his proposal would be those who pointed to the excessive government of France as an example of what resulted from such an alliance. To forestall their objections, he enunciated, in 'Democracy,' what was to become one of his cardinal principles of political reasoning:

> One may save one's self from much idle terror at names and shadows if one will be at the pains to remember what different conditions the different characters of two nations must necessarily impose on the operation of any principle.

In one instance, say that of France, Arnold argued, state action would only strengthen the already strongly entrenched tendency of the French to overgovernment; in another instance, say that of England, state action would serve as the much-needed corrective to the national characteristic of working individually. Here, exclaimed Arnold, is just 'the great use which two unlike characters may find in observing each other. Neither is likely to have the other's faults, so each may safely adopt as much as suits him of the other's qualities.' The highly individualistic English nation could never run the danger of having too much state action; nor could the highly collectivized and overgoverned French nation run the danger of too much encouraging individual action.[54]

Arnold's sanguine conception of the usefulness of having nations compare themselves with one another rested on an assumption of the deep-rootedness and permanence of national character, and of its imperviousness to the modifying influences of culture. Yet earlier in this very essay Arnold had noticed the way in which the movement towards democracy was softening so tough a thing as English individualism; and at the end of the essay he admitted that the modern spirit was 'even modifying national character.' Nevertheless, his standard reply to those who, like Mill, insisted that the trend towards over-government was accelerating a decline, already begun, in English individualism was: 'There is no danger at all that the native independence and individualism of the English character will ever belie itself, and become either weakly prone to lean on others, or blindly confiding in them.'[55]

Arnold had overstated his argument, and, by deserting his own principle of relativism, weakened his case. It is simply not true that, as he so positively said, there is 'no danger at all' of national character being transformed by alien influences. One of the most striking characteristics of our own day is the relative ease with which national characters and ancient cultures are being completely transformed.[56] It would have been more in tune with Arnold's habitual relativism, and more true, for him to have said that national characters could stand a certain, perhaps a considerable, amount of leavening by alien influences, without being changed beyond recognition.

Mill considered the differences between national character the stumbling block which every political philosophy had to surmount before it could be taken seriously. Whereas Arnold's toleration—and even encouragement—of diversity among nations was at odds with his tireless insistence upon unity and uniformity for his own country, Mill's welcome recognition of the diversity of European nations was the natural outgrowth of his desire for variety and diversity in his own society.

We get some sense of the qualities with which Mill identified the leading European nations of his day from Caroline Fox's account of a talk she had with Mill on the subject in 1840. She reports how Mill stressed 'the differences in national character' as a vital subject for investigation. He then pointed out that an outstanding characteristic of the French was their possession of 'so much nationality'—every great man in the country considering himself a Frenchman before all else. The English, on the other hand, were characterized by individuality, for 'each takes his own road and succeeds by his own merits.' The French were very receptive to new ideas, though few of these originated in France. The Germans Mill found an extremely speculative people who assimilated new ideas with perfect equanimity. The English, on the contrary, were so thoroughly practical that they resisted new truths, 'lest they should force them to admit that they had hitherto lived in vain.'[57]

Mill's first detailed exposition of the need for a philosophy of national character appeared in the onslaught on Bentham. Bentham, as Halévy has described him, 'was possessed by one fixed idea: to secure the drawing up and the promulgation of his entire Code, everywhere, somewhere, no matter where.' Bentham offered his projected *Pannomion*, or *Complete Body of Laws*, impartially to the American President and to the Russian Emperor. 'He dreamed of setting out,' says Halévy, 'for Switzerland, for Spain, for Mexico, for Venezuela, and of landing among a people whose traditional and local prejudices he ignored, like Epimenides at Athens or Plato at Syracuse.'[58] No wonder, then, that Mill accused Bentham of attempting the impossible by prescribing a philosophy of laws and institutions without reference to national character. It is, after all, argued Mill, national character which makes such a thing as society possible, and which, to a large extent, determines the difference between one society and another:

> The true teacher of the fitting social arrangements for England, France, or America, is the one who can point out how the English, French, or American character can be improved, and how it has been made what it is. A philosophy of laws and institutions, not founded on a philosophy of national character, is an absurdity.[59]

Mill's philosophy of national character was the basis of his political relativism. Laws and political and social institutions, he argued, cannot be evaluated without reference to a particular national character. They are not to be judged absolutely, but relatively, in terms of the wisdom or folly of applying them in particular countries at particular times. A country of slaves, Mill pointed out, requires training in self-government; a country of savages needs to learn submission to the government of others. The English do not necessarily benefit from laws which may suit the French very well. 'Very different institutions,' Mill asserted, 'are needed to train to the perfection of their nature' the peoples of different European nations.[60]

Mill's theory of the relation between political or social institutions and national character could justify opposite practical policies regarding the adoption of foreign institutions. On the one hand, it might be said—and this was the line of argument Mill pursued in attacking Bentham—that a French institution founded on general principles ought not to be imported into England because it would jar with the English national character, so suspicious of practices founded on general principles. On the other hand, it might be argued—and Mill tended to pursue this line more and more once he had buried the ghost of Bentham—that there is a presumption in favor of adopting any foreign institution which is at odds with English national character precisely because that character wants leavening by new and alien elements.[61] One reason why Mill never finally decided between the two views—any more than he did between the organic and mechanical theories of society[62]—was that he was trying to transform English character while preserving what was best in it:

> Though we have not, like so many of our contemporaries, made it our grand occupation, to impress our countrymen with a deep sense of their own wisdom and virtue, and to teach them how proud they ought to be of every thing English, more especially of every thing that is English and bad; we are far from being unconscious how much they have really to be proud of, and in how many respects they might be taken as models by all the nations of the world. If we saw them in any danger of forgetting their own merits, we too might preach them a sermon on that hacknied text. But it is not their failing to underrate themselves, or to overrate other nations. They are more in need of monitors than of adulators; and we cannot but think that it may be of some use to them to know, that if there are some points in which they are superior to their neighbours, there are others in which they are inferior; that they may learn something from other nations, as well as other nations from them.[63]

France was the modern European nation of greatest importance to Arnold and Mill. Its importance to them arose largely from the fact that France was the only nation in Europe which was attempting to organize society democratically. It was France which kindled their youthful enthusiasm for political and artistic ideals, and retained their mature admiration for intellectual and social achievement. When they spoke of the Continent in general as a place where things were better managed than in England, it was usually France that they had in mind.

Before the French Revolution, England had been, for European Liberals, the home of progress and enlightenment. Even during the political stagnation of the eighteenth century, England seemed to Voltaire the carrier of scientific and philosophical light into the cobwebs of dark superstition that still enveloped France. In England, Locke, Newton, and smallpox inoculations had displaced Aristotle, Descartes, and medieval superstition. In politics, the same contrast between England and France was apparent. The English, Voltaire maintained, had fought for liberty in their civil wars, whereas 'les guerres civiles de France ont été plus longues, plus cruelles, plus fécondes en crimes que celles d'Angleterre; mais, de toutes ces guerres civiles, aucune n'a eu une liberté sage pour objet.'[64] But the French Revolution, though captured by Napoleon and declared null and void by the settlement of the Congress of Vienna, was to reverse the relative positions of England and France. France, however reactionary her governments might thereafter be, stood in the vanguard of Europe while England brought up the rear.

Ever since Burke's onslaught upon the French Revolution, it had been a commonplace among English patriots—who readily forgot their old title of Europe's most ungovernable people— that the great virtues of England were largely attributable to the fact that England never had a revolution. English freedom, English stability, England's amicable relations between classes: all testified to the blessings of continuity, as France's misfortunes testified to the bad effects of a violent break with the past. But Mill and Arnold were rather inclined to think that many of England's worst shortcomings were due to her not having had, like France, a revolution which propelled her irrevocably into the modern world. In a letter of 1847, Mill replied to John Austin's strictures on the revolutions in France by arguing that, although revolutionary convulsions had given the French the unpleasant characteristics of high ambition and adventurism, the French Revolution had also given France institutions and habits of mind which England could well afford to emulate. Perhaps, he added, England needed a violent revolution 'to give that general shake-up to the torpid mind of the nation which the French Revolution gave to Continental Europe. England has never had any general break-up of old associations & hence the extreme difficulty of getting any ideas into its stupid head.'

Of all countries in Europe, Mill asserted, only France—witness her redistribution of property after the Revolution—had taken her fate into her own hands and fashioned a state of society that had as its chief object the welfare and civilization of the great mass of its people.[65]

For Arnold, too, the great importance of the French Revolution lay in its revelation of a whole people's desire to rule its affairs by reason rather than by custom, by ideas rather than by established facts. It was all very well, he wrote in *Friendship's Garland*, for the English aristocracy to pride itself upon its conquest of the French Revolution. It had won the respect of Europe in the early part of the nineteenth century because of its energetic and effective suppression of French aspirations to empire. But the English aristocracy, and its middle-class successors, made the fatal error of confusing a conquest of the French Revolution with a conquest of the ideas of the French Revolution. England no longer commanded the respect of the Continent because she failed to see the way the world was going —namely, in the direction of the dominant idea of that very French Revolution which she had crushed, the idea of 'making human life more natural and rational.' Once intelligence rather than energy became the one thing needful, England lost her primacy among the nations.[66] Arnold persistently recommended Voltaire to his countrymen because Voltaire was the most effective agent of the French quality of lucidity: '. . . the perception of the want of truth and validness in notions long current; the perception that they are no longer possible, that their time is finished and they can serve us no more.'[67]

Thus it was not merely the French Revolution but the fact that it resulted from the French allegiance to ideas which impressed Arnold and Mill. Since France's allegiance to reason rather than to custom or prejudice had enabled her, alone among the European nations, to make the final break with the past, it was in France that the great questions of the future would pose themselves soonest and most clearly. Mill predicted that the 'whole problem of modern society . . . will be worked out . . . in France and nowhere else.'[68] Arnold prophesied that 'the French spirit is destined to make its influence felt,—as an element, in alliance with the native spirit, of novelty and movement.'[69] Both believed that France, by virtue of her devotion to ideas and to reason, was the *avant-garde* spirit of the modern world.

Although they were more insistent upon intellectual integrity than most of their contemporaries, Arnold and Mill were typically Victorian in their desire for a union of the intellectual and social motives; and they observed the ideal marriage of the intellectual with the reforming impulse in France.

In an 1833 article called 'Comparison of the Tendencies of French and English Intellect,' Mill contrasted the dogmatic practicality of England, at one extreme, with the scientific speculativeness of Germany at the other, and decided that France, 'having an equal turn for framing general theories and reducing them into practice,' represented the happy union of both qualities. He found it a shortcoming of English intellect that English political passions were never roused by abstractions. The English people, he said, would fight for particular laws but not for a principle of law; they would campaign furiously for a change in the way members were elected to Parliament, but they remained indifferent to doctrines of popular sovereignty or the rights of man.[70]

Returning to the same theme four years later, Mill wrote that, although the typical English statesman prided himself on being void of large political principles and guiltless of purposes rationally conceived and pursued, his country was none the better for his vaunted purity. It was, in fact, for want of ideas and of purpose that the English government had not a single notable achievement to show for the fifty-year period from 1780 to 1830—a period when statesmen conceived the Code Napoléon in France, the Federal Constitution in the United States, and systems of land reform, municipal organization, and public education in Prussia.[71] In 1845, Mill said that the English mind—with the sole exception of the Oxford theologians—was distinguished from that of the Continent by its lack of any conception of human or social destination.[72]

In 1861, Arnold took up Mill's theme in 'Democracy.' He claimed, in this essay (which introduces nearly all the themes more fully and rhetorically developed in *Culture and Anarchy*), that France was the great power she was in Europe because she had made the ideas of 1789 the rationale of her state. All European nations, he said, had felt the ideas of 1789 to a lesser or greater degree, but France had capitalized upon them with unequaled thoroughness and rationality by making them the basis of the state and its organizations. France alone had 'remodelled her institutions with an eye to reason rather than custom, and to right rather than fact.'[73] A year later, in *Friendship's Garland*, Arnold called the intellect of England 'at this moment, to an almost unexampled degree, without influence on the intellect of Europe.' France, he argued, influenced the world because she understood ideas and the way in which they move the world; England neither understood nor believed in ideas but only played with them 'like counters, taking them up and laying them down at random.'[74]

Arnold and Mill believed that the happy union of the intellectual and the moral passion which characterized French intelligence arose from the fact that, in France, ideas appealed not only to the intellectual elite but to all classes of society. As Arnold put it, intelligence in France was '*wide and deepspread*' and ideas captured the imagination of 'the commonplace man as well as . . . the Genius.'[75]

In 1865, Arnold applied Mill's distinction between the causes which arouse political passion in France and in England to the English 'Revolution' of 1642 and the French Revolution of 1789. The first, he maintained, was motivated by men's practical sense, the second by their intelligence. '1789 asked of a thing, Is it rational? 1642 asked of a thing, Is it legal?' Because ideas are naturally more universal and permanent than are laws, the French Revolution was of far greater significance than the English. In fact, Arnold concluded, it was 'the passion with which it could inspire a multitude for [its] ideas' that made the French Revolution 'the greatest, the most animating event in history.'[76]

One of Mill's earliest and strongest declarations about the French Revolution was that no one could hope to understand it who did not grasp at the outset that what made it a new and unique phenomenon was that it was 'emphatically the work of the people.' The French Revolution, he asserted in 1828, revealed for the first time the existence and the significance of 'that force which converts a whole people into heroes, which binds an entire nation together as one man.'[77] Over twenty years later, in a letter of 1852, Mill wrote: 'The French working men and women contended for a principle, for an idea of justice, and they lived on bread and water till they gained their purpose. It was not more and costlier eating and drinking that was their object, as it seems to be the sole object of most of the well-paid English artisans.'[78]

Thus, both Mill and Arnold believed that, as the latter wrote, 'it is the brightest feature in [French] civilisation that her common people can understand and appreciate language which elsewhere meets with a response only from the educated and refined classes.'[79] It was of the greatest importance for Arnold and Mill to discover the reasons why the common people of France were so much more amenable to reason than were the common people of England; for the common people of England were about to assume the rule of their country.

Arnold and Mill gave three reasons for the healthy condition of the French common people: French appreciation of the idea of society itself; French social equality; and French education. They agreed in recommending English adoption of the first two, but parted ways over the question of English adoption of the French system of state education. Their disagreements over the relevance of certain French institutions to England were essentially disagreements over how far England ought to imitate the French version of democracy.

It was the view of Arnold and Mill that the idea of society and of social intercourse was the strain of continuity which connected prerevolutionary with postrevolutionary France. For Arnold, the cause of the French Revolution was not the spirit of philanthropy, or the spirit of envy, or the love of abstract ideas, but 'the spirit of society.' Voltaire, Arnold pointed out, had rightly fixed upon '*l'esprit de société*' as the special gift of the great age of Louis XIV to the world. This French ideal of social intercourse, said Arnold, 'brings men together, makes them feel the need of one another, understand one another.' But, he argued, once the spirit of society is abroad, the spirit of equality cannot be far off, since universality of manners will not long tolerate gross inequalities of property and social position.[80] Once the ideal of society was embraced by even a small group of Frenchmen, it was destined to inspire a whole people with the desire to make the idea of society genuinely national.

England, never having had the spirit of society, had never had the spirit of equality, and had never had a revolution. Their want of the 'sympathetic and social virtues' explained why Englishmen, unlike Frenchmen, had never succeeded in establishing a 'vital union' between themselves and races they had conquered.[81]

Mill, too, looked upon the 'sociability and demonstrativeness—the . . . natural refinement of manners down to the lowest rank' of the French as a heritage from prerevolutionary times, though he thought it a quality inherent in French national character rather than a contribution of the age of Louis XIV. What especially impressed Mill about eighteenth-century France was its appreciation that thought and the pursuit of knowledge are in some sense social and public rather than purely individual and private acts. When he organized the Utilitarian Society in 1823, Mill was conscious of reviving an institution far better known in France than in England: the school of thinkers who produce ideas by discussion and mutual criticism. When Mill sought a prototype for the idea of organized, almost socialized intellect, he hit upon the French *philosophes* of the eighteenth century as a group foreshadowing the character and aims of the Utilitarians. The *philosophes*, Mill remarked, were 'the example we sought to imitate, and we hoped to accomplish no less results.' Mill said in his *Autobiography* that it was only by living in France and entering into French society that he had come to understand how low was the moral tone of English society, which seemed to him characterized by a hostility to, and embarrassment at the expression of, lofty sentiments. The French, on the other hand, made such sentiments 'the current coin of human intercourse, both in books and in private life.' Mill argued that it was by reason of this 'habitual exercise of the feelings' that the 'general culture of the understanding' was 'carried down into the most uneducated classes . . . in a degree not equalled in England among the so-called educated.'[82]

Arnold and Mill believed that the spirit of society already present in the French people was translated by the French Revolution into the fact of social equality—which, in turn, enhanced the ideal of society. For both of them, the achievement of social equality was the most important practical result of the French

Revolution; and it was the chief reason why the common people of France were the most civilized common people in the world.

There was much evidence to support Arnold's and Mill's belief that the egalitarian institutions brought into being after the French Revolution had drastically changed the relative positions of the French and English common people on the scale of well-being. Voltaire, looking at the English peasant in the third decade of the eighteenth century, was impressed by the fact that he, unlike his French counterpart, 'n'a point les pieds meurtris par des sabots, . . . mange du pain blanc, . . . est bien vêtu, . . . ne craint point d'augmenter le nombre de ses bestiaux ni de couvrir son toit de tuiles, de peur que l'on ne hausse ses impôts l'année d'après.'[83] In 1811, a French visitor to England could still come to the conclusion that, although English political practices were among the most corrupt and disgusting he had ever witnessed, England's government was the best that ever existed; for 'the great mass of the people [were] richer, happier, and more respectable than any other with which I am acquainted.'[84]

But in 1848, Mill cited as a typical, and wholly justifiable, Continental opinion the following remarks of a Swiss industrialist upon the English working classes:

> Whilst in respect to the work to which they have been specially trained they are the most skillful, they are in conduct the most disorderly, debauched, and unruly, and least respectable and trustworthy of any nation whatsoever whom we have employed; and in saying this, I express the experience of every manufacturer on the continent to whom I have spoken, and especially of the English manufacturers, who make the loudest complaints. . . .
> When the uneducated English workmen are released from the bonds of iron discipline in which they have been restrained by their employers in England, and are treated with the urbanity and friendly feeling which the more educated workmen on the continent expect and receive from their employers, they completely lose their balance.[85]

Arnold expressed his agreement with a Frenchman, writing in the seventies, who said of the English working class:

> I consider this multitude to be absolutely devoid, not only of political principles, but even of the most simple notions of good and evil. Certainly it does not appeal, this mob, to the principles

of '89, which you English make game of; it does not insist on the rights of man; what it wants is beer, gin, and *fun*.[86]

Mill thought he knew the reason why the artisans of Paris formed 'the most intelligent and best-conducted labouring class . . . to be found on the earth's surface,'[87] and why the French peasant was, unlike the typical English day laborer, on the same level of civilization as the middle classes of his country, fully capable of sharing their objects and pursuits.[88] He noticed how, in France, respectability did not depend upon money: 'All agree that any man who can dress decently may dine with or go to the soirées of anybody, & mix on terms of perfect equality with all whom he meets.'[89] In England, on the other hand, 'the distribution of what may be called social dignity is more unequal . . . than in any other civilized country of Europe, and the feeling of communion and brotherhood between man and man more artificially graduated according to the niceties of the scale of wealth.'[90]

Mill also recognized how the spirit of social equality had given impetus to, and had in turn been reenforced by, the more equal distribution of property which took place after the revolution. He devoted an entire chapter of his *Principles of Political Economy* to the collection and presentation of evidence from a variety of sources testifying to 'the state of cultivation, and the comfort and happiness of the cultivators, in those countries and parts of countries, in which the greater part of the land has neither landlord nor farmer, other than the labourer who tills the soil.' Mill, trying to persuade an England devoutly attached to the unequal system of land distribution founded on primogeniture (and strict settlement), argued for peasant proprietorship by collecting testimonials (especially from English observers) upon the beneficent workings of the institution in France and other European countries. It was generally agreed, Mill observed, that peasant properties fostered efficiency, industry, self-respect, and—perhaps most important of all—respect for the institution of property.[91] Republicanism in France, Mill once wrote, could never jeopardize the institution of property; for 'where almost every peasant has his piece of land,' and landowners form more than half the adult male population, 'the respect for the right of property amounts to a superstition.'[92]

The lesson about the security which democracy gave for property was one of many which Mill had learned from Tocqueville.[93] Mill understood that for Tocqueville the essential part of the natural tendency towards democracy was the inevitable movement towards equality of conditions, and 'the absence of all aristocracy, whether constituted by political privileges, or by superiority in individual importance and social power.' But he also understood that the English, who had little faith in irresistible tendencies, had still less faith in equality, and would therefore find Tocqueville's prediction incredible. Indeed, Mill remarked, England really did seem to be an exception to the general movement towards equality, for the 'passion for equality' which Tocqueville saw as the dominant moral force of the modern world was hardly even known among the English, who possessed, on the contrary, 'a passion for inequality.' Yet, Mill argued, England was no exception. Already the power, the influence, even the quality of the English aristocracy had been sapped, and the aristocratic regime was giving way to the regime of the middle class.[94] The triumph of equality was inevitable. The crucial question was whether Englishmen would understand in time that 'the only school of genuine moral sentiment is society between equals'[95] and would prepare themselves for the acceptance of what would in any case become the general rule of modern society.

Arnold also investigated the relation between the quality of working-class life and the degree of equality in a country with the help of Tocqueville. He had read in George Sand endless eulogies of the French peasant, and expressions of what she called the 'holy doctrine of social liberty and fraternal equality'; and he agreed that 'the French peasant is really, so far as I can see, the largest and strongest element of soundness which the body social of any European nation possesses.'[96] He noticed that Tocqueville, by no means in love with democracy, had written that the common people were 'plus grossier dans les pays aristocratiques que partout ailleurs';[97] and he tried to confirm Tocqueville's assertion by contrasting aristocratic England with democratic France. In 'Democracy,' Arnold argued that a community—as opposed to an individual or a class—which desired to expand and develop would instinctively choose equality. For a community which resisted equality sacrificed the contribution to the community which its common people might otherwise have made. Great inequalities, he maintained, tended to depress rather than excite the energies of the common people as a class; in a society characterized by vast inequalities, the common people seemed to forsake even the modest amount of amelioration available to them when they saw the absolute futility of trying to raise themselves to the level, so far above their own, of the highest class. But in France, where social equality prevailed, the common people had 'a self-respect, an enlargement of spirit, a consciousness of counting for something in their country's action' which made them the superior of the common people of any other country.[98]

In 'Equality,' published seventeen years after 'Democracy,' Arnold translated the general recommendation of equality as a civilizing force into the explicit assertion that England could not do away with her religion of inequality without forsaking her superstitious belief in the sanctity of primogeniture and freedom of bequest. He insisted, as Mill had done, that the community of tastes which existed among peasant, tradesman, gentleman, and scholar in France was the result of equality. He supported his contention that English inequality was not a divine mandate promulgated as eternal law but a state of things established by law when inequality was the most expedient arrangement for society and therefore alterable by law when inequality was no longer expedient, by noting that 'the right of bequest was in early times, as Sir Henry Maine and Mr. Mill have pointed out, seldom recognised.' He even considered, momentarily, Mill's practical proposal for curing English inequality: 'Mr. Mill and others have shown that a law of bequest fixing the maximum . . . which any one individual may take by bequest or inheritance, but in other respects leaving the testator quite free, has none of the inconveniences of the French law, and is in every way preferable.' But having gone so far with Mill, Arnold would go no farther. Abruptly casting aside all talk of practical proposals as being in an insufficiently lofty tone for a lecture before the Royal Institution, he fell back upon his habitual nostrum and urged his audience to take thought.[99]

Yet the agreement in principle between Arnold and Mill is clear. Both enjoined their countrymen to adopt the French ideal of equality if they truly desired to realize the English ideal of the greatest happiness of the greatest number.[100]

The agreement between Arnold and Mill over the desirability of English adoption of French institutions designed to civilize the common people ended where the question of public education arose. Both were profoundly dissatisfied with the civilization of the English middle class and with the educational system that it had devised. But where Arnold thought that the French system of state education was the cure for the shortcomings of the English middle class, Mill believed that the middle-class Englishman's individualism, destructive as it might often be, was too valuable to be sacrificed for the advantages of uniformity and regulation.

Arnold believed that French public schools had done for the French middle class what social equality had done for the working class. Every advantage which France had over England—superior cities, theater, recreations, food—was attributable, Arnold argued, to the high demands which the vast French middle class made upon life, demands made elsewhere only by a small upper class.[101] The contrast between this French middle class and its English counterpart was as striking as that between the lower classes of the two countries. Arnold expressed full sympathy with the Frenchman who said of the English middle class:

> To understand the success of Messrs. Moody and Sankey, one must be familiar with English manners, one must know the mind-deafening influence of a narrow Biblism, one must have experienced the sense of acute ennui, which the aspect and the frequentation of this great division of English society produce in others, the want of elasticity and the chronic ennui which characterise this class itself, petrified in a narrow Protestantism and in a perpetual reading of the Bible.[102]

Despite all the shortcomings of the English middle class, Arnold expected and, in one sense, even wanted it to rule democratic England. But he maintained that the middle class was unfit to rule as long as it remained uneducated.[103] He insisted that the middle-class principle of supply and demand could not be relied on to call into existence a sound system of education. Men generally know pretty well, he said, the distinction between good and bad butter, and between tainted and fresh meat; and so

> the principle of supply and demand may, perhaps, be relied upon to give us sound meat and butter. But the mass of mankind do not so well know what distinguishes good teaching and training from bad; they do not here know what they ought to demand, and, therefore, the demand cannot be relied on to give us the right supply.[104]

As Arnold looked at the Licensed Victuallers' schools and Commercial Travellers' academies which the principles of the market place had produced when applied to education, he found concrete proof that the English supply of middle-class education was neither right nor adequate.

Arnold was so convinced of the urgency of his country's need for a state system of education that he entitled an essay in which he recommended it: 'Porro Unum est Necessarium.' In this essay he reminded readers that in 1859 he had submitted to the government a blue-book report urging England to follow the French example and organize a system of public secondary education. Such a measure would rescue England from the plight in which she found herself as a result of having the worst-educated middle class in Europe, and would secure for her, as it had for France, a great social good by 'fusing all the upper and middle classes into one powerful whole.' Arnold then quoted from another report, submitted in 1865, which stressed the fact that the English middle class was rendered socially and intellectually underprivileged by the education it received. Its private schools had made it a class *brought up on the second plane,* and thus deprived it of the qualities requisite for governing. Arnold placed the reward for the public organization of its secondary education clearly before the eyes of the English middle class when he told it that in France 'the government is composed entirely of men from the professional and middle classes.'[105]

Arnold proposed a practical plan for the establishment of secondary schools—upon the French model—to be financed and inspected by the state. His plan required the provision throughout England of an adequate number of properly supplied secondary schools whose teachers would give guarantees of their proficiency in the form of a university degree or a certificate for secondary education.[106] He asked England to follow the example of France in making it the duty of the state to maintain standards in both public and private secondary education.

Arnold believed that the success of French education was due to the French genius for organizing the idea of democracy in the institutions of the state; and he thought Napoleon the most notable example of that genius. He held the organization and administration of education by the French state to be one of the great achievements of the Revolution and of 'the great Napoleon.'[107] His private remarks about Napoleon indicated to what a great extent he considered the ideas of Napoleon to have been those ideas which the English aristocracy thought it had discredited by defeating the French Revolution in the shape of Napoleon's armies.[108] Whatever Napoleon's shortcomings, his elaborate attempt to imitate a Roman Republic in his dictatorial regime was bound to touch a soft spot in Arnold's heart.

Mill, on the other hand, bore a grudge against Napoleon just because he had incorporated some principles of the Revolution in the state administration. Mill even blamed the well-meaning Louis XVIII for preserving 'that vast net-work of administrative tyranny which did not exist under the old French government, which the Convention created for a temporary purpose, and which Napoleon made permanent; that system of bureaucracy, which leaves no free agent in all France, except the man at Paris who pulls the wires.'[109] The difference in their attitudes towards Napoleon's achievements symbolized the divergence between Arnold's and Mill's views of the French system of education.

They reacted very differently to a story about a French Minister of Instruction which was current in England during the sixties and seventies. Mill's version of the story appeared in 1865 in the course of his attack upon Comte's proposal of an intellectual dictatorship to direct all the mental resources of a nation to the solution of one question at a time:

> We should then see [said Mill] the whole speculative intellect of
> the human race simultaneously at work on one question, by

orders from above, as a French minister of public instruction once boasted that a million of boys were saying the same lesson during the same half-hour in every town and village of France.[110]

Arnold, writing in 1877, saw neither the humor nor the serious import of the anecdote—especially when it was used by Englishmen to illustrate the dangers of state education. He himself had 'never been able to see that it was in itself so very lamentable a thing that all these French boys should be saying the same lesson at the same time' because the only question worth considering was what the lesson was. So far from uniformity in instruction being the great evil, Arnold retorted,

> I lament nothing more in our actual instruction than its multiformity,—a multiformity, too often, of false direction and useless labour. I desire nothing so much for it as greater uniformity,—but uniformity in good.[111]

Mill illustrated his critique of Comte's plan to combat intellectual anarchy with the anecdote about French educational uniformity because most of Comte's aberrations from sanity appeared to Mill to result from the fact that Comte carried 'the mania for regulation by which Frenchmen are distinguished among Europeans'[112] to its utmost extreme. When Mill was forced to choose between France's 'mania for uniformity' and England's 'unbounded toleration for every description of anomaly,' he unhesitatingly chose the latter.[113] In 1867, he wrote that 'I have long thought that while French schoolboys are better taught and learn more than English boys, the freer system of the English schools has much to do with the superiority of England in the love and practice of personal and political freedom.'[114]

Mill was not unmindful of the poor state of English education or of the inability of the free enterprise principle to provide a better. As early as the first Reform Bill, he began to insist that education was not a commodity, like any other, which should depend for its maintenance upon the vicissitudes of the market place; and he

> urged strenuously the importance of having a provision for education, not dependent on the mere demand of the market, that is, on the knowledge and discernment of average parents, but calcu-

lated to establish and keep up a higher standard of instruction than is likely to be spontaneously demanded by the buyers of the article.[115]

In 1833, Mill defended the principle of government educational endowments against the attacks which had been made upon them by such revered fathers as Turgot and Adam Smith. He argued that a people might be perfectly free, perfectly secure, and yet 'in an abject state of degradation, both physical and mental'; and he directed the eyes of his countrymen to the success and efficiency of the endowed universities of France and Germany.[116] Thirty-six years later, in 1869, Mill was still maintaining that education was emphatically not 'one of those marketable commodities which the interest of rival dealers can be depended on for providing, in the quantity and of the quality required.'[117]

Mill, like Arnold, warned of the specially dangerous effects of bad private education upon the middle classes, who would never of themselves demand a kind of learning which did not seem conducive to business success. All who are interested in the welfare of society, Mill maintained, must wish 'that the education of those who are above poverty, but who are not, for their own bane and that of others, predestined to idleness, should have [some] better guide than an extremely narrow conception of the exigencies of a business life.'[118] Mill also saw that the middle class was not merely destined for something other than idleness, but that it had already become, as he wrote in 1840, 'the arbiter of fortune and success.'[119] He knew that its predominance in government was inevitable, knew also that knowledge is 'the one thing needful in every concern of life, and pre-eminently in government,' and insisted, in 1866, that government was something for which no person was suited who did not have 'a large and liberal general education.'[120]

Mill was even prepared to go a considerable distance with Arnold in combating the English prejudice against state interference in education. He proposed the establishment of 'a certain number of places of education with the *prestige* of public sanction, giving, on a large and comprehensive scale, the best teaching which it is found possible to provide.'[121] But he pulled up short at the prospect of the state directing education. The state-established and state-controlled schools which he spoke of as providing a certain standard of excellence against which others might measure themselves were to be few in number and only existed, as he explained in *On Liberty*, 'as one among many competing experiments.'[122]

Mill supported government enforcement of compulsory education but resolutely opposed government operation and control of schools:

> I have never conceived compulsory education in that sense. What I understood by it is that all parents should be required to have their children taught certain things, being left free to select the teachers, but the efficiency of the teaching being ensured by a Government inspection of schools, and by a real and searching examination of pupils.[123]

Mill held that 'diversity of education' was an essential element in the development of individuality in conduct and thought. Uniform state education, consequently, was the greatest enemy of individual variety and social pluralism.

> A general State education is a mere contrivance for moulding people to be exactly like one another: . . . in proportion as it is efficient and successful, it establishes a despotism over the mind, leading by natural tendency to one over the body.[124]

The conflict between Arnold and Mill over whether the object lesson of French education ought to stand as an example or as a warning to England symbolized their disagreement over the form which democracy ought to take in England. They were in full agreement about the desirability of the social equality which democracy brought, but they fell out over the question of whether democracy ought to be organized in the state. All the disagreements between Arnold and Mill about the relevance of certain French institutions[125] to England are ultimately explainable by a blunt observation which Mill made in *Considerations on Representative Government*:

> In England there has always been more liberty, but worse organization, while in other countries there is better organization, but less liberty.[126]

France was not the only country which presented to England an example of democracy which she could either imitate or reject. Democracy also prevailed in the United States of

America; but there it had been given a very different interpretation. Arnold's and Mill's disagreements about French institutions were paralleled by their disagreements about American institutions, and showed how each man, when he urged his country to accept democracy, had a different working model in mind.

Arnold and Mill were often inclined to look upon America as nothing else but England with certain elements or ingredients left out, and others exaggerated; they expected that, if England did not become more European, she would become more American. Mill, in 1840, asked whether 'the American people as a whole, both in their good qualities and in their defects, resemble anything so much as an exaggeration of our own middle class?'[127] He pointed to the similarity between the active and energetic temperaments of both nations,[128] and called them 'the only two first-rate Powers who are also free nations.'[129] Arnold, in 1865, complained that 'to be too much with the Americans is like living with somebody who has all one's own bad habits and tendencies,'[130] and, in 1882, called America 'just ourselves, with the Barbarians quite left out, and the Populace nearly'—which left only the Philistine middle class.[131]

Yet Arnold and Mill knew that America was also different— both from aristocratic England and from democratic France. Neither man could quite get over the fact that America lacked certain institutions which were taken for granted in England. Mill noticed how there were more built-in counterweights to the dominant middle class in England than in America. England had an agricultural class that was, unlike America's, stable and rooted in a locality. England also possessed two classes almost unknown in America: the leisured class and the learned class.[132] In *Considerations on Representative Government*, Mill deplored the manner in which American character had been harmed by American institutions, which undermined the idea of distinction by inculcating the belief 'that any one man (with a white skin) is as good as any other.'[133]

Arnold also blamed America because she was without any protection against middle-class domination and because she lacked respect for individual distinction. The fact that America had never had either a priesthood or an aristocracy was for Arnold sufficient explanation of her middle-class character, her failure to respect distinction and elevation, and her religion of the *'average man.'*[134] Thus, he shared Mill's dissatisfaction with certain characteristics of American society, but explained them in a different way.

Arnold denied that he was being unfair to America by blaming her for the absence of an established aristocracy and church, which she could not help. He argued that America, without having inherited an established aristocracy and an established church, need not have suffered the evils which usually attend the absence, or the abrupt departure, of such institutions:

> The greatest men of America, her Washingtons, Hamiltons, Madisons, well understanding that aristocratical institutions are not in all times and places possible; well perceiving that in their Republic there was no place for these; comprehending, therefore, that from these that security for national dignity and greatness, an ideal commanding popular reverence, was not to be obtained, but knowing that this ideal was indispensable, would have been rejoiced to found a substitute for it in the dignity and authority of the State.[135]

Arnold, when he made this statement, was trying to persuade his countrymen that, although democracy itself was inevitable, England still had the freedom to choose between the French version of democracy and the American. The rhetorical flourish with which he capped all his arguments in favor of organizing democracy, as the French had done, 'with a certain indisputable grandeur and success,' in the institutions of the state, came in the form of a question—and its answer:

> On what action may we rely to replace . . . that action of the aristocracy upon the people of this country, which we have seen exercise an influence in many respects elevating and beneficial, but which is rapidly, and from inevitable causes, ceasing? In other words, and to use a short and significant modern expression which every one understands, what influence may help us to prevent the English people from becoming, with the growth of democracy, *Americanised*? I confess I am disposed to answer: On the action of the State.

Democracy, Arnold argued, need not be interpreted as the Americans interpreted it. The Americans had had the opportunity to organize their state in such a way that it might have given the law to human life as authoritatively as the aristocracy and priesthood had done in other countries; the Americans had missed their opportunity, and were suffering the consequences in their national life. The question which Englishmen had to answer therefore was:

> When the inevitable course of events has made our self-government something really like that of America, when it has removed or weakened that security for national dignity, which we possessed in *aristocracy*, will the substitute of the *State* be equally wanting to us?

'If it is,' Arnold promptly answered, 'then the dangers of America will really be ours; the dangers which come from the multitude being in power, with no adequate ideal to elevate or guide the multitude.'[136]

Mill did not favor the French form of democracy over the American. Far from belittling American education, as Arnold frequently did,[137] Mill said there was 'a superiority of mental development' in even the lowest class of Americans not to be found in any other country.[138] He contrasted America, where all citizens participated in the administration of the business of society, with France, which had democratic society without democratic government. Far from insisting, with Arnold, that American democracy needed a strong central government, Mill argued that 'society in America requires little but to be let alone':[139]

> Let them be left without a government, every body of Americans is able to improvise one, and to carry on that or any public business with a sufficient amount of intelligence, order, and decision. This is what every free people ought to be; and a people capable of this is certain to be free: it will never let itself be enslaved by any man or body of men because these are able to seize and pull the reins of the central administration.[140]

Yet Mill, too, in a letter written to Henry Fawcett fifteen months before the appearance of Arnold's 'Democracy,' uttered a warning against the Americanization of democracy. He praised Fawcett for promoting Hare's plan of proportional representation, which 'contains the true solution of the political difficulties of the future,' but warned that

> it is an uphill race, and a race against time, for if the American form of democracy overtakes us first, the majority will no more

relax their despotism than a single despot would. But our only chance is to come forward as Liberals, carrying out the democratic idea, not as Conservatives, resisting it.[141]

Mill, like Arnold, proposed measures which England had to take if she was to be preserved from American democracy. But where Arnold's warning against Americanism was a warning against anarchy, Mill's was a warning against despotism.

In his 1840 review of *Democracy in America*, Mill expounded Tocqueville's doctrine of the 'tyranny of the majority.' This peculiarly American brand of tyranny, Mill said, was exercised less over the body than over the mind. In America, the land of freedom and of great intellectual activity on the part of the individual, less independence of thought existed than in any other country. For when the collective voice of the majority in America had made up its mind upon a question, hardly a single American dared to question its conclusion. Having rejected the authority of the past, of the philosopher, of the priest, Americans prostrated themselves before the God of public opinion. Each American found himself incapable of imagining that an enormous mass of individuals all very much like himself could be in the wrong.[142] Mill feared that America, for want of a strong center of resistance to popular will, would fall under the tyranny of the majority.

Mill's fears of 1840 seemed to have been partially confirmed by 1861. The misgivings which Mill confided to Fawcett in this year were publicly reflected by his plea to his countrymen to avoid the despotism of the majority which prevailed in the United States. Where Arnold, holding aloft the spectre of 'Americanization,' asked England to substitute for the action of the nearly defunct aristocracy the action of the state, Mill, brandishing the same red flag, asked his countrymen to prevent the establishment of a new despotic class by instituting proportional representation and weakening the action of the state:

> In the United States, where the numerical majority have long been in full possession of collective despotism, they would be as unwilling to part with it as a single despot or an aristocracy. But I believe that the English democracy would as yet be content with protection against the class legislation of others, without claiming the power to exercise it in their turn.[143]

Not everyone understood that 'short and significant modern expression' as well as Arnold had hoped. Both Arnold and Mill deplored that dominance of the average man over the mind of all which they detected in American democracy. Arnold, however, thought the American perversion of democracy was the failure to replace the action of the aristocracy upon the average man with the action of the state. Mill feared that the state, in a democracy ruled solely by the numerical majority, would merely institutionalize the despotic control which the average man already exercised through public opinion. No wonder, then, that the threat of Americanization of English democracy meant to Arnold the threat of anarchy, and to Mill the threat of tyranny.

It must not be thought that either France or America or any modern nation, democracy or not, could have won Arnold's or Mill's complete allegiance. In fact, the only country which they ever admitted preferring, in an absolute sense, to England, was an ancient and partly imaginary entity: Greece of the fifth century.

Their deep sympathy for ancient Greece connected their cosmopolitan ideal of culture with their concern for the proper form modern democracy ought to take. For Greece symbolized both the ideal of culture and the ideal of democracy. For England to ignore France was for England to ignore manners and ideas; for England to ignore Italy was for England to ignore beauty, and so on with other modern European countries; but for England to ignore ancient Greece was for England to lose sight of the ideal of culture itself. Similarly, in politics, France and America could never be recommended to England as anything more than imperfect imitations of the Platonic ideal of democracy which prevailed in fifth-century Athens.

Athens represented the ideal union of culture and democracy which Arnold and Mill were seeking to establish in the modern world. Mill, who asserted that 'an average Athenian was a far finer specimen of humanity on the whole than an average Englishman,'[144] and Arnold, who saw faults in English translations of Homer as faults in English character,[145] believed that ancient Greece offered not only the highest philosophical ideal of human perfection ever conceived, but a citizenry whose standards of conduct, taste, and intelligence were far above those of the citizenry of nineteenth-century England.

It was because Greek society embodied their cultural ideal and because it was the model of a democratic society founded upon equality that Arnold and Mill urged their countrymen to study it. Arnold, in 'Democracy,' said that Athens would always be interesting because it provided 'the spectacle of the culture of a *people*.' It embodied, he said, the highest development of the humanity of the middle and lower classes that had ever been reached, and was therefore the ideal of a state based upon social equality. In Athens, Arnold pointed out, shopkeepers and tradesmen as well as philosophers could participate in refined philosophic discussion. This is why 'a handful of Athenians of two thousand years ago are more interesting than the millions of most nations our contemporaries.'[146] Mill, in 1846, called the ancient Greeks 'the most remarkable people who have yet existed,' and proclaimed their history more relevant to an Englishman of the middle of the nineteenth century than the history of his own country.[147] When he wanted to bring home to the mind of the average Englishman an idea of what representative government could achieve as an agent of national education, Mill observed that 'the practice of the dicastery and the ecclesia raised the intellectual standard of an average Athenian citizen far beyond anything of which there is yet an example in any other mass of men ancient or modern.'[148]

Arnold and Mill could recommend the example of Athenian democracy far more freely than they could French or American democracy because in it, according to them, a powerful state action existed side by side with full individual liberty. Thus Arnold maintained that 'it is in ancient Greece, where state action was omnipresent, that we see the individual at his very highest pitch of free and fair activity.'[149] And Mill asserted that the 'intellectual and moral pre-eminence' of Athens was attributable to the organization of democracy in Athenian institutions, and that along with the spirit of liberty Athenian democracy inculcated a powerful feeling that the interests of individuals and those of the state were identical.[150]

Their recommendation of the Greek ideal of democracy to England showed how truly English Arnold and Mill, for all their cosmopolitanism, were. For they both believed that, as Arnold wrote, the English had, 'more than any modern people, . . . the power of renewing, in [their] national life, the example of Greece.'[151] 'It is hardly an accident,' G. M. Young has written, 'that . . . the most conspicuous memorial of the Utilitarians is a History of Greece. Across the ages, the modern Englishman recognized his peers.'[152] The Greece which Arnold and Mill invoked to judge English character, English art, and English society was, in part, an imaginary Greece. It was the fulfillment of the desire, by which they were ruled, for harmony and completeness. It was the native home of their ideal of democratic culture as the harmonious development of human nature in all classes of society. It was the imaginary destination towards which the injunction to know the best that was thought and known in the world urged individuals and nations.

VII

CULTURE AND LIBERTY

———————◦———————

Freedom and not servitude is the cure of anarchy; as religion, and not atheism, is the true remedy for superstition.

EDMUND BURKE

You know it is an old maxim of mine, that interest, as love and religion, and so many other pretty things, should be free.

JEREMY BENTHAM

Almost all the projects of social reformers of these days are really *liberticide*.

JOHN STUART MILL

Those who cannot read Greek should read nothing but Milton and parts of Wordsworth: The State should see to it.

MATTHEW ARNOLD

THE divergence between the paths which Arnold and Mill chose to follow in pursuit of a single ideal of culture appeared even more clearly in their views on English domestic politics than it did in their discussions of the cultures of foreign nations. Both men favored democracy for England, but feared that, unless it were prepared for properly, it would become the enemy of culture instead of its ally. Both believed the essence of democracy to be equality rather than liberty, but whereas for Mill this meant that liberty had to be jealously protected to prevent democracy from becoming tyrannical, for Arnold it meant that liberty had to be carefully circumscribed in order to make democracy successful. Mill, unlike Arnold, thought liberty an essential element of culture. Therefore, he resisted the strengthening of the state which Arnold believed to be the indispensable agent of culture in a democratic society.

Arnold and Mill had three main reasons for favoring the introduction of democracy in England. They believed, with Tocqueville, that democracy was inevitable; they argued that ultimately democracy was the only way in which the world could be ruled by right rather than force; they saw that the aristocracy was no longer fitted to rule and that, in any case, the principle of *noblesse oblige*, which was used to justify aristocratic rule, was false.

Both Arnold and Mill took to heart Tocqueville's assertion, reiterated throughout the first volume of *Democracy in America*, that the most important modern problem was not how to resist democracy, which was 'the will of God,'[1] but how to prepare for it. According to Mill, the most important lesson and the inescapable conclusion to be drawn from Tocqueville's study was that democracy was as inevitable, its ultimate triumph in the modern world as certain, as a law of nature, but that it still remained to human control to decide whether the irresistible natural force should work for good or for evil.[2] In 1861, Arnold wrote that 'at the present time, almost every one believes in the growth of democracy, almost every one talks of it, almost every one laments it; but the last thing people can be brought to do is to make timely preparation for it.'[3]

Arnold and Mill appreciated the morality as well as the expediency of Tocqueville's defense of democracy. Tocqueville maintained that the world ought to be ruled by right, and not force:

> Do you not see that religious belief is shaken and the divine notion of right is declining, that morality is debased and the notion of moral right is therefore fading away? Argument is substituted for faith, and calculation for the impulses of sentiment. If, in the midst of this general disruption, you do not succeed in connecting the notion of right with that of private interest, which is the only immutable point in the human heart, what means will you have of governing the world except by fear?[4]

Mill, in 1837, defended representative institutions from Carlyle's attacks upon them by asserting that, although democratic institutions would not by themselves provide a people with a faith, they would give to people in possession of a creed 'the only regular and peaceable mode in which that faith can quietly declare itself.' The real pre-eminence of the representative form of government, according to Mill, arises from the fact that 'it alone is government by consent—government by mutual compromise and compact; while all others are, in one form or another, governments by constraint.'[5] Arnold adopted Joubert's pernicious maxim that force governs the world until right is 'ready' in order to defend Burke's reaction to the French Revolution, but he recognized that, since Burke's day, democracy had become the decree of Providence and was therefore not only right but 'ready.' He argued that, in France, democracy had had the effect of removing the hostility between citizens and the state because the ordinary man now felt that the state represented himself: 'The enthusiasm of the French people for the Army,' Arnold reported in a letter of 1859, 'is remarkable; almost every peasant we passed in the diligence took off his hat to this officer, though you never see them salute a gentleman, as such; but they feel that the army is the proud point of the nation and that it is made out of themselves.'[6]

Arnold and Mill charged that, for a variety of causes, the aristocratic class of England was no longer fitted to rule. Arnold maintained that the culture of the aristocracy had seriously declined from what it was in the eighteenth century, and that the common people, sensing this, no longer recognized the right of the aristocracy to lead. But even if the English aristocracy had not declined, Arnold knew that aristocracies were, by nature, helpless in the presence of ideas because they were used to resting 'on all which is most solid, material, and visible.' Thus, whatever might be said for the rule of aristocracies in general, an era of intellectual ferment was no time to leave government in the hands of a class blind, if not hostile, to ideas and unconscious of their power. To put democracy (by which Arnold meant both the abstract idea and the *demos*), with its openness to ideas, under the tutelage of aristocracy at such a time would be, he argued, to retard progress.[7] Mill, too, believed that the aristocracy was less alive intellectually than either of the other classes. In a letter of 1847, he remarked that

every year shows more & more their *pitoyable* absence of even that very moderate degree of intellect, & that very moderate amount of will & character which are scattered through the other classes but of which they have certainly much less than the average share, owing to the total absence of the habit of exerting their minds for any purpose whatever.[8]

The aristocracy's want of intellect incapacitated it for rule, but its excessive materialism, Arnold and Mill believed, actually had a demoralizing influence upon the people. For Arnold the aristocratic ascendancy was not merely ineffectual but positively harmful in its action upon the people. For the aristocracy, he argued, was inevitably materialistic, and its materialistic ideal had the effect of vulgarizing the middle class and brutalizing the lower class.[9] Mill deplored the corrupting example which a materialistic upper class set for the lower classes, and he decried the predominance, in an undemocratic nation, of private and selfish (that is, aristocratic) interests over the public interest in the management of the state. Aristocratic rule tended to corrupt the whole life of society

> because the respect of the multitude always attaching itself principally to that which, in the existing state of society, is the chief passport to power; and under English institutions, riches, hereditary or acquired, being the almost exclusive source of political importance; riches, and the signs of riches, were almost the only things really respected, and the life of the people was devoted to the pursuit of them.[10]

Arnold and Mill rejected the defense of aristocratic rule which was made by people like Ruskin on the principle of *noblesse oblige*. Arnold and Mill not only saw how little the theory corresponded to the world it pretended to describe; they rejected the theory itself as unsound. Mill, in the *Autobiography*, implied that all doctrines of *noblesse oblige* were delusory and impossible of fulfillment when he said that 'while the higher and richer classes [hold] the power of government, the instruction and improvement of the mass of the people [are] contrary to the self-interest of those classes, because tending to render the people more powerful for throwing off the yoke.'[11] In 'Thoughts on Parliamentary Reform,' one of the two reasons he gave why everyone should have the vote was that the interests of those who lack political influence are always postponed by governments in the interest of those who have it.[12] Arnold, in

'The Future of Liberalism,' gave a sprightly defense of the Utilitarian doctrines of enlightened self-interest and universal suffrage by boldly asserting that

> if experience has established any one thing in this world, it has established this: that it is well for any great class and description of men in society to be able to say for itself what it wants, and not to have other classes, the so-called educated and intelligent classes, acting for it as its proctors, and supposed to understand its wants and provide for them. They do not really understand its wants, they do not really provide for them.

In fact, Arnold added, the belief that a governing class would cater to the interests of classes without power or representation was 'the last left of our illusions.'[13] In 'Numbers,' he insisted once again that the mass of the people, whatever its short-comings, should be allowed to manage its own affairs, and not be forced to stand aside in favor of 'a so-called superior class, possessing property and intelligence.'[14]

The implied corollary of the theory of *noblesse oblige*—the principle of social paternalism—was also rejected by Arnold and Mill. In his *Principles of Political Economy*, Mill maintained that the paternalistic attitude towards the poor, which had never been effective in practice, should no longer be retained as an ideal. 'It is on a far other basis,' he warned, 'that the well-being and well-doing of the labouring people must henceforth rest. The poor have come out of leading-strings, and cannot any longer be governed or treated like children. To their own qualities must now be commended the care of their destiny.'[15] Arnold, in *A French Eton*, preceded his usual definition of the relation of the state to individuals as that of men in their corporate to men in their individual capacity with some remarks upon what that relation is not. 'Is a citizen's relation to the State,' he asked, 'that of a dependant to a parental bene-factor?' 'By no means,' he answered, 'it is that of a member in a partnership to the whole firm.'[16]

The stock of opinions about democracy which Arnold and Mill held in common included, finally, the belief that the essence of democracy is equality rather than liberty. Arnold said explicitly that it is not political freedom—which may be established and maintained under a variety of forms of government—but social freedom or equality which is the special 'field of the conquests of democracy.'[17] But where Mill saw democracy's indifference to liberty as a danger signal, requiring to be answered by the hasty erection of fortifications about the independence and integrity of individuals, Arnold saw democracy's preoccupation with the cooperative virtues and the demands of society as a whole as the ideal corrective to English individualism.

In his 1838 essay on Jeremy Bentham, Mill, with admirable incisiveness, defined the 'three great questions in government: First, to what authority is it for the good of the people that they should be subject? Secondly, how are they to be induced to obey that authority? . . . [Thirdly,] by what means are the abuses of this authority to be checked?'[18] Mill, as we have seen, agreed with Bentham that democracy provided adequate answers to the first two questions by saying that the people should be responsible to themselves as represented in the state, which they would obey once they knew that it was the instrument of their will and not that of some privileged class. But Mill accused Bentham of having enshrined majority rule in the authority of the state without bothering to provide an answer to the third essential question; for Mill opposed the establishment of democracy under what he called the absolute and unfettered authority of the numerical majority.

From 1832 on, the circumstances of English society seemed to compel Mill to qualify his essential faith in democracy in order to mitigate democracy's harmful tendencies without neutralizing its beneficial effects. His study of Tocqueville turned him away from allegiance to absolute or 'pure' democracy—the Radical ideals of one man, one vote, and of simple majority rule—towards advocacy of a modified form of democracy which would have built-in safeguards against the absolute predominance of the numerical majority.[19]

Mill insisted on the distinction, which he said Bentham had overlooked, between the people and the majority of the people. He said that Bentham, instead of exhausting all his ingenuity 'in devising means for riveting the yoke of public opinion closer and closer round the necks of all public functionaries,' ought to have occupied himself, as Tocqueville had done, with finding the means for making democratic institutions conducive to the preservation and encouragement of respect for individual personality and for the 'superiority of cultivated intelligence.'[20]

Mill believed that the establishment of democracy would be detrimental to culture if its passion for equality were allowed to override individuality. Mill accepted the rule of the majority, but insisted on limiting and thwarting the action of the majority sufficiently to prevent one type of imperfection from being universally imposed:

> The numerical majority of any society whatever, must consist of persons all standing in the same social position, and having, in the main, the same pursuits, namely, unskilled manual labourers; and we mean no disparagement to them: whatever we say to their disadvantage, we say equally of a numerical majority of shop-keepers, or of squires. Where there is identity of position and pursuits, there also will be identity of partialities, passions, and prejudices; and to give to any one set of partialities, passions, and prejudices, absolute power, without counter-balance from partial-ities, passions, and prejudices of a different sort, is the way to render the correction of any of those imperfections hopeless; to make one narrow, mean type of human nature universal and perpetual, and to crush every influence which tends to the further improvement of man's intellectual and moral nature.

In the interests of human possibility and the ideal of steady improvement towards perfection and wholeness, Mill urged that 'the institutions of society should make provision for keeping up, in some form or other, as a corrective to partial views . . . a perpetual and standing Opposition to the will of the majority.'[21] Mill's attack upon Bentham's political philosophy, though it was accompanied by no practical proposals for thwarting absolute majority rule, was the forerunner of Mill's later advocacy of proportional representation, plural voting, and, in general, most measures designed to prevent the state from becoming the instrument of a monolithic majority.

For Arnold, it was precisely English individualism and hostil-ity to the state which cast doubt upon the successful establish-ment of democracy. He defined democracy as

> a force in which the concert of a great number of men makes up for the weakness of each man taken by himself; democracy accepts a certain relative rise in their condition, obtainable by this concert for a great number, as something desirable in itself, because though this is undoubtedly far below grandeur, it is yet a good deal above insignificance.

But how would such a force, Arnold wondered, appeal to the traditionally self-reliant and individualistic English people who did not like to work in concert or to work for any prize but the highest, or to contemplate sharing that prize with anyone? For a people committed to working as rugged individualists is not, asserted Arnold, a people working democratically.[22]

Arnold said that he did not want to deprive England of those qualities which impel people to work individually: 'May it never lose them! A people without the salt of these qualities, relying wholly on mutual co-operation, and proposing to itself second-rate ideals, would arrive at the pettiness and stationariness of China.' He believed that England's individualistic national character was beyond the reach of alien cultural and political influences, and so rocklike in its strength and permanence that any apprehension of its being endangered by ubiquitous state action was illusory. He treated with levity the Englishman's qualms about his personal liberty, his constitutional rights, and his ultimate control over the actions of his representatives in government. Ironically, he tried to reassure his individualistic countrymen by invoking the doctrine of identity between government and people which Mill saw as the future basis of the tyranny of the majority which threatened to destroy individualism:

> Here the people will always sufficiently keep in mind that any public authority is a trust delegated by themselves, for certain purposes, and with certain limits. . . . Here no one dreams of removing a single constitutional control, of abolishing a single safeguard for securing a correspondence between the acts of government and the will of the nation.[23]

Arnold's preparations for the inevitable advent of democracy consisted not in hedging freedom and individualism against the assaults which the passion for equality seemed likely to make upon them, but in refurbishing the state in order that it might serve as the guardian of culture in a democratic society. For it was culture and not liberty that Arnold worried about preserving—or, rather, establishing. The American version of democracy was inadequate to England's needs: 'Nations are not truly great solely because the individuals composing them are numerous, free, and active'; national greatness, Arnold maintained, arises when natural resources serve a higher ideal than that which the ordinary man proposes to himself. Liberty is all very well, but 'all the liberty and industry in the world will not ensure . . . a high reason and a fine culture.'[24]

Every question raised in 'Democracy' received the identical answer: culture cannot survive in democratic society without the state. Once he had disposed of the question concerning the dangers incident to state action, Arnold addressed himself to the question of what special gifts the state had for the preservation of culture, and what qualified the men who formed the state executive to exercise powers so much greater than those given to the mass of citizens. He began his answer by quoting Burke's definition of the state as *the nation in its collective and corporate character.* Yet he recognized that, in practice, the state must be composed of men; and he knew that granting large powers to men is not so easily justified as granting the same powers to the abstract entity, 'the nation.' He argued, therefore, that even men of ordinary intellectual and moral strength were transformed when they received great power and high position. They gained, merely by virtue of their position, two enormous advantages: 'access to almost boundless means of information, and the enlargement of mind which the habit of dealing with great affairs tends to produce.' Besides, these men could be shamed into virtue simply by being given, and being made aware that they had been given, grave responsibility as the representatives of nothing less than the collective will of the nation.[25]

But the traditional justification of state action, Arnold believed, was strengthened in a democracy. Perhaps sensing the weakness of the argument that power tends to make people better, and absolute power to make them perfect, Arnold ventured a second reply to his question by way of consolation in the event that state action should prove to be clumsy and maleficent:

> If the executive government is really in the hands of men no wiser than the bulk of mankind, of men whose action an intelligent man would be unwilling to accept as representative of his own action, whose fault is that? It is the fault of the nation itself, which, not being in the hands of a despot or an oligarchy, being free to control the choice of those who are to sum up and concentrate its

action, controls it in such a manner that it allows to be chosen agents so little in its confidence, or so mediocre, or so incompetent, that it thinks the best thing to be done with them is to reduce their action as near as possible to a nullity. Hesitating, blundering, un-intelligent, inefficacious, the action of the State may be; but, such as it is, it is the collective action of the nation itself, and the nation is responsible for it.[26]

If you pretend to have chosen democracy as your form of government, Arnold said, why not commit yourself to it whole-heartedly? The action of the state was, after all, the action of the nation coming back to flatter or to haunt it in another form —whatever virtues or faults the collective nation had would be mirrored in the state.

Here was consolation indeed! Arnold did not admit that the state could multiply and aggravate the faults of what he would later call the unsound majority, faults which, in other circum-stances, would have been at least partially counteracted by the reforming efforts of Arnold's righteous minority.[27] Arnold thus provided an apology for democracy which Tocqueville had warned against when he said:

Our contemporaries are constantly excited by two conflicting passions: they want to be led, and they wish to remain free. As they cannot destroy either the one or the other of these contrary propensities, they strive to satisfy them both at once. They devise a sole, tutelary, and all-powerful form of government, but elected by the people. They combine the principle of centralization and that of popular sovereignty; this gives them a respite: they console themselves for being in tutelage by the reflection that they have chosen their own guardians. Every man allows himself to be put in leading-strings, because he sees that it is not a person or a class of persons, but the people at large who hold the end of his chain.[28]

Of course, Arnold reminded his readers, almost as an after-thought, the state power must represent the best self rather than the inferior self of the nation if it is to become in practice what it always is ideally: the genius of the English people.[29] But this reservation, important in itself, came rather weakly after Arnold had, in effect, said that the way to transform a man's ordinary self into his best self is to entrust him with a position of power in the state; and it only amounted to saying that individual culture is impossible without the state, and that the state cannot be legitimately established except upon a basis of individual culture.

Mill, like Arnold, was aware of the need for continuity between democracy and the form of polity it was replacing. In his 1840 essay on Coleridge, he wrote that one absolute requisite of civil society is loyalty to '*something* which is settled, something permanent, and not to be called in question; something which, by general agreement, has a right to be where it is, and to be secure against disturbance, whatever else may change.' For Arnold this something was the state, which he believed the sacred framework of society. Mill, to be sure, spoke with fondness in this essay of the 'old ideal' of the state 'as a concentration of the force of all the individuals of the nation in the hands of certain of its members, in order to the accomplishment of whatever could be best accomplished by systematic cooperation.' But Mill also asserted that once the requisites of civil society had been lost, they should not, indeed they could not, be restored 'in connexion with the same institutions or the same doctrines as before.' When society must be rebuilt, he said, 'there is no use in attempting to rebuild it on the old plan.' In the future, he maintained, the feeling of loyalty he had spoken of could exist only insofar as it attached itself 'to the principles of individual freedom and political and social equality.'[30]

Mill rejected the argument that democracy reenforced the traditional justification of the authority of the state. He maintained, in the Introduction to *On Liberty*, that the external aspect of the conflict between liberty and authority had changed so drastically with the advent of more or less representative government as nearly to disguise the fact that such a conflict was still possible (if not, in fact, taking place). In times past, he said, whether in Greece, Rome, or England, it was customary, and justifiable, to think of the rulers of a country as being in necessary antagonism to the ruled because they did not govern by the consent of the people but by virtue of inherited or usurped power; and therefore this conflict stood as the type of the conflict between liberty and authority. As a result, patriots made it their goal to limit the power of the ruler over the people and referred to the limitations of power which they were able to effect as liberty. In time, however, Mill continued, there arose approximations to representative government, in which the functionaries of the state were made delegates of, and responsible to, the people themselves. No sooner had this great change in the form of government become general than men began to think that the old conflict between liberty and authority no longer existed:

> As the struggle proceeded for making the ruling power emanate from the periodical choice of the ruled, some persons began to think that too much importance had been attached to the limitation of the power itself. *That* (it might seem) was a resource against rulers whose interests were habitually opposed to those of the people. What was now wanted was, that the rulers should be identified with the people; that their interest and will should be the interest and will of the nation. The nation did not need to be protected against its own will. There was no fear of its tyrannising over itself. Let the rulers be effectually responsible to it, promptly removable by it, and it could afford to trust them with power of which it could itself dictate the use to be made. Their power was but the nation's own power, concentrated, and in a form convenient for exercise.[31]

Mill said that the sophistries to which he referred had been characteristic of the preceding generation of European liberals and still remained articles of faith among Continental liberals. Could Mill have read the essay in which Arnold presented the action of the state as 'the collective action of the nation itself,' whose wishes it could 'sum up and concentrate,'[32] and argued that in a democracy it was absurd for the nation to put limitations upon the state, i.e., itself, he would have known that democratic statism still had a powerful advocate in the British Isles.

On Liberty and *Culture and Anarchy* were attempts to prepare for the advent of democratic reform in such a way as to make democracy the preserver rather than the destroyer of culture. They differed over the question of whether culture in a democratic society depends upon authority and the state or upon liberty and individuality. By comparing the treatments of certain questions raised in both works, I shall try to show that their disagreement about whether it is more liberty or more

243

authority which is needed to make democracy a force for good caused Arnold and Mill to espouse what we now think of as opposed political philosophies.

The way in which *On Liberty* and *Culture and Anarchy* follow divergent paths in pursuit of a single ideal of culture is illustrated by the different roles which Wilhelm von Humboldt, the German statesman and man of letters, plays in them. In the *Autobiography*, Mill stated his indebtedness to Humboldt for the leading idea of *On Liberty*—the doctrine of individuality and the right and obligation of people to develop themselves fully and freely.[33] He opened *On Liberty* by quoting the words from Humboldt's *The Sphere and Duties of Government* which announced that 'the grand, leading principle, towards which every argument unfolded in these pages directly converges, is the absolute and essential importance of human development in its richest diversity.'[34] Humboldt played a less prominent but equally important role in *Culture and Anarchy*. Arnold, in order to prove that in foreign countries full awareness of the evil uses to which state action might be put could coexist with realistic acquiescence in a considerable amount of state action, pointed to the example of Humboldt. He attacked a writer in the *Westminster Review* who dwelt upon Humboldt's warnings against excessive reliance upon the state for overlooking the fact that it was the immediate object of Humboldt's life to extend the action of the German state. Arnold maintained that Humboldt was flexible enough to see 'that for his purpose itself, of enabling the individual to stand perfect on his own foundations and to do without the State, the action of the State would for long, long years be necessary.' To prove his contention, Arnold pointed out that Humboldt became Prussian Minister of Education soon after he wrote *The Sphere and Duties of Government*, 'and from his ministry all the great reforms which give the control of Prussian education to the State . . . take their origin.'[35]

The admiration which Arnold and Mill had for Humboldt arose, in the first instance, because he shared their ideal of human perfection. He stated, in his treatise on government, that the end of a man's existence is 'the highest and most harmonious development of his powers to a complete and consistent whole.' But his book justified two different means of pursuing this end, and each of his admirers chose the means which he preferred. Through most of his book, Humboldt insisted that the two conditions for human perfection are freedom and variety. He condemned all state institutions designed 'to elevate the positive welfare of the nation' as 'positively hurtful in their consequences, and wholly irreconcilable with a true system of polity.' His lengthy discussion of education was a refutation of every argument which supported the principle of national education. But in the conclusion to his book he suddenly decided that the theory which he had passionately expounded through fifteen chapters should not be prematurely applied to reality; for the principle of freedom must always give way, he argued, to the exigencies of political 'necessity.'[36] Humboldt's book thus embodied not only the ideal of culture as a harmonious development of human nature which was espoused by Arnold and Mill, but also the two possible ways in which that ideal might be realized.

The difference between *Culture and Anarchy* and *On Liberty* can be exaggerated if it is forgotten that Mill defended liberty not as an end in itself, but as an indispensable means to the end of human perfection. 'I forego any advantage,' Mill said in his Introduction, 'which could be derived to my argument from the idea of abstract right, as a thing independent of utility.' Liberty had to justify itself in terms of utility, but 'utility in the largest sense, grounded on the permanent interests of a man as a progressive being.' Mill's defense of liberty and individuality was based upon his belief that 'mankind are greater gainers by suffering each other to live as seems good to themselves, than by compelling each to live as seems good to the rest.'[37]

There are reasons why many critics of Mill, perhaps including Arnold, have accused him of making liberty an end in itself. Mill's inclination to blame the great thinkers of the past for their irresponsibility in having 'occupied themselves rather in inquiring what things society ought to like or dislike, than in questioning whether its likings or dislikings should be a law to individuals'[38] stands in marked contrast to Arnold's opinion that 'our being able to say what we like is . . . absolutely nothing to boast of or exult in, unless we are really made better by it, and more able to think and say such things as be rightful. We may like it and imagine it impossible to do without it; but it is, in itself, no *virtue*, it confers no excellence.'³⁹ But Mill did not go farther toward making liberty an end in itself than Arnold did toward making the state an end in itself. As Arnold thought the state was essential to human perfection, so Mill thought liberty was indispensable for the same end. We must remember that it was in *On Liberty* that Mill proffered Pericles as the ideal representative of a human nature complete on all sides, and recited with approval Humboldt's definition of man's purpose as 'the highest and most harmonious development of his powers to a complete and consistent whole.'⁴⁰

Mill hoped to show that liberty was an element of culture by proving that freedom of opinion and individuality were essential to human development. Arnold, in *Culture and Anarchy*, asserted that human perfection was possible without freedom of expression and without freedom of action but not without the state.

Mill contended that human development had been retarded by the suppression of opinions. He pointed to the executions of Socrates and of Jesus, and to the persecution of Christianity by Marcus Aurelius as the outstanding instances of the grave fallibility of those—usually the moral and religious models of the community—who persecuted the carriers of ideas. Mill chose his examples with a view to linking the doctrine of free thought and discussion with his conception of the necessary elements of human perfection. For Socrates was the father of Greek philosophy, and Jesus the founder of Christianity. The successful suppression of the opinions of either man would have deprived humanity of half its heritage.

But the critics of free thought had always protested that, although the forces of order and conservatism *did* put Socrates and Jesus to death, the truths they defended lived and flourished. Dr. Johnson had actually defended the persecutors of Christianity by saying that truth needs to survive the test of persecution, and that Marcus Aurelius provided such a test. Mill replied by calling it the merest sentimentality to suppose that truth, as truth, was more impervious than error to the ordeals of the dungeon and the stake. 'History,' he said, 'teems with instances of truth put down by persecution. If not suppressed for ever, it may be thrown back for centuries.' Every reasonable

246

person, he maintained, knew that Christianity might have been destroyed if it had been persecuted more severely and continuously in the Roman Empire.[41] We can never know, he implied, what we lose by persecution and suppression of ideas. Mill believed that, as F. A. Hayek, a modern disciple of Mill, has argued,

> liberty . . . is an ideal that will not be preserved unless it is accepted as an overriding principle governing all particular acts of legislation. Where no such fundamental rule is stubbornly adhered to as an ultimate ideal about which there must be no compromise for the sake of material advantages . . . freedom is almost certain to be destroyed by piecemeal encroachments. For in each particular instance it will be possible to promise concrete and tangible advantages as the result of a curtailment of freedom, while the benefits sacrificed will in their nature always be unknown and uncertain.[42]

Mill dwelt on the character and actions of the persecutor Marcus Aurelius longer than he did upon the figures of the two most notable victims of persecution, Socrates and Jesus, because Marcus presented the classic case of well-intentioned persecution hindering the development of a truly complete ideal of human nature. The 'extreme admiration' which, in a letter of 1855,[43] Mill claimed to have for Marcus Aurelius showed itself clearly in *On Liberty*. A man of the highest rectitude and 'tenderest heart,' Marcus' ethical writings, Mill asserted, were hardly distinguishable from the best teachings of Jesus. Yet Marcus' admirers were confronted with the paradoxical fact that 'this man, a better Christian in all but the dogmatic sense of the word than almost any of the ostensibly Christian sovereigns who have since reigned, persecuted Christianity.'[44]

Mill suggested extenuating circumstances for Marcus' error. Responsible for the maintenance of the entire civilized world of his day, he firmly believed that his world was sustained by its religion and by its devotion to that religion. Christianity, which sought to overthrow the prevailing religion, seemed to him a dark, dissolving force whose victory would plunge the world into barbarism and chaos. Christianity's nonrational foundations appalled him, and made him incapable of imagining that any good might come of it. Consequently, 'the gentlest and most amiable of philosophers and rulers, under a solemn sense of duty, authorized the persecution of Christianity.'[45]

The immediacy of Mill's regret at Marcus' great error resulted not from his outrage at a violation of civil liberties but from his recognition that Marcus' policy had prevented that union of the best in the pagan and Christian ideals of human nature which it was Mill's lifelong object to foster:

> To my mind this is one of the most tragical facts in all history. It is a bitter thought, how different a thing the Christianity of the world might have been, if the Christian faith had been adopted as the religion of the empire under the auspices of Marcus Aurelius instead of those of Constantine.[46]

The significance of Marcus Aurelius' action in Mill's argument for freedom of opinion depended upon the loss to humanity occasioned by Marcus' refusal to adopt Christianity.

Mill considered that nothing would have been learned from Marcus Aurelius' enormous blunder in persecuting the early Christians if modern Christians did not recognize their own proneness—and with less justification—to a similar error. When Christians are tempted, as they so often are, to suppress the opinions and destroy the lives, of those whose beliefs they abhor, they ought, said Mill, to recall that

> no one plea which can be urged for punishing anti-Christian teaching was wanting to Marcus Aurelius for punishing, as he did, the propagation of Christianity. No Christian more firmly believes that Atheism is false, and tends to the dissolution of society, than Marcus Aurelius believed the same things of Christianity; he who, of all men then alive, might have been thought the most capable of appreciating it.[47]

Marcus Aurelius was, for Mill, the supreme example of a man of the highest wisdom and virtue who commits the error of persecuting those who promulgate what he believes to be false, dangerous, and subversive ideas. Moreover, Marcus proved how necessary liberty is to culture because his particular violation of liberty had detrimental effects upon the ideal of human nature which was to be adopted by a large portion of the human race. If a man of Marcus' consummate moral and intellectual purity could err so grievously, Mill warned, then it is

unlikely that any mortal can take for granted his infallibility
in punishing men who promote opinions he thinks pernicious.[48]

Arnold seems to have read *On Liberty* shortly after it appeared,
and his immediate reaction to it was favorable. 'Have you seen
Mill's book on Liberty?' he asked his sister in a letter of June,
1859. 'It is,' he noted, 'worth reading attentively, being one of
the few books that inculcate tolerance in an unalarming and
inoffensive way.'[49]

But certain things in *On Liberty* must, inevitably, have disturbed Arnold, and in 1863 one of them came to the surface.
Arnold opened his essay on Marcus Aurelius, published in that
year, by noting that

> Mr. Mill says, in his book on Liberty, that 'Christian morality
> is in great part merely a protest against paganism; its ideal is
> negative rather than positive, passive rather than active.' He
> says that, in certain most important respects, 'it falls far below the
> best morality of the ancients.'

Arnold attempted briefly to refute Mill's charge—although in
their proper context Mill's remarks were really part of an
attempt to expound something nearly identical to Arnold's idea
of Hebraism and Hellenism as the constituents of human
completeness—by asserting that the superiority of a religious
to a philosophical morality lay in the greater power of the
former to arouse emotion. A purely rational morality like that
of Epictetus or Marcus Aurelius, Arnold argued, can appeal
only to the few, not to the many. Morality in the hands of
religion commands more respect than philosophical morality
because religion lights up morality by supplying it with 'the
emotion and inspiration needful for carrying the sage along
the narrow way perfectly, for carrying the ordinary man along
it at all.' Arnold offered a few comparisons between religious
and philosophical moral injunctions which were supposed to
prove the superiority of the former, and then, turning back to
Mill, said—in something of a *non sequitur*—that

> it is because Mr. Mill has attained to the perception of truths of
> this nature, that he is,—instead of being, like the school from which
> he proceeds, doomed to sterility,—a writer of distinguished mark
> and influence, a writer deserving all attention and respect; it is

(I must be pardoned for saying) because he is not sufficiently leavened with them, that he falls just short of being a great writer.[50]

Arnold now passed on to his consideration of Marcus Aurelius, and had, ostensibly, finished with Mill, who was not again mentioned in the essay. Yet Arnold was acutely conscious of Mill from the beginning of the essay to the end. For although the remarks about Christianity which peeved Arnold were not directly related to Mill's remarks about Marcus Aurelius, they did appear in the same chapter with Mill's discussion of the Roman Emperor's persecution of Christianity and they helped to complete the argument which that discussion served. Arnold's reading of *On Liberty* was, I believe, the immediate cause of his decision to discuss Marcus Aurelius in terms of the difference between pagan and Christian morality.

Arnold's reverence for Marcus Aurelius was comparable to Mill's. G. W. E. Russell, Arnold's friend, recalled seeing Arnold, on the morning after he had lost his eldest son, 'consoling himself [with] Marcus Aurelius.'[51] In one of his poems, Arnold referred to Marcus Aurelius as 'the imperial sage, purest of men.'[52] His 1863 essay on Marcus Aurelius is an admiring, even a worshipful tribute. In it the Emperor's ethical writings are held to possess a good deal of that power of lighting up morality which Arnold called characteristic of religion rather than philosophy. Marcus' character prompted Arnold to call him 'perhaps the most beautiful figure in history.' Among sovereigns, said Arnold, only Saint-Louis and Alfred can compare to him in goodness; and his interest for modern man is far greater than theirs because 'he lived and acted in a state of society modern by its essential characteristics, in an epoch akin to our own, in a brilliant centre of civilisation.'[53] Marcus Aurelius is thus not only supremely great, but supremely relevant.

Yet Arnold, like Mill, was impeded in his praise of Marcus by his recollection of the fact of Marcus Aurelius' persecution of Christianity, and he had to come to terms with that fact before he could proceed. It would not do, Arnold said, to ignore or try to discredit the evidence of Marcus' persecution of the Christians. 'Of his humanity, of his tolerance, of his horror of cruelty and violence, of his wish to refrain from severe measures against the Christians, of his anxiety to temper the severity of these measures when they appeared to him indispensable, there is no doubt. . . .'[54] But, Arnold added, there is also no doubt that Marcus Aurelius ordered Christians to be punished because they were Christians.

Like Mill, Arnold enumerated the circumstances which mitigated Marcus' guilt, and said that people unaware of them were likely to have a false impression of the moral significance of his action. First of all, it had to be remembered in what light early Christianity appeared to the Roman emperors. It seemed to them not the visible embodiment of saintliness, but rather 'something philosophically contemptible, politically subversive, and morally abominable.' That none of his modern readers might be under any misapprehension about the image which early Christianity presented to Marcus Aurelius, Arnold said that Marcus and his contemporaries 'regarded it much as well-conditioned people, with us, regard Mormonism.' Moreover, as the leader of a vast empire, Marcus Aurelius saw Christianity as a disruptive and subversive force; and thus 'it was inevitable that Christianity in the Roman world, *like democracy in the modern world*, like every new spirit with a similar mission assigned to it, should at its first appearance occasion an instinctive shrinking and repugnance in the world which it was to dissolve.' (Italics mine.) Marcus Aurelius and his friends looked at Christianity through colored glasses because their concern for political stability, their dislike of associations unauthorized by the state, and their tendency to confuse the Christians with the Jews, 'that isolated, fierce, and stubborn race,' led them to attribute to the Christians 'a thousand faults not their own.'[55]

Arnold once again resembled Mill in seeing the wider implications for humanity and for its ideal of perfection of Marcus Aurelius' actions. The shortcomings of early Christianity led him to speculate upon what might have been the fate of Christianity had it been adopted and not rejected by Marcus Aurelius. 'Who,' asked Arnold, 'will venture to affirm that by the alliance of Christianity with the virtue and intelligence of men like the Antonines,—of the best product of Greek and Roman civilisation, while Greek and Roman civilisation had yet life and power,—Christianity and the world, as well as the Antonines themselves, would not have been gainers?'[56] For

Arnold, just as for Mill, Marcus Aurelius' rejection of Christianity was a fact of momentous importance because it was the historical event which confirmed the divorce between Hebraism and Hellenism, or the Christian and Greek ideals of perfection.

But for Arnold the circumstances in which Marcus Aurelius acted not only mitigated his guilt; they removed it. Mill, who believed that the real life of a creed was coextensive with the period when it was fighting for its existence,[57] traced Christianity's decline as a power in men's inner lives from the time of its adoption by Constantine; therefore, he never considered the possibility that Marcus Aurelius' opinion of Christianity might have been true. But Arnold, who maintained that without the help of Constantine 'Christianity might have lost itself in a multitude of hole-and-corner churches like the churches of English Nonconformity,'[58] pointed out that although the early Christians may not have had all the faults Marcus Aurelius ascribed to them, they nevertheless were amply supplied with faults:

> Who can doubt that among the professing Christians of the second century, as among the professing Christians of the nineteenth, there was plenty of folly, plenty of rabid nonsense, plenty of gross fanaticism?

Arnold had not forgotten his analogy between the early Christians and the Mormons. Whereas the history of Marcus Aurelius proved to Mill the inextricable connection between culture and liberty, Arnold, though he admitted that Marcus Aurelius 'did Christianity an immense injustice and *rested in an idea of State-attributes which was illusive*,' though he recognized that Marcus' error had resulted in narrowing humanity's ideal of perfection, yet failed to grasp what Mill thought the hard lesson of the whole affair. (Italics mine.) For he concluded that Marcus Aurelius 'incurs no moral reproach by having authorised the punishment of the Christians' and proclaimed him 'blameless.'[59]

It is likely that Mill's work suggested to Arnold the analogy between early Christianity and Mormonism. Mill, as we have seen, used the incident of Marcus Aurelius' persecution of Christianity to sharpen his moral injunction against any modern Christian who took it upon himself to suppress teachings which in his opinion tended to the dissolution of civilized society. But many modern Christians thought they discerned just such teachings in the doctrines of the Mormons, and were prepared to inflict upon the Mormons just such cruelties as Mill had warned against.

In the fourth chapter of *On Liberty*, Mill presented as his last example of the propensity of the English public to delve into matters which were not its proper concern 'the language of downright persecution which breaks out from the press of this country whenever it feels called on to notice the remarkable phenomenon of Mormonism.' Saying that no one disapproved of Mormonism more strongly than he did, Mill nevertheless insisted on the right of the Mormons to follow their chosen course of existence free from outside interference. Watching the persecution of the Mormons and even hearing of proposals to exterminate them, Mill deplored the fact that the world had learned nothing from the error of Marcus Aurelius. It is true, he admitted, that Mormonism is 'the product of palpable imposture, not even supported by the *prestige* of extraordinary qualities in its founder,' and lamentable that it should be believed by hundreds of thousands of people. Nevertheless, the parallel between Mormonism and early Christianity was unmistakable:

> What here concerns us is that this religion, like other and better religions, has its martyrs: that its prophet and founder was, for his teaching, put to death by a mob; that others of its adherents lost their lives by the same lawless violence; that they were forcibly expelled in a body, from the country in which they first grew up.[60]

For Arnold, as we have seen, the most significant similarity between Mormonism and early Christianity lay not in their persecution by the forces of respectable conservatism but in the presence, among the devotees of both groups, of plenty of folly, nonsense, and fanaticism. Thus, when the opportunity came to Arnold to show that he had learned something about the importance of liberty from Marcus Aurelius' error, he merely reacted, as one of the 'well-conditioned people' of his age, to Mormonism in the same spirit in which Marcus Aurelius had reacted to Christianity.

In *Culture and Anarchy*, Arnold considered the existence of the Mormons as symptomatic of the absence of recognized, authoritative standards of quality in religion and of the tendency to replace them with standards dictated by a respect for quantity. The claims which sects like the Mormons made for themselves struck Arnold as a compound of impudence and madness. He replied to the Mormon Hepworth Dixon's boast that his sect possessed 200,000 souls and 20,000 rifles by asserting that

> if the followers of a doctrine are really dupes, or worse, and its promulgators are really fanatics, or worse, it gives the doctrine no seriousness or authority the more that there should be found 200,000 souls—200,000 of the innumerable multitude with a natural taste for the bathos,—to hold it, and 20,000 rifles to defend it.[61]

Like Mill, Arnold was not impressed but appalled by the fact that a religion so devoid of intellectual and moral substance could command so large a following. But of those persecutions inflicted on the Mormons which aroused Mill's moral passion, Arnold had nothing to say. For he was certain that liberty is not an essential element of culture, and Mormonism seemed to him to have as little to do with human perfection as Christianity did to Marcus Aurelius.

Culture and Anarchy and *On Liberty* differed as sharply over the necessity of individuality to culture as they did over the indispensability of liberty. Whereas Mill believed that reason and perfection were attainable only through the free efforts of individuals to approximate them, Arnold opposed individual reason to a 'right reason' defined by the state, and held that the insistence on individuality was incompatible with human perfection.

Mill asserted that individuality, like freedom, was a requisite of complete and harmonious human development. He contended that the reasons which justified freedom of opinion also supported the individual's claim to translate his opinions into practice—up to the point where his actions affected persons other than himself. Human action, he argued, is as fallible as human opinion, and just as premature unity of opinion precludes the possibility of discovering the whole truth, so the premature imposition of a uniform pattern upon the conduct of human life narrows and impoverishes humanity's ideal of perfection. Yet, he lamented, few people recognize unfettered individual development for what it is: 'a necessary part and condition' of 'civilisation, instruction, education, culture.'[62]

Mill said that it was not only the individual's right but his duty to consciously choose his own way of life. If he failed to do so, his genuinely human qualities would atrophy, for 'the mental and moral, like the muscular powers, are improved only by being used.' The value of human life, he claimed, depends not upon what man produces but upon what he becomes. However correct his conduct and productive his work, an individual who allows his way of life to be dictated by another will be no more than a machine. But, Mill insisted, 'human nature is not a machine to be built after a model, and set to do the work prescribed for it, but a tree, which requires to grow and develop itself on all sides, according to the tendency of the inward forces which make it a living thing.'[63]

Apparently without knowing it, Mill had committed himself simultaneously to two incompatible defenses of individualism. On the one hand, he wished to show that individuality is an indispensable means to human perfection because it encourages every possibility which might contribute to an ideal of human excellence and thus prevents a premature synthesis of human powers; on the other hand, he tried to justify individuality as an end in itself, because it is natural, because growth should not be thwarted. The latter defense, being based on an anarchic principle, inevitably overshadowed the former.

Mill seemed to be losing sight of the harmonious 'Greek ideal of self-development' which he had espoused at the outset of his chapter on 'Individuality, as One of the Elements of Well-Being' when he said that 'individuality is the same thing with development, and . . . it is only the cultivation of individuality which produces, or can produce, well-developed human beings.' Although he presented many persuasive arguments for the constructive powers of individuality, Mill could not resist falling back upon the argument that new and unusual modes of existence should be tolerated because 'there is no reason that all human existence should be constructed on some one or small number of patterns.' Not only should there be various ways of achieving 'spiritual development,' there should be various ideals of spiritual perfection, and perhaps as many ideals as there are persons: 'If a person possesses any tolerable amount of common sense and experience, his own mode of laying out his existence is the best, not because it is the best in itself, but because it is his own mode.'[64]

If any part of *Culture and Anarchy* may be thought of as a criticism of the corresponding part of *On Liberty*, then Arnold's attack upon 'British Atheism' may be taken as a criticism of Mill's doctrine of individuality. For Arnold spoke of

> a kind of philosophical theory . . . widely spread among us to the effect that there is no such thing at all as a best self and a right reason having claims to paramount authority, or at any rate, no such thing ascertainable and capable of being made use of; and that there is nothing but an infinite number of ideas and works of our ordinary selves . . . pretty nearly equal in value, which are doomed either to an irreconcilable conflict, or else to a perpetual give and take.[65]

Yet, as we have seen, Mill had a fairly definite idea of what a 'best self' should be, and he proposed individuality as a means, like liberty, of ascertaining the best self. He can be extricated from the quandary into which he plunged himself with his organic argument for individuality if it is remembered that, at the outset of his discussion, he qualified all his arguments for individuality by saying that they applied 'while mankind are imperfect.'[66] Mill was prepared to admit that uniformity in perfection is preferable to diversity in imperfection. But he believed that perfection was a long way off and that therefore an infinite variety of experiments in living had to be tolerated in order that all the elements required for the perfection of human existence might be discovered. In 1838 he had warned (in a passage quoted earlier) that 'the field of man's nature and life cannot be too much worked, or in too many directions; until every clod is turned up the work is imperfect; no whole truth is possible but by combining the points of view of all the fractional truths, nor, therefore, until it has been fully seen what each fractional truth can do by itself.'[67] In 1859, Mill was not yet convinced that the powers of humanity had developed to the point where they provided adequate materials for a perfect and final synthesis. Therefore he continued to insist upon liberty of thought and action as 'the only unfailing and permanent source of improvement . . . since by it there are as many possible independent centres of improvement as there are individuals.'[68]

The question of timing, of when analysis should give way to synthesis, diastole to systole, is, as I have suggested previously, a crucial one in comparing Arnold and Mill. Arnold rejected Mill's doctrine of individuality in favor of what he thought was a faster as well as a surer way of ascertaining the best self. As Mill's fondness for endless experimentation tempted him to forget that individuality was but a means to perfection, Arnold's impatient desire for synthesis led him to confuse the state with the noble end he thought it could serve.

Arnold's attitude towards individuality was nearly identical to his attitude towards freedom of opinion. Mill had argued, in *On Liberty*, for the right of 'doing as we like, subject to such consequences as may follow.'[69] Arnold maintained that the light of culture 'shows us that there is nothing so very blessed in merely doing as one likes, that the really blessed thing is to like what right reason ordains, and to follow her authority.'[70] But who or what embodies right reason, the principle of authority? Arnold's answer was the state. But since the state, as he defined it in 'Democracy,' rested upon a foundation of individuals who thought and acted in accordance with right reason, Arnold had to show, in *Culture and Anarchy*, how the state could be something other than the imperfect instrument of sect or party when the people who composed it were, by his own admission, seriously deficient in sweetness and light. He had to define the relation between the state and the 'best self' which culture tries to produce.

Arnold charged that the average Englishman was suspicious of giving the state much power because he thought of it as an instrument to be manipulated by the class in power for selfish ends. He thought this way precisely because he was deficient in culture, and his ordinary self thought strictly in terms of class interest, in terms of each class, like each individual, doing as it likes. As long as men live in accordance with the beliefs and desires of their ordinary selves, Arnold granted, no power can exist which will not be tyrannical. But to do away with all power and to be thus saved from the abuses of power is not to be rescued from the danger of anarchy.[71]

The need for the state, Arnold argued, could not be denied. But what was to be its foundation, its justification? What else, he replied, but the '*best self*' which culture seeks to create, a self which takes no pleasure 'in doing what it likes or is used to do,' but which tries to act according to the best light available. Culture provided the only alternative to anarchy: 'We want an authority, and we find nothing but jealous classes, checks, and a deadlock; culture suggests the idea of *the State*. We find no basis for a firm State-power in our ordinary selves; culture suggests one to us in our *best self*.'[72]

Once again Arnold's argument was revolving in an eternal circle. He persistently argued that the attainment of the best self through culture was impossible without the state. Yet he now proposed to establish the state upon the basis of the best self, to build it upon a foundation which did not yet exist. Arnold probably believed that the state could serve as a kind of visible paradigm for the disinterestedness which the individual needed to develop. Once the disinterested and classless best self was developed, it would in turn make the state, in substance and spirit as well as in form, a national best self. As so often in Arnold's writings, the frame was to make the picture possible, doing to precede being, and right action to provide a signpost to right belief.

Arnold proposed for society what he had once proposed for poetry: a rigid framework which had to be kept intact at whatever cost to the development of a larger ideal of perfection than that which inspired creation of the frame itself:

> For us the framework of society, that theatre on which this august drama has to unroll itself, is sacred; and whoever administers it, and however we may seek to remove them from their tenure of administration, yet, while they administer, we steadily and with undivided heart support them in repressing anarchy and disorder; because without order there can be no society, and without society there can be no human perfection.[73]

For Arnold the state seemed as indispensable to perfection as individuality did to Mill; and as Mill recognized the threat which the state posed to individuality, Arnold looked upon individuality as the greatest threat to the state.

In dealing with society as in dealing with poetry, Arnold

resembled those thinkers whom Mill criticized for synthesizing before they completed their analyses. Mill, convinced that the ideal of human perfection was not yet complete, warned that a 'Chinese stationariness'[74] was the certain way to prevent perfection ever being reached, and championed individuality as the guarantee of progress towards true perfection. Arnold, at the end of 'Democracy,' had said that 'perfection will never be reached.'[75] But in the concluding section of *Culture and Anarchy*, he anticipated a millennium in which the state would be the expression, the instrument, and the enforcer of a universal perfection. Almost the grand culmination of Arnold's most important work was the vision of a closed, static, uniformly perfect society in which the framework of the state, having been conscientiously preserved for the use of democracy, would at last be filled with the precepts of right reason and would organize 'its internal composition and all its laws and institutions conformably to them.' The state would finally become the expression of the 'best self,' which is not manifold, and vulgar, and unstable, and contentious, and ever-varying, but one, and noble, and secure, and peaceful, and the same for all mankind.'[76] Arnold put the final touch to his Utopian vision by warning, somewhat superfluously, that any symptoms of anarchy arising in the era of universal perfection would be suppressed with the greatest urgency and severity.

Though the irony of his admission that dissent could arise in an era of universal perfection escaped Arnold, it revealed that he was not placing his Utopia as far off in the future as such places are usually expected to be. Arnold seemed to believe that the best way of making something come true was to pretend that it already was true. No sooner had he described the apotheosis of the state than he saw in various London disturbances connected with the failure of the second Reform Bill an opportunity for the state to show that it was the expression of the best self by repressing the ordinary selves of contentious individuals:

> Our Barbarian Secretaries of State let the Park railings be broken down, and our Philistine Alderman-Colonels let the London roughs rob and beat the bystanders. But we, beholding in the State no expression of our ordinary self, but even already, as it were, the appointed frame and prepared vessel of our best self,

and, for the future, our best self's powerful, beneficent, and sacred expression and organ—we are willing and resolved, *even now*, to strengthen against anarchy the trembling hands of our Barbarian Home Secretaries and the feeble knees of our Philistine Alderman-Colonels; and to tell them, that it is not really in behalf of their own ordinary self that they are called to protect the Park railings, and to suppress the London roughs, but in behalf of the best self both of themselves and of all of us in the future.[77] (Italics mine.)

The doctrine that the state could prove itself to be the expression of culture's 'best self' by repressing ordinary selves was fraught with dangers, but Arnold was not the man to see them. He had become so intent upon suppressing individualism with right reason that he came to believe that the act of suppression was itself proof of the possession of right reason.

Neither was Arnold able to see that even if the state is the agent of the best self there may be an objection to its coercing individuals into conformity with right reason. For, unlike Mill, he recognized no contradiction between force and reason.

Arnold insisted that the state had to do more than inform or persuade: it had to coerce. The end, he believed, was always 'to make right reason act on individuals'; but the end was not the same as the means. Coercion by law had to precede persuasion by reason, for the second was not always possible without the first. When the *Daily News* charged that his support of authority had a 'non-intellectual root' because, instead of relying upon the common reason of society to check individual eccentricity by working upon individual reason, it resorted to force, Arnold had a ready retort. In making such a charge, he said, the *Daily News* merely proved, once again, the inflexibility of the English race, for

> it being admitted that the conformity of the individual reason of the Rev. W. Cattle or Mr. Bradlaugh with right reason is our true object, and not the mere restraining them, by the strong arm of the State, from Papist-baiting or railing-breaking,—admitting this, we English have so little flexibility that we cannot readily perceive that the State's restraining them from these indulgences may yet fix clearly in their minds that, to the collective nation, these indulgences appear irrational and unallowable, may make them pause and reflect, and may contribute to bringing, with time, their individual reason into harmony with right reason.[78]

Mill, on the other hand, believed that the imposition of reason through force is both self-defeating and inconsistent with the idea of perfection as an inward condition. He never denied that society, if it fails to influence its members through the moral power it exercises over them during the whole period of their youthful education, can still enforce obedience to an established code of conduct superior, in many cases, to that which individuals would follow of their own accord. But in doing so, he said, society would be sacrificing its true goal to expediency, since nothing 'tends more to discredit and frustrate the better means of influencing conduct than a resort to the worse.'[79] People who are constrained to act in a certain way do not, Mill argued, come in time to like it and to attain a harmony between inward assent and outward obedience. On the contrary, they chafe against the imposed constraints and are moved to violent reaction, when they have the power, against both the constraints and the men who have imposed them.

Mill would never admit that reason, truth, or right conduct can be forcibly imposed upon individuals without losing their meaning. In the interest of the true ideal of human perfection, in the interests of culture, and even in the interests of the state, Mill condemned the shortsighted opportunism which, in its obsession with machinery, loses sight of the true object of life:

> The worth of a State, in the long run, is the worth of the individuals composing it; and a State which postpones the interests of *their* mental expansion and elevation to a little more of administrative skill, or of that semblance of it which practice gives, in the details of business; a State which dwarfs its men, in order that they may be more docile instruments in its hands even for beneficial purposes—will find that with small men no great things can really be accomplished; and that the perfection of machinery to which it has sacrificed everything will in the end avail it nothing, for want of the vital power which, in order that the machine might work more smoothly, it has preferred to banish.[80]

The force which Arnold thought indispensable to spiritual perfection seemed to Mill destructive of the spiritual life itself.

The actions of the Reform League which, as we have seen, so agitated Arnold in *Culture and Anarchy*, also engaged the attention of John Stuart Mill. The second Reform Bill was to commit England irrevocably to democracy, and the different ways in which Arnold and Mill reacted to the disturbances connected with passage of the bill epitomized their opposite views of the way in which democracy might be so organized as to make it the ally of culture.

The Hyde Park affair began in July of 1866, shortly after the defeat of Gladstone's reform bill of that year and the substitution of a Tory for a Liberal government. The Reform League, led by Edmond Beales, Colonel Dickson, Charles Bradlaugh, and Mill's friend George Jacob Holyoake, organized a mass meeting of protest which they planned to hold in Hyde Park.

But Hyde Park was not, in 1866, as it is today, a place of refuge and opportunity for all people with heterodox opinions to express and unpopular creeds to propagate. Rather, it was looked upon as a place set aside for the amusement and recreation of the respectable classes. For this reason, among others, Spencer Walpole, the Home Secretary, ordered the gates of the park to be closed about two hours before the Reformers were due to arrive. The leaders of the procession, when it arrived at Marble Arch, demanded entry and were refused. At this point most of them decided to settle for second best and redirected the procession towards Trafalgar Square. But a part of the crowd, especially, it is assumed, Bradlaugh's charges, remained near Hyde Park and began tearing down some of the railings in order to gain entrance. Once the breach in the wall was achieved, a large crowd composed of observers as well as Reformers trampled the flower beds and gamboled with delight all around the forbidden park, pausing at intervals to throw stones at homes in Belgravia. Troops were called in, but by the time they arrived at Hyde Park whatever slight damage had been done was already completed.

On the following day, Beales and his friends paid a visit to the Home Secretary, impressing upon him the restraint which the Reformers had shown in the face of the government's refusal of their eminently reasonable request and demanding, once again, permission to assemble in Hyde Park. In response, Spencer Walpole, the official representative of the state, Arnold's strong-armed instrument for enforcing right reason and suppressing anarchy, began to cry. The members of the

Reform League, hearing nothing to the contrary, interpreted Walpole's tears as the expression of a contrite heart anxious to make up for past injustices, and at once set in motion plans for another monster rally at Hyde Park.

But they had misinterpreted Walpole's display of emotion. When he heard of Beales's new plan, he at once asked the Reform leaders to consult with him again and alerted the troops for the impending assault upon Hyde Park. But the assault, for reasons that I shall examine presently, did not materialize.

Arnold's reaction to the Hyde Park 'riots' must be viewed in perspective. It will not seem excessive or hysterical if we measure it against Carlyle's reaction to the same affair. In 'Shooting Niagara: And After?' Carlyle wrote:

> Perhaps the consummation may be now nearer than is thought. It seems to me sometimes as if everybody had privately now given-up serious notion of resisting it. Beales and his ragamuffins pull down the railings of Her Majesty's Park, when Her Majesty refuses admittance; Home-Secretary Walpole (representing England's Majesty), listens to a Colonel Dickson talking of 'barricades,' 'improvised pikes,' etc.; does *not* order him to be conducted, and if necessary to be kicked, down stairs, with injunction never to return, in case of worse; and when Beales says, 'I will see that the Queen's Peace is kept,' Queen (by her Walpole) answers, 'Will you, then; God bless *you*!' and bursts into tears. Those 'tears' are certainly an epoch in England; nothing seen, or dreamt of, like them in the History of poor England till now.[81]

The Hyde Park episode seemed to Carlyle to prove, what he had long asserted, that democracy was the final disaster, the descent into the bottomless pit—in short, 'shooting Niagara.'

The same episode seemed to Arnold proof that democracy could be successful only if allied with a strong state action. The Hyde Park riot and its aftermath had a strong effect upon Arnold—who had stood on the balcony of his Belgravia home watching the rioters fling stones at the house across the square. A few days after the working-class invasion of the Philistine sanctuary, Arnold wrote to his mother about various aspects of the affair, especially Spencer Walpole's 'absurd behaviour and talking and shilly-shallying and crying.' It was, he wrote, a bad thing in itself that the principle of authority in England had proven to be so weak. Yet, he added, it was the very absence of the democracy which the Reformers desired that prevented the state from exercising its true authority:

> Whereas in France, since the revolution, a man feels that the power which represses him is the *State*, is *himself*, here a man feels that the power which represses him is the Tories, the upper class, the aristocracy, and so on; and with this feeling he can, of course, never without loss of self-respect accept a formal beating, and so the thing goes on smouldering. *If ever there comes a more equal state of society in England, the power of the State for repression will be a thousand times stronger.* (Italics mine.)

The Hyde Park riot rankled in Arnold's mind. At the end of 1867, eighteen months after it had occurred, he wrote to his mother: 'You know I have never wavered in saying that the Hyde Park business . . . was fatal, and that a Government which dared not deal with a mob, of any nation or with any design, simply opened the flood-gates to anarchy.'[82] Throughout *Culture and Anarchy*, which appeared in *The Cornhill Magazine* from July, 1867, through August, 1868, the pulling down of the railings in Hyde Park was presented as one of the most perfect specimens of the anarchy rampant in England. Even as he recognized the justice of the Reformers' claims, Arnold insisted upon keeping the sacred framework of the state intact. For what he ultimately desired was to persuade the common people that a state founded upon political democracy and social equality was a state they could trust. The best self of each man, he argued,

> knows that it is stablishing the *State*, or organ of our collective best self, of our national right reason; and it has the testimony of conscience that it is stablishing the State on behalf of whatever great changes are needed, just as much as on behalf of order; stablishing it to deal just as stringently, when the time comes, with Sir Thomas Bateson's Protestant ascendency, or with the Rev. W. Cattle's sorry education of his children, as it deals with Mr. Bradlaugh's street-processions.[83]

Mill's interpretation of the Hyde Park affair differed almost as much from Arnold's as Arnold's did from Carlyle's. One reason for the difference was that Arnold chose to ignore that part of the Hyde Park episode in which Mill played a crucial role.

Mill stepped into the affair at the point when the government, already making military preparations, and the Reform League, bent on a second attempt to meet in Hyde Park, seemed headed towards a violent collision. The leaders of the Reform League, despite Arnold's picture of them, were moderate men; therefore they invited Mill and other Radical members of Parliament to try to dissuade them from their intended course. Mill, one of the few members of Parliament known to have taken the side of workingmen, later claimed that with the exception of Gladstone and Bright, neither of whom was available, no one but himself then had sufficient influence with the working classes to be capable of restraining them.[84]

Mill used a double-edged argument to persuade the workingmen to hold their meeting in a place other than Hyde Park. He told them that a clash with government troops was justified only if conditions were so desperate that revolution seemed desirable, and if, this being so, they thought they could carry out the revolution successfully. 'To this argument, after considerable discussion,' Mill later recalled, 'they at last yielded: and I was able to inform Mr. Walpole that their intention was given up. I shall never forget the depth of his relief or the warmth of his expressions of gratitude.'[85] As a consolation, Mill agreed to address the mass meeting, originally scheduled for Hyde Park, at the Agricultural Hall in Islington. Speaking with some difficulty to a wild crowd that gave what the *Daily News* called 'probably the most numerous and imposing demonstration of popular feeling that was ever exhibited under a single roof,' Mill said that the demonstration had lost little of its effect by being held indoors. What was of primary importance, he reminded his audience, was that 'the countries where the people are allowed to show their strength are those in which they are not obliged to use it.'[86] Still, the government was wrong to deny the use of the park, and Mill's speech implied his intention to right the wrong.

The promise of the speech was not long in being fulfilled. In May of 1867, the government, having suddenly been made aware that it had no legal right to proscribe meetings in Hyde Park, proposed to acquire that right by legislation. In August, when the bill seemed certain to gain approval, Mill organized a meeting with the leaders of the Reform League, at their request, in the tearoom of the House of Commons. The government accused Mill of holding conspiratorial meetings in the very seat of state, but the furor it raised about this petty incident kept the house from getting to the main business of the bill itself long enough to enable Mill and some of his followers to talk the bill to death.[87] The bill was never renewed, and, largely as the result of Mill's efforts, Hyde Park became, what it has ever since remained, a symbol of English liberty.

The Hyde Park affair illustrates both the agreement which existed between Arnold and Mill about ends and their disagreements over the means by which those ends were to be achieved. Both sympathized with the ultimate aims of the Reform League which precipitated the riot—Arnold more so than Mill because Mill disliked the League's acceptance of the ballot and its objection to female suffrage. Both saw that the democracy for which the Reformers contended would do good only if the right preparations were made for its establishment. But whereas Arnold, confronted with a popular democratic movement, hastened to reaffirm the idea of the state and saw the incursion into Hyde Park as a defeat for the state, Mill dealt with the same movement in such a way as to postpone democracy's triumph until it could be gained legitimately, and brought about instead a victory for the principle of liberty. When the time to institute democracy arrived, Arnold still looked upon the state, and Mill upon liberty, as the only instrument which could make democracy conducive to human perfection. Their argument was to continue after their deaths, and it has not yet been settled.

NOTES

(Books listed in the Bibliography under GENERAL WORKS are referred to from the outset by the names of their authors.)

CHAPTER ONE

1. *Lectures and Essays in Criticism*, p. 289.
2. He refused to involve himself in controversy with thinkers like the Benthamites. 'Why,' he asked in *Theory of Religious Belief* (London, 1843), p. 351, 'should we vex ourselves to find out whether our own deductions are philosophical or no, provided they are religious?' The task of carrying the battle to the enemy was left to men like W. G. Ward, another Oxford convert to Rome, who carried on a friendly correspondence with Mill. See William Irvine, *Apes, Angels, & Victorians* (London, 1955), pp. 251–55.
3. Walt Whitman, *Leaves of Grass and Selected Prose*, ed. by John Kouwenhoven (New York, 1950), p. 460.
4. Bliss Perry, *Walt Whitman* (Boston and New York, 1906), p. 178.
5. F. Stephen, 'Mr. Matthew Arnold and his Countrymen,' *Saturday Review* (December 3, 1864), p. 684.
6. *Mill on Bentham and Coleridge*, p. 40.
7. *Ibid.*, p. 101.
8. *Ibid.*, pp. 101–3.
9. Carlyle, *Works*, XXVIII, 133–35.
10. *Unpublished Letters*, pp. 65–66.
11. Leslie Stephen, *An Agnostic's Apology*, 2nd ed. (London, 1903), pp. 168–82. Neff maintains, p. 54, that 'the lives of Carlyle and Mill are largely representative of the intellectual and spiritual history of the age of transition into our twentieth century world.' Bonnerot declares, p. 134, that 'entre Carlyle et Arnold les points de contact sont si nombreux que seule une étude particulière et détaillée pourrait les relever tous, et pareille étude serait indispensable si l'on se proposait d'examiner les idées d'Arnold.' If we were to count votes, the Carlyle-Mill division would be the correct one. In addition to Neff's work, we have Edward Jenks, *Thomas Carlyle and John Stuart Mill* (Kent, 1888), and Patrick P. Alexander, *Mill and Carlyle: An Examination of J. S. Mill's doctrine of causation in relation to moral freedom. With an occasional discourse on Sauerteig, by Smelfungus* (Edinburgh, 1866).
12. *Discourses in America*, p. 139.
13. Anschutz, p. 5.
14. *Spirit of the Age*, p. vii. On the subject of Mill's representativeness, see

267

also Harold Laski's introduction to the World's Classics edition of the *Autobiography*, pp. xiii–xiv; Humphry House, *The Dickens World*, 2nd ed. (London, 1960), p. 70; and Williams, *Culture and Society*, p. 49.

15. H. V. Routh, *Towards the Twentieth Century* (Cambridge, 1937), p. 171.

16. Trilling, *Arnold*, pp. 193–94. Nevertheless, in the year before Trilling's book appeared, a critic could argue that Arnold's independent line had only isolated him from his contemporaries. 'Prophet of European Unity,' *Times Literary Supplement*, April 16, 1938, pp. 257–58.

17. There is at least a half-truth in Crane Brinton's assertion that 'you cannot get a more representative definition of the areas a good Victorian liberal thought should be sacred to the individual than John Mill's essay *On Liberty*.' *Ideas and Men* (London, 1951), p. 432.

18. *Autobiography*, p. 88.

19. Newman, *Apologia Pro Vita Sua*, p. 237.

20. *Culture and Anarchy*, p. 41.

21. *Irish Essays*, pp. 141–42.

22. *Culture and Anarchy*, p. 99.

23. *Lectures and Essays*, p. 288.

24. *Culture and Anarchy*, p. 106.

25. *Autobiography*, p. 172.

26. *Ibid.*, p. 90.

27. *Ibid.*, p. 100.

28. *Ibid.*, p. 1.

29. *Dissertations and Discussions*, I, iv.

30. *Letters of Arnold*, I, 59; II, 10. In February, 1876, Arnold wrote to his sister that 'George Eliot says . . . that of all modern poetry mine is that which keeps constantly growing upon her,' and in June: 'I am going to dine with the Bishop of Derry on the 3rd of July. I could not refuse a man who told me that my poems were the centre of his mental life, and that he had read many of them hundreds of times.' *Letters of Arnold*, II, 146, 151.

31. *System of Logic*, p. 596.

32. *Dissertations and Discussions*, III, 196.

33. *Essays in Criticism: Second Series*, p. 308.

34. *Autobiography*, pp. 38, 59.

35. M. Woods, 'Matthew Arnold,' *Essays and Studies by Members of the English Association*, XV (1929), 10.

36. *Uncollected Essays*, p. 41.

37. *Culture and Anarchy*, pp. 44–45.

38. Mueller, pp. 230–31.

39. 'Inaugural Address,' in Cavenagh, pp. 182–83.

40. *Autobiography*, p. 91.

41. Morley, *Recollections*, I, 56.

42. *Poetical Works*, p. 212, ll. 35–37; pp. 302–3, ll. 114–16.

43. *Letters of Arnold*, I, 225–26, 282, 233–34. Stephen's criticism is on p. 683 of 'Mr. Matthew Arnold and his Countrymen,' *Saturday Review*, December 3, 1864.

44. Morley, *Critical Miscellanies*, III, 42.

45. *Autobiography*, pp. 14–15.

46. *Culture and Anarchy*, p. 211.

47. *Lectures and Essays*, p. 275. See J. Dover Wilson's introduction to *Culture and Anarchy*, p. xxxi.

48. *Culture and Anarchy*, p. 208.

49. *Letters of Arnold*, I, 249, 456.

50. Quoted in Packe, p. 447.

51. W. D. Christie, 'Mr. John Stuart Mill for Westminster,' *Macmillan's Magazine*, XII (May–October, 1865), 96.

52. *Autobiography*, p. 199.

53. *Letters of Arnold*, II, 313, 412. See the essay 'Copyright' in *Irish Essays*.

54. *Autobiography*, p. 195. The cheap copies sold so well that his publishers decided to allow Mill half the profits of all volumes over a certain number sold.

55. Holyoake, p. 5.

56. Morley, 'Matthew Arnold,' *Nineteenth Century*, XXXVIII (July–December, 1895), 1044.

57. Morley, *Critical Miscellanies*, III, 40–41.

58. Bain, *J. S. Mill*, p. 184.

59. *Dissertations and Discussions*, III, 338–39.

60. *Lectures and Essays*, p. 230.

61. *Ibid.*, p. 381.

62. *Letters to Clough*, p. 51.

63. *Ibid.*, pp. 110, 116.

64. *Note-Books*, p. 198. The quotation is from the *Autobiography*.

65. Morley, *Critical Miscellanies*, III, 92.

66. T. Woods, *Poetry and Philosophy*, p. 66.

67. Morley, *Critical Miscellanies*, IV, 159–60.

68. B. Russell, 'John Stuart Mill,' *Proceedings of the British Academy*, XLI (1955), 46.

69. *Spirit of the Age*, p. vii.

70. G. K. Chesterton, *The Victorian Age in Literature* (London, 1955), p. 47.

71. *A French Eton*, pp. 386, 389. Huxley himself was forward in crediting Arnold with 'true sympathy with scientific thought.' *Science and Education*, p. 142.

72. 'Inaugural Address,' in Cavenagh, pp. 141–42, 138.

73. 'Some Early Impressions,' *The National Review*, XLII (October, 1903), 217. See Anschutz, p. 1.

74. R. A. Scott-James, *The Making of Literature* (New York, n.d.), p. 262.

75. Hallam Tennyson, *Alfred Lord Tennyson: A Memoir* (2 vols., London, 1897), II, 225.

76. Hunt, 'Matthew Arnold and his Critics,' *Sewanee Review*, XLIV (October, 1936), 449–56.

77. F. L. Lucas, 'Matthew Arnold,' in *Victorian Literature: Modern Essays in Criticism*, ed. by Austin Wright, p. 55.

78. Fox, p. 124.

79. Graham Wallas, *Francis Place* (London, 1898), p. 91.

80. Leslie Stephen, *The Life of Sir James Fitzjames Stephen* (London, 1895), p. 308.

81. Ruskin, *Works*, XVII, 79.

82. Chesterton, *The Victorian Age in Literature*, pp. 24–25.

83. For an exception with regard to Mill, see the argument of W. J. Ong, 'Mill's Pariah Poet,' *Philological Quarterly*, XXIX (July, 1950), that the weaknesses of Mill's poetic theory are due to his inability to completely disavow his Utilitarian and mechanistic past associations. For an example of extreme harshness on the part of a social scientist toward Arnold, see Ernest Barker, *Political Thought in England: 1848 to 1914*, 2nd ed. (London, 1928), pp. 198–99.

84. Karl Marx, *Capital*, trans. by S. Moore and E. Aveling (3 vols., Chicago, 1906–09), I, 20.

85. 'John Stuart Mill,' *Proceedings of the British Academy*, XLI (1955), 43.

86. Anschutz, p. 6.

87. Nesbitt, pp. 170–71.

88. Trilling, *Arnold*, pp. 259–65; 'Wordsworth and the Rabbis,' in *The Opposing Self*, p. 136.

89. Houghton, pp. 284, 287–91.

90. Bonnerot, p. 254. Bonnerot also sees, pp. 121–22, how Mill's description of Vigny, in *Dissertations and Discussions*, I, 290–96, as the prototype of the conservative poet born into a progressive age fits Arnold.

91. Culler, p. xvii.

92. Introduction to *Bentham and Coleridge*, pp. 5–6, 12–15, 36–37.

93. Meyer H. Abrams, *The Mirror and the Lamp* (New York, 1953), p. 334. Raymond Williams has written in *Culture and Society*, pp. 181–82, that 'in attaching himself to Fabianism, Shaw was . . . telling Carlyle and Ruskin to go to school with Bentham, telling Arnold to get together with Mill.'

94. *Letters of Mill*, II, 93.

95. *Letters to Clough*, p. 75. It is an ironic comment upon Arnold's remark that John Butler Yeats, in planning a figure of Job, should have hit upon Mill's face as the perfect model for it. Richard Ellmann, *Yeats, the Man and the Masks* (New York, 1948), p. 12.

96. *A French Eton*, p. 122. See *God and the Bible*, p. 146.

97. *Lectures and Essays*, pp. 133–57.

98. *St. Paul*, pp. xxxvii–xxxviii.

99. *Culture and Anarchy*, p. 68.

100. *A French Eton*, p. 100.

101. *Mixed Essays*, p. 102. Few questions bring out the similarities in temperament between Arnold and Mill as well as the Irish question. Both believed that England ought to maintain her connection with Ireland, but both warned England that she must make concessions and institute reforms in Ireland out of a sense of justice and therefore immediately rather than at the last possible moment, out of a fear of military insurrection. *England and Ireland*, pp. 27–37; *Irish Essays*, p. 18. Their agreement about a solution to the Irish land problem is even more striking than their agreement about the religious problem. Both recommended for application to Ireland the Prussian land reforms worked out by Stein and Hardenberg, which required large landed properties to be broken up and distributed as peasant properties; Mill in *England and Ireland*, pp. 15–16; Arnold in *Friendship's Garland*, pp. 39–40.

102. *A French Eton*, pp. 281, 369n.
103. *Letters of Arnold*, I, 111.
104. *Lectures and Essays*, p. 136.
105. *Uncollected Essays*, p. 91.

CHAPTER TWO

1. For Mill's low opinion of Hegel, see *Dissertations and Discussions*, III, 281.
2. 'Inaugural Address,' in Cavenagh, p. 177. Mill's speculations on the possibility of constructing a science of history and society form one of the vital strands of his thought. Keys to his view of the subject may be found in *Dissertations and Discussions*, II, 128–29; *System of Logic*, pp. 553–54, 564; *Bentham and Coleridge*, pp. 54, 129, 131; and *Auguste Comte and Positivism*, pp. 39, 52, 106.
3. *Literature and Dogma*, p. 352.
4. *Lectures and Essays*, p. 268.
5. *Spirit of the Age*, p. 15.
6. *Autobiography*, pp. 115–16.
7. *Ibid.*, p. 122.
8. In March, 1831, Mill wrote that 'although I am not a St Simonist nor at all likely to become one, *je tiens bureau de St Simonisme chez moi.*' *Earlier Letters*, I, 71.
9. *Spirit of the Age*, p. 15.
10. *Ibid.*, pp. 12, 20–21.
11. *Ibid.*, p. 36. Along with Athens and Rome, Mill named the United States as one of the superior examples of the natural states of society. Years later, Arnold said that 'politically and socially the United States are a community living in a natural condition.' *Uncollected Essays*, p. 31.
12. *Spirit of the Age*, pp. 52, 58.
13. *Autobiography*, pp. 116–17.
14. Bonnerot, p. 123.
15. *The George Eliot Letters*, ed. by Gordon S. Haight (7 vols., London, 1954), I, 253.
16. *Lectures and Essays*, p. 266.
17. *Ibid.*, pp. 266–67.
18. *Letters of Arnold*, II, 192.
19. *Lectures and Essays*, p. 269.
20. *Mixed Essays*, pp. vi–viii.
21. *Irish Essays*, pp. 161–62.
22. *Democratic Education*, p. 274.
23. *Spirit of the Age*, p. 6.
24. *Lectures and Essays*, pp. 109–10.
25. *Ibid.*, pp. 268–69.
26. Voltaire, *Lettres Philosophiques ou Lettres Anglaises* (Paris, 1956), pp. 23, 127.
27. *Bentham and Coleridge*, p. 104.

28. T. L. Peacock, 'An Essay on Fashionable Literature,' *Notes and Queries*, Series XI, II, 62.

29. *Autobiography*, pp. 149–50.

30. 'Periodical Literature: *Edinburgh Review*,' *Westminster Review*, I (April, 1824), 516.

31. *Earlier Letters*, I, 37–38. Morley, *Recollections*, I, 57, said Mill had an 'aversion to sect and the spirit of sect.'

32. *Early Essays*, p. 241.

33. *Autobiography*, p. 144.

34. Bain, *J. S. Mill*, p. 57.

35. *Earlier Letters*, II, 370–71.

36. *Lectures and Essays*, pp. 270–71, 267–68. Burke is a strange choice for the role of foil to English sectarians. As Halévy points out, 'according to Burke [England], like the Roman republic of old, owed its greatness to the party spirit.' Burke, he adds, was 'a sociologist, indifferent to questions of truth and principle,' who believed not in discovering prejudices and untying the bonds of selfish interest which attached men to parties but in confirming the former and securing the latter. Halévy, pp. 145–46.

37. *Letters of Arnold*, I, 157, 183–84.

38. Henry Adams, *The Education of Henry Adams* (Boston and New York, 1918), p. 126.

39. *Earlier Letters*, I, 46.

40. *Friendship's Garland*, p. 147.

41. *Earlier Letters*, I, 29. See also I, 153–54, 204–8.

42. *Bentham and Coleridge*, pp. 103–4. The implicit equation which Mill made between the dialectics of controversy and the dialectics of history is apparent in his remarks about 'the fight between the nineteenth century and the eighteenth' as being similar to 'the battle about the shield, one side of which was white and the other black.' *Autobiography*, p. 114.

43. Young, p. 186.

44. *Culture and Anarchy*, pp. 138–39.

45. *Letters of Arnold*, II, 13, 37.

46. *Culture and Anarchy*, pp. 130–35.

47. *Literature and Dogma*, p. 57.

48. *Culture and Anarchy*, pp. 54–55, 141–43.

49. *Ibid.*, p. 158.

50. *Ibid.*, p. 204.

51. *Utilitarianism*, pp. 43–44.

52. *Three Essays on Religion*, p. 99.

53. *On Liberty*, pp. 108–11. Arnold disagreed with this passage, but he was irked by the idea of a 'positive' morality and not by the charge of Christian incompleteness, which he accepted. *Lectures and Essays*, p. 133.

54. *On Liberty*, p. 120.

55. *Bentham and Coleridge*, pp. 130–31, 140, 108.

56. *Subjection of Women*, p. 221.

57. *Bentham and Coleridge*, pp. 40, 99, 155.

58. *Autobiography*, p. 153.

59. William Hazlitt, *The Spirit of the Age* (London, 1960), p. 6.

60. *Bentham and Coleridge*, p. 61. Charles W. Everett, *The Education of Jeremy Bentham* (New York, 1931), p. 90, has tried to give the lie to Mill's picture of the narrow peculiarity of Bentham's nature. He relates the agonies of Bentham's choice between marriage to Mary Dunkly and the great work of reforming the law, and concludes that 'the fact that he chose the rational course rather than the romantic one should not lead us into the romantic idea that his choice meant weak feelings and insensitiveness.'

61. *Bentham and Coleridge*, pp. 59–61.

62. *Ibid.*, pp. 60–61.

63. *Culture and Anarchy*, pp. 67–68.

64. *Bentham and Coleridge*, pp. 58–59, 47, 64–65, 74–75.

65. *Ibid.*, p. 65.

66. *On Liberty*, pp. 105–6. See *Bentham and Coleridge*, pp. 107–9.

67. *Ibid.*, p. 58.

68. *Comte*, pp. 128–29.

69. *Ibid.*, pp. 119–20, 170–71.

70. *Culture and Anarchy*, pp. 130, 146–47.

71. *Lectures and Essays*, pp. 261, 263.

72. *Letters to Clough*, pp. 142–43.

73. Bonnerot, p. 204.

74. See Houghton, pp. 14–15.

75. *Culture and Anarchy*, p. 149. See also p. 37.

76. *On Liberty*, p. 107. See also *System of Logic*, p. 572.

77. *Comte*, p. 4.

78. *Dissertations and Discussions*, I, iv–v. For the discussion of endowments, see *Dissertations and Discussions*, I, 1–41, and IV, 1–24.

79. *Discourses in America*, pp. 186–89.

80. *Democratic Education*, p. 29.

81. *Dissertations and Discussions*, I, 234.

82. Tocqueville, I, 7.

83. *Comte*, pp. 118–19.

84. *Dissertations and Discussions*, II, 9.

85. *Mixed Essays*, pp. vii–viii.

86. *Irish Essays*, pp. 111–12.

87. *Democratic Education*, p. 29.

88. *Letters to Clough*, pp. 86, 95. For further examples of Arnold's use of the notion of the *Zeitgeist*, see 'Bishop Butler and the Zeitgeist,' in *St. Paul*, pp. 288, 333; and *Culture and Anarchy*, pp. 60–61.

89. *Lectures and Essays*, pp. 274, 276.

90. *Comte*, p. 115. Mill said in *On Liberty*, p. 73, that until men are capable of being improved by freedom, 'there is nothing for them but implicit obedience to an Akbar or a Charlemagne, if they are so fortunate as to find one.' See *Considerations on Representative Government*, p. 197.

91. *Ibid.*, p. 207. See Mueller, p. 229.

92. Fox, p. 196.

93. *J. S. Mill and Harriet Taylor*, p. 216.

94. *Spirit of the Age*, p. 48.

95. *Bentham and Coleridge*, pp. 99–100, 126–29.

96. *Culture and Anarchy*, pp. 29, 142–43.

97. Arnold Toynbee, *The Industrial Revolution* (Boston, 1956), p. 31.

98. *Subjection of Women*, p. 225.

99. *Irish Essays*, p. 141.

100. *On Liberty*, p. 117.

101. *Lectures and Essays*, p. 348.

102. *Three Essays on Religion*, pp. 56, 54.

103. *Poetical Works*, p. 5.

CHAPTER THREE

1. Strachey, p. 191.

2. Arnold and Mill were not involved with the London University at the same time. James Mill was on the Council of the London University in 1828 when it was still equivalent to University College. What is today the University of London was chartered in 1836, under a chancellor and a Senate of 36 fellows. Dr. Arnold was a member of the first Senate. See Augustus D. Waller, *A Short Account of the Origins of the University of London* (London, n.d.).

3. 'The great end of liberal principles is indeed the "greatest happiness of the greatest number," if we understand that the happiness of man consists more in his intellectual well-doing than in his physical; and yet more in his moral and religious excellence than in his intellectual.' Thomas Arnold, *Miscellaneous Works*, p. 364.

4. Wilfrid Ward, *W. G. Ward and the Oxford Movement* (London, 1889), pp. 109–10. 'Around him [Bentham] were many practical reformers, besides such figures as James and John Stuart Mill. With their hatred of tradition, they seemed to provide a rational basis for revolution in a time of unrest, and their habit of thinking everything out afresh and taking nothing for granted, was very dear to the heart of Arnold.' Bamford, p. 191. Ironically, W. G. Ward was accused by the *Quarterly Review* of having drawn more of *his* principles from the school of Mill than from the Anglican theologians. *Earlier Letters*, II, 665.

5. Bain, *James Mill*, p. 11n.

6. *Ibid.*, p. 21.

7. *Autobiography*, p. 2.

8. Bain, *James Mill*, pp. 50, 52.

9. Mill did not plunge to the radical depths at once, but descended gradually from the Tory *Anti-Jacobin Review* to the Whig *Edinburgh* (for which he wrote from 1808 until 1813) and finally to the *Westminster*.

10. *Bentham and Coleridge*, pp. 63, 134. See Arnold's remarks on Gray in *Essays in Criticism: Second Series*, pp. 91–93.

11. Halévy, pp. 75–76.

12. Bain, *James Mill*, p. 138.

13. L. Stephen, *English Utilitarians*, II, 6–7.

14. Halévy, p. 307. 'He [J. S. Mill] spoke with such admiration of his father's character, saying he never cared about getting the credit of doing anything, as long as the thing itself was done, that he inspired everyone but

himself kept in the background & Mrs. G[rote] said no one would ever know what a moving power he had been at the time of the Reform Bill.' *The Amberley Papers*, ed. by Bertrand and Patricia Russell (2 vols., London, 1937), I, 370. It was probably James Mill's capacity for discipleship as much as his physical impressiveness that led Carlyle to speak fondly of him even after his friendship with John Mill had ended.

15. Halévy, p. 309.

16. L. Stephen, *English Utilitarians*, II, 36.

17. W. H. Burston, 'James Mill on the Aims of Education,' *Cambridge Journal*, VI (October, 1952–September, 1953), 101.

18. *Autobiography*, pp. 33–34. J. S. Mill overlooked the same contradiction in himself.

19. Bain, *James Mill*, p. 465.

20. Courtney, p. 16.

21. Bain, *James Mill*, pp. 74, 181–82, 211.

22. *Ibid.*, pp. 422–23.

23. Morley, *Critical Miscellanies*, III, 56.

24. L. Stephen, *English Utilitarians*, II, 34.

25. Bain, *James Mill*, p. 422.

26. Stanley, p. 3.

27. *Ibid.*, pp. 21, 14–15.

28. Arnold Whitridge, *Dr. Arnold of Rugby* (London, 1928), p. 15. Stanley, p. 26, refers to the 'prosaic and matter of fact element' of Arnold's life at Oxford.

29. Stanley, pp. 18–20.

30. Strachey, pp. 178–79.

31. *Miscellaneous Works*, American Edition (New York and Philadelphia, 1845), p. 266. (All other references to this work cite the English edition.)

32. E. L. Woodward, *The Age of Reform: 1815–1870* (Oxford, 1958), p. 488.

33. Stanley, p. 484. Arnold feared that 'Newmanism . . . will grow and grow, till it provokes a reaction of infidelity, and then infidelity will grow and grow, till up starts Newmanism again in such form as it may wear in the twentieth or twenty-first century.'

34. *Ibid.*, p. 31.

35. Thomas Hughes, *Tom Brown's Schooldays* (London, 1952), p. 260.

36. Young, p. 70.

37. Stanley, pp. 77, 272.

38. Tocqueville, I, 321–22, 325.

39. For evidence of Mill's Manicheanism, see 'Southey's *Book of the Church*,' *Westminster Review*, III (January, 1825), 176. J. S. Mill wrote, *Autobiography*, p. 28, of his father's religious beliefs: 'The Sabaean, or Manichean theory of a Good and Evil Principle, struggling against each other for the government of the universe, he would not have equally [with the orthodox Christian explanation] condemned; and I have heard him express surprise, that no one revived it in our time.'

40. Stanley, pp. 42, 64.

41. *Lectures on Modern History*, pp. 36, 39.

42. G. P. Gooch, *History and Historians of the Nineteenth Century*, 2nd ed.

(London, 1961), p. 299, points out that emulation of his master, Niebuhr, combined with his abhorrence of Gibbon to move Arnold to write the history of Rome.

43. Stanley, pp. 267–68.

44. *Miscellaneous Works*, p. 349. In his *Lectures on Modern History*, p. 33, Arnold said: 'We derive scarcely one drop of our blood from Roman fathers; we are in our race strangers to Greece, and strangers to Israel. But morally how much do we derive from all three: in this respect their life is in a manner continued in ours; their influences, to say the least, have not perished.'

45. Stanley, pp. 119–20.

46. *Ibid.*, pp. 426, 181–82. On the subject of the Syracusan expedition, see J. S. Mill in *J. S. Mill and Harriet Taylor*, p. 229, and Matthew Arnold in *Classical Tradition*, p. 30.

47. *Dissertations and Discussions*, II, 130.

48. *History of British India*, I, xxiii.

49. *Auguste Comte and Positivism*, pp. 110–11.

50. Bain, *James Mill*, pp. 369, 326–27.

51. William Hazlitt, *Complete Works*, ed. by P. P. Howe (21 vols., London and Toronto, 1930–34), XII, 50.

52. *Ibid.*

53. L. Stephen, *English Utilitarians*, II, 23–24.

54. Gooch, p. 287.

55. Quoted from manuscript letter of Stanley in Lowry's edition of *Letters to Clough*, p. 166.

56. Young, p. 69.

57. Stanley, pp. 259, 307.

58. *Ibid.*, pp. 173, 222, 249.

59. *Earlier Letters*, I, 92.

60. Stanley, p. 306.

61. *Ibid.*, pp. 431, 233. For some indication of the difference in religious taste between father and son, see Matthew's remarks on Milton's tracts in *Mixed Essays*, pp. 233–34. Matthew, unlike his father, made a terrible fuss about uniformity in such matters as burial services, and was inclined to blame those who deviated from uniformity all the more where no principle was involved.

62. Stanley, p. 297.

63. *Ibid.*, p. 333.

64. See Bain, *James Mill*, pp. 353–54; and Stanley, pp. 385, 394–95, and *passim*.

65. 'Ecclesiastical Establishments,' *Westminster Review*, V (April, 1826), 505.

66. Bain, *James Mill*, pp. 387–88. On the subject of Utilitarianism and especially Bentham not being liberal, see Halévy, p. 144.

67. *Autobiography*, pp. 74–75.

68. *Essays*, p. 5.

69. *Ibid.*, pp. 9, 16–17.

70. Bain, *James Mill*, p. 222. The simplicity of Mill's notion of govern-

ment contrasts with that of his son. James Mill, as a follower of Bentham, showed only scorn for the idea of balanced government, believing that built-in antagonism between equally powerful groups must either paralyze the government or end with the members of one group swallowing those of the other. J. S. Mill was committing apostasy when he espoused the idea of balance and antagonisms in government, for it was the idea of Burke, not Bentham.

71. *Miscellaneous Works*, pp. 171, 184–85.

72. Bain, *James Mill*, pp. 220–21, 363–64.

73. *Miscellaneous Works*, p. 453.

74. Stanley, pp. 527–28. Arnold held, p. 528, that 'the hopes entertained by many of the effects to be wrought by new churches and schools, while the social evils of their [the common people's] condition are left uncorrected, appear to me to be utterly wild.' What Arnold thought the downright evil of the Newmanite or 'antichrist' movement was only compounded in his eyes by the indifference of the Oxford Movement to the conditions of the laboring classes. Many of the worst slums in the city of Oxford were located on property belonging to colleges dominated by the Tractarians. Woodward, p. 502.

75. Stanley, p. 66.

76. James Mill's emphasis on liberty, which is not a necessary corollary of the Utilitarian principles, should not be overlooked. Bain pointed out that among the great variety of subjects dealt with in Mill's commonplace book, 'Liberty of the Press' is the one returned to most frequently. *James Mill*, p. 464. As for Dr. Arnold, on the other hand, it is hard to escape the conviction that he will always postpone the interests of liberty to considerations of state. Did not Matthew Arnold proudly, if only temporarily, adopt his father's policy for dealing with mobs in 'the old Roman way' by forceful suppression and punishment? *Culture and Anarchy*, p. 203.

Another instructive comparison of Arnold's and Mill's views on a particular political question may be made with respect to Ireland. Mill said England, after all the outrages she had committed against Ireland, could do nothing better than to sever the connection with her neighbor. Bain, *James Mill*, p. 312. Arnold proposed sending missionaries. Stanley, p. 64.

77. *Ibid.*, pp. 501, 606.

78. Bain, *James Mill*, p. 302n.

79. Stanley, pp. 608–9.

80. H. V. Routh, *Towards the Twentieth Century* (Cambridge, 1937), p. 234.

81. Stanley, pp. 86–87.

82. Thomas Arnold the Younger, *Passages in a Wandering Life* (London, 1900), p. vi.

83. Stanley, p. 37.

84. Hughes, *Tom Brown's Schooldays*, p. 105.

85. 'Inaugural Address,' in Cavenagh, p. 140.

86. Stanley, p. 406.

87. Young, p. 71.

88. *The Poems of Arthur Hugh Clough*, ed. by H. F. Lowry, A. L. P. Norrington, F. L. Mulhauser (Oxford, 1951), p. 295.

89. *Miscellaneous Works*, p. 377.
90. Stanley, pp. 34, 103.
91. Hughes, *Tom Brown's Schooldays*, pp. 63, 122, 249, 151.
92. *Ibid.*, pp. 182, 271.
93. *Letters and Verses of Arthur Penrhyn Stanley*, ed. by R. E. Prothero (New York, 1895), p. 74.
94. *Poems of Clough*, p. 295.
95. *Miscellaneous Works*, p. 368.
96. Stanley, p. 75.
97. Hughes, *Tom Brown's Schooldays*, p. xii.
98. *Ibid.*, p. 92.
99. Halévy, p. 159.
100. Stanley, p. 175. See Arnold's remarks, p. 606, on Falkland as a victim of sect. They foreshadow his son's sympathy for the Civil War hero.
101. 'Education,' in Cavenagh, pp. 1, 60.
102. *Ibid.*, pp. 8, 11.
103. *Autobiography*, p. 75.
104. 'Education,' in Cavenagh, pp. 11–12, 17, 20.
105. *Ibid.*, pp. 27–29, 48–50.
106. *Ibid.*, p. 52.
107. *Ibid.*, p. 71.
108. *Ibid.*, p. 72.
109. Quoted in Mueller, p. 9, from an unpublished letter in the British Museum.
110. L. Stephen, *English Utilitarians*, II, 17–23.
111. 'Southey's *Book of the Church*,' *Westminster Review*, III (January, 1825), 192.
112. *Autobiography*, p. 33.
113. 'Education,' in Cavenagh, p. 22.
114. *Autobiography*, p. 47.
115. David Masson, *Memories of London in the Forties* (London, 1908), p. 35.
116. Bain, *James Mill*, pp. 189–90.
117. *Ibid.*, pp. 200, 205.
118. *Letters of Mill*, I, xv–xvi.
119. *Earlier Letters*, I, 128.
120. *Autobiography*, p. 126.
121. Bain, *James Mill*, p. 334.
122. *Autobiography*, pp. 6, 21.
123. Fox, p. 84.
124. *Earlier Letters*, II, 457.
125. 'Education,' in Cavenagh, p. 24.

CHAPTER FOUR

1. *Autobiography*, p. 94.
2. *Ibid.*, p. 95.

3. *Ibid.*, p. 96.

4. *Ibid.*, pp. 96, 97.

5. *Ibid.*, p. 98.

6. *Ibid.*, p. 99.

7. *Ibid.*, pp. 99–100.

8. *Earlier Letters*, I, 221.

9. L. Stephen, *English Utilitarians*, II, 37–38.

10. *Bentham and Coleridge*, pp. 62–63. Yet Everett maintains that 'it was in the feverish intensity of analysis that Bentham managed to escape from the world of feeling. His emotions were sensitive to a degree only to be accounted for by his illnesses in childhood and from . . . sharp feeling of the world, the quivering response of his senses to the sounds, sights, odors thrown at them in bewildering rapidity and complexity, his intuitive grasp of the pains, sorrows, hopes, loves, and fears of those about him,—from all this complexity and threatened pain of sympathy, he took refuge in intellectual analysis.' *The Education of Jeremy Bentham* (New York, 1931), p. 86.

11.   For not to think of what I needs must feel,

        But to be still and patient, all I can;

        And haply by abstruse research to steal

        From my own nature all the natural man—

        This was my sole resource, my only plan:

        Till that which suits a part infects the whole,

        And now is almost grown the habit of my soul.

                      'Dejection: An Ode,' ll. 87–93.

12. *Shakespeare Criticism: A Selection*, ed. by D. Nichol Smith (London, 1923), p. 289.

13. *J. S. Mill and Harriet Taylor*, p. 43. After reading Mill's criticism, Browning forsook the Shelleyan mode and turned to the dramatic monologue. See L. F. Haines, 'Mill and "Pauline": The "Review" that "Retarded" Browning's Fame,' *Modern Language Notes*, LIX (June, 1944), 410–412.

14. *Earlier Letters*, I, 149. See also I, 154.

15. *Utilitarianism*, pp. 7–9.

16. *Dissertations and Discussions*, I, 283.

17. 'Inaugural Address,' in Cavenagh, p. 153.

18. *Utilitarianism*, pp. 21–22. Tocqueville, I, 11, 225, gave powerful if reluctant support to Mill's seemingly presumptuous view of Utilitarianism as the creed of a new organic age.

19. *The Education of Henry Adams* (Boston and New York, 1918), p. 192.

20. Morley, *Critical Miscellanies*, III, 56–57.

21. Stanley, p. 424.

22. Lowry, Introduction to *Letters to Clough*, p. 7.

23. *Goldwin Smith's Correspondence*, ed. by Arnold Haultain (London, 1913), p. 269.

24. Wilfrid Ward, *W. G. Ward and the Oxford Movement* (London, 1889), p. 110.

25. 'Recent English Poetry,' *North American Review*, LXXVII (July, 1853), 20, 22.

26. Despite Arnold's later professions of indebtedness to Newman, he went on only two or three occasions to hear Newman preach at Oxford. Then again, his brother Tom went but once and was later converted to Roman Catholicism. F. L. Wickelgren, 'Matthew Arnold's Literary Relations with France,' *Modern Language Review*, XXXIII (April, 1938), 209.

27. E. M. Sellar, *Recollections and Impressions* (Edinburgh and London, 1907), pp. 151–52.

28. *Arnold*, pp. 18, 21–22.

29. *Letters to Clough*, p. 111.

30. *Poetical Works*, p. 4, ll. 3–4.

31. *Unpublished Letters*, p. 18.

32. *Letters to Clough*, pp. 136, 126. Bracketed commas are Lowry's.

33. *Poetical Works*, p. 417, ll. 159–61.

34. *Ibid.*, p. 425, ll. 382–86.

35. *Ibid.*, p. 426, ll. 422–26.

36. *Ibid.*, p. 429, ll. 5–10, 15.

37. *Ibid.*, p. 431, ll. 90–91.

38. *Ibid.*, p. 436, ll. 248–49.

39. *Ibid.*, p. 438, ll. 327–30.

40. *Ibid.*, p. 439, ll. 351–54.

41. Bonnerot, pp. 137, 138, 155. See also p. 177.

42. *Classical Tradition*, pp. 1–3. Arnold said, p. 32, that Lucretius was an inadequate poetical interpreter of his age because he was afflicted by feelings of depression and *ennui*, feelings, Arnold added, 'stamped on how many of the representative works of modern times!'

43. *Letters to Clough*, pp. 20, 128. See also p. 125.

44. *Arnold*, p. 22.

45. *Chateaubriand et son Groupe Littéraire sous l'Empire*, 2nd ed. (2 vols., Paris, 1861), I, 356.

46. Bain, *J. S. Mill*, p. 69n. According to Morley, Mill used to say that 'the Oxford men had at least brought argument, learning, and even philosophy of a sort, to break up the narrow and frigid conventions of reigning system in church and college, in pulpits and professorial chairs.' *The Life of William Ewart Gladstone* (3 vols., New York and London, 1903), I, 163–64. See also *Earlier Letters*, II, 509; and two letters by Mill in the *Morning Chronicle*, January 1 and 13, 1842.

47. J. A. Symonds, 'Arthur Hugh Clough,' *Fortnightly Review*, X (1868), 602.

48. *Letters to Clough*, pp. 56, 84.

49. *Ibid.*, p. 142.

50. *Letters of Arnold*, I, 16–17.

51. *Letters to Clough*, p. 129.

52. *Ibid.*, p. 130. In a subsequent letter, p. 146, Arnold wrote: 'You certainly do not seem to me sufficiently to desire and earnestly strive towards—assured knowledge—activity—happiness. You are too content to *fluctuate*—to be ever learning, never coming to the knowledge of the truth. This is why, with you, I feel it necessary to stiffen myself—and hold fast my rudder.' For a possible gloss on Arnold's use of the word *assiette*, see Michel de Montaigne, *Essais*, ed. by A. Thibaudet (Paris, 1950), p. 641.

53. *Poetical Works*, p. 239, l. 2.
54. *Ibid.*, p. 240, ll. 17–20.
55. *Ibid.*, ll. 31–32.
56. Arnold copied the following quotation from Mill's *Examination of Sir William Hamilton's Philosophy* into his *Note-Books*, p. 197: 'analytic psychology —that most important branch of speculation, on which all the moral and political sciences ultimately rest.'
57. Halévy, p. 195.
58. *Areopagitica* (Cambridge, 1940), p. 43.
59. 'Formation of Opinions,' *Westminster Review*, VI (July, 1826), 13–14, 20.
60. T. H. Huxley, *Method and Results* (New York, 1898), pp. 40–41.
61. *On Liberty*, pp. 79, 82.
62. *Ibid.*, p. 83.
63. *Ibid.*, p. 97.
64. Fox, p. 347.
65. Harriet Martineau, *Autobiography* (3 vols., London, 1877), II, 367.
66. *Auguste Comte and Positivism*, p. 197.
67. *Culture and Anarchy*, p. 61.
68. *Comte*, pp. 112–13.
69. *Culture and Anarchy*, pp. 21, 30.
70. Fox, p. 225.
71. *Autobiography*, p. 177.
72. *On Liberty*, p. 111.
73. *Three Essays on Religion*, p. 117.
74. *Dissertations and Discussions*, I, 294–96. See Bonnerot, pp. 121–22.
75. *Poetical Works*, p. 301, ll. 67–72.
76. *Autobiography*, p. 99.
77. J. H. Buckley, *The Victorian Temper* (Cambridge, Mass., 1951), p. 11.
78. W. H. Mallock, *Is Life Worth Living?* (New York, 1879), pp. 25–26.
79. *Works*, I, 131–33.
80. *Ibid.*, I, 152–53.
81. *Ibid.*, I, 153, 157.
82. *Ibid.*, XXVIII, 5.
83. *Ibid.*, XXVIII, 76, 7, 8, 13. Of those Sophists who drove Empedocles to distraction, Carlyle wrote: '. . . When Virtue, properly so called, has ceased to be practised, and become extinct, and a mere remembrance, we have the era of Sophists descanting of its existence, proving it, denying it, mechanically "accounting" for it; as dissectors and demonstrators cannot operate till once the body be dead.' *Works*, XXVIII, 10. Mill, on the other hand, wrote a long apology for the Sophists in *Dissertations and Discussions*, III, 293–318.
84. *Works*, XXVIII, 26–27.
85. *Ibid.*, XXVIII, 104–5.
86. *Ibid.*, X, 117.
87. Mill compared the throes of his spiritual depression to that mood in which the Methodist is smitten with the conviction of sin. *Autobiography*, p. 94.

88. *Works*, X, 159. Ruskin, though a disciple of Carlyle, parted with his master on the question of thoughtful workmen. He said it is an easy matter to train a workman to thoughtless efficiency; to get him 'to strike a curved line, and to carve it; and to copy and carve any number of given lines or forms, with admirable speed and perfect precision. . . .' But, he added, 'if you ask him to think about any of those forms, to consider if he cannot find any better in his own head, he stops; his execution becomes hesitating; he thinks, and ten to one he thinks wrong; ten to one he makes a mistake in the first touch he gives to his work as a thinking being. But you have made a man of him for all that. He was only a machine before, an animated tool.' Ruskin, *Works*, X, 191–92.

89. *Letters to Clough*, p. 47. Emerson must have agreed, for he replied: 'Clough, I consecrate you Bishop of all England.'

90. *Letters of Mill*, II, 220–21.

91. *Discourses in America*, p. 142.

92. *Letters of Arnold*, II, 222. On the title page of *Past and Present* stands Goethe's motto: 'Ernst ist das Leben.' In a letter of 1858, Arnold called Carlyle 'part man of genius, part fanatic—and part tom-fool.' Quoted by Trilling, *Arnold*, p. 202, from a letter in the Morgan Library.

93. *Discourses in America*, pp. 198–99.

94. Houghton, in his long and generously documented chapter on dogmatism in Victorian England, does not once mention Newman, the Victorian who, by his own profession, devoted his life to defending the dogmatic principle, as an example of the vice.

95. *The Tamworth Reading Room*, p. 33.

96. *Ibid.*, p. 34. Oliver Elton has asked whether, in the *Grammar of Assent*, Newman 'does not offer us a psychology under the guise of logic.' *A Survey of English Literature: 1830–1880* (2 vols., London, 1920), I, 197.

97. *The Tamworth Reading Room*, p. 34.

98. Wilfrid Ward, *The Life of Cardinal Newman* (2 vols., London, 1912), II, 90.

99. *Apologia Pro Vita Sua*, p. 216.

100. Hallam Tennyson, *Alfred Lord Tennyson: A Memoir* (2 vols., London, 1897), I, 396.

101. *Works*, XVIII, 186.

102. *Ibid.*, V, 334.

103. The poem is often thought to be a portrait of Cardinal Wiseman because it appeared shortly after the 'Papal Aggression' of 1850 and the appointment of Wiseman as Cardinal and Archbishop of Westminster, but it also contains thinly veiled references to Newman.

104. Charles Kingsley, *Letters and Memories* (2 vols., New York, 1900), II, 165.

105. Leslie Stephen, *The Life of Sir James Fitzjames Stephen* (London, 1895), pp. 453–54.

106. Young, p. 75.

107. *Discourses in America*, p. 139. See also *Lectures and Essays*, p. 290.

108. *Irish Essays*, p. 191. Cf. *Dissertations and Discussions*, II, 525.

109. *Letters of Arnold*, I, 289–90.

110. *Poetical Works*, p. 320, ll. 237–38.

111. *Culture and Anarchy*, pp. 208, 151.

112. 'Culture: A Dialogue,' in *The Choice of Books*, pp. 110, 111.

113. *Culture and Anarchy*, pp. 73–74.

114. *Letters of Arnold*, I, 456.

115. *System of Logic*, pp. 585–86.

116. *The Philosophical Works of Francis Bacon* (London, 1905), p. 59.

117. *Spirit of the Age*, p. 30.

118. *Earlier Letters*, I, 30.

119. 'The education which my father gave me, was in itself much more fitted for training me to *know* than to *do*.' *Autobiography*, p. 26.

120. *On Liberty*, p. 115.

121. *Ibid.*, p. 116.

122. Fox, p. 347.

123. *Poetical Works*, p. 182, ll. 1–4. See 'The Buried Life,' ll. 16–22.

124. *Culture and Anarchy*, pp. 108–9.

125. *Autobiography*, pp. 103–5. See T. Woods, *Poetry and Philosophy*, p. 51.

126. *Poetical Works*, p. 270, ll. 8–9.

127. *Ibid.*, pp. 271–72, ll. 42–57, 60–67.

128. *Essays in Criticism: Second Series*, pp. 153–54.

129. *Ibid.*, p. 203.

130. *Letters of Arnold*, II, 182, 191.

131. *Autobiography*, p. 105.

132. *Earlier Letters*, I, 80–82. To his further surprise Mill found that his differences with the 'philosophic Tory' Wordsworth were 'differences of matter-of-fact or detail' whereas his differences with Utilitarians and Radicals were matter of principle. See also Anna Jean Mill, 'John Stuart Mill's Visit to Wordsworth,' *Modern Language Review*, XLIV (July, 1949), 341–50.

133. *Early Essays*, p. 256.

134. *Earlier Letters*, II, 474.

135. 'Wordsworth and the Rabbis,' in *The Opposed Self*, p. 136.

136. *Culture and Anarchy*, pp. 55–56.

137. *Areopagitica*, p. 30.

138. *On Liberty*, p. 117. Walter Pater, a follower of Arnold, praised Mill as one who had learned from Wordsworth that the perfection of human life consists 'rather in *being* than *doing*.' He called Mill a man 'who had meditated very profoundly on the true relation of means to ends in life, and on the distinction between what is desirable in itself and what is desirable only as machinery.' *Appreciations* (London. 1927), pp. 61–62.

139. *On Liberty*, p. 108.

140. *Essays in Criticism: Second Series*, pp. 295–99. Only think, said Arnold, what havoc would be wrought upon an English village if its upper-class inhabitants decided to follow Tolstoy and earn their bread by the work of their hands. Cf. Mill's remarks on the gulf between Christian professions and Christian practice in *On Liberty*, p. 101.

141. *Poetical Works*, p. 60, ll. 275–78.

142. *A History of Western Philosophy* (New York, 1945), p. xiv.

143. 'John Stuart Mill,' *Proceedings of the British Academy*, XLI (1955), 43.
144. *Arnold*, p. 11.
145. Charles Kingsley wrote: 'There are . . . only two deliverances from Werterism possible in the nineteenth century; one is into Popery, and the other is—

> Forward, forward, let us range;
> Let the peoples spin for ever down the
>   ringing grooves of change;
> Through the shadow of the world we
>   sweep into the younger day:
> Better fifty years of Europe than a cycle of Cathay.'

Literary and General Essays (London, 1880), p. 115. More recently, T. S. Eliot has warned us that 'there are two and only two finally tenable hypotheses about life: the Catholic and the materialistic.' *Essays, Ancient and Modern* (London, 1936), p. 172.
146. 'Matthew Arnold,' in *Victorian Literature: Modern Essays in Criticism*, ed. by Austin Wright, p. 65.
147. Richard Chase, 'Christian Ideologue,' *The Nation* (April 8, 1950), p. 330.

CHAPTER FIVE

1. *Dissertations and Discussions*, I, 79.
2. 'On the Present State of Literature,' *The Adelphi*, I (October, 1923–January, 1924), 682. This speech was given in 1827 or 1828 but not published until this century.
3. Stillinger, p. 199.
4. *Dissertations and Discussions*, I, 83–84.
5. Mill remained as rigid on this point as Coleridge or Poe. In 1841 he wrote to G. H. Lewes: 'I do *not* think that epos *quâ* epos, that is *quâ* narrative, is poetry, nor that the drama *quâ* drama is so. I think Homer & Aeschylus poets only by virtue of that in them which might as well be lyrical.' *Earlier Letters*, II, 466.
6. *Dissertations and Discussions*, I, 87.
7. *Ibid.*, I, 93.
8. *Early Essays*, p. 259.
9. In 1834 Mill himself had written to Nicholl that Tennyson's poems were 'the best poems . . . which have appeared since the best days of Coleridge.' *Earlier Letters*, I, 245.
10. *Early Essays*, pp. 259–60, 261, 265–66.
11. *Ibid.*, pp. 260–61. Later in the essay, pp. 266–67, Mill denied the existence of any natural incompatibility between intellectual endeavor and the poetical gift: 'Whoever, in the greatest concerns of human life, pursues truth with unbiased feelings, and an intellect adequate to discern it, will not find that the resources of poetry are lost to him because he has learnt to use and not to abuse them. They are as open to him as they are to the sentimental weakling, who has no test of the true but the ornamental.' In a

letter written to Lewes six years later, Mill suggested that one part of a definition of poetry might be, 'feeling expressing itself in the forms of thought.' *Earlier Letters*, II, 471.

12. *Early Essays*, p. 261.

13. *Lectures and Essays*, p. 262. See *Essays in Criticism: Second Series*, pp. 184–185.

14. *Lectures and Essays*, p. 34.

15. *Essays in Criticism: Second Series*, p. 165.

16. *Letters of Arnold*, I, 147.

17. *Ibid.*, I, 241–42.

18. *Letters to Clough*, p. 63.

19. *Essays in Criticism: Second Series*, p. 4.

20. *Lectures and Essays*, pp. 30–31.

21. *Ibid.*, pp. 33–34. Both Arnold and Mill approved Milton's maxim that poetry, unlike rhetoric, ought to be simple, sensuous, and passionate. See *Discourses in America*, p. 154; and *Early Essays*, p. 262n.

22. *Lectures and Essays*, pp. 262–63, 260–61.

23. *Letters to Clough*, p. 65.

24. *Lectures and Essays*, p. 261. For further illustrations of Arnold's cultural determinism, see the remarks on Gray in *Essays in Criticism: Second Series*, pp. 85, 91–93, and his explanation of the absence of a modern English drama in *Irish Essays*, p. 222.

25. *Lectures and Essays*, pp. 261, 285.

26. *Ibid.*, p. 263.

27. *Conversations with Eckermann and Soret*, trans. by John Oxenford (London, 1874), p. 254.

28. *Classical Tradition*, p. 8.

29. *Lectures and Essays*, pp. 380–81.

30. *Mixed Essays*, p. 294.

31. *Classical Tradition*, p. 8. See also *Mixed Essays*, p. 292.

32. *Letters to Clough*, p. 143.

33. *Ibid.*, p. 65.

34. *Ibid.*, pp. 97–99.

35. A letter of 1858 suggests that for Arnold a choice had become necessary. Writing of his stiff Neoclassical tragedy, *Merope*, which had been poorly received, he spoke of a temptation 'to transfer your operations to a region where form is everything.' For in the nineteenth century, he said, 'to attain perfection in the region of thought and feeling, and to unite this with perfection of form' requires either spiritual self-mutilaton or a total consecration of one's life to one's work. *Letters of Arnold*, I, 72–73.

36. *Classical Tradition*, p. 15.

37. *Lectures and Essays*, p. 275. In 1864, the year before this essay appeared, Arnold wrote: 'One is from time to time seized and irresistibly carried along by a temptation to treat political, or religious, or social matters, directly; but after yielding to such a temptation I always feel myself recoiling again, and disposed to touch them only so far as they can be touched through poetry.' *Letters of Arnold*, I, 270–71.

38. *Earlier Letters*, II, 446.

39. Arnold denied Carlyle greatness as a writer 'because the materials furnished to him by that devouring eye of his, and that portraying hand, were not wrought in and subdued by him to what his work, regarded as a composition for literary purposes, required.' *Discourses in America*, pp. 166–168.

40. 'On the Present State of Literature,' *The Adelphi*, I, 683.

41. *Earlier Letters*, II, 484.

42. *J. S. Mill and Harriet Taylor*, pp. 225–26. Cf. Pater's remarks in his essay on Winckelmann: 'Certainly, for us of the modern world, with its conflicting claims, its entangled interests, distracted by so many sorrows, so many preoccupations, so bewildering an experience, the problem of unity with ourselves, in blitheness and repose is far harder than it was for the Greek within the simple terms of antique life. Yet, not less than ever, the intellect demands completeness, centrality.' *The Renaissance* (London, 1919), p. 227.

43. *J. S. Mill and Harriet Taylor*, p. 225. See Houghton, pp. 290–91.

44. *Conversations with Eckermann and Soret*, p. 236.

45. *Letters to Clough*, p. 133.

46. *Classical Tradition*, pp. 4, 6–7.

47. 'Age of Chivalry,' *Westminster Review*, VI (July, 1826), 63.

48. 'On the Present State of Literature,' *The Adelphi*, I, 689.

49. *Early Essays*, p. 255.

50. 'Inaugural Address,' in Cavenagh, p. 154.

51. *Ibid.*, p. 153. In the 1853 Preface, Arnold mimicked the arguments of his opponents by asking: 'What then, . . . are the ancients to be our sole models? the ancients with their comparatively narrow range of experience . . . ?' *Classical Tradition*, p. 12. Yet in 1879 Arnold wrote: 'In many respects the ancients are far above us, and yet there is something that we demand which they can never give.' *Essays in Criticism: Second Series*, p. 160.

52. 'Inaugural Address,' in Cavenagh, p. 156.

53. *Dissertations and Discussions*, I, 302–3. To illustrate this assertion, Mill said that the writings of Vigny fall 'within a far other category than that of the Beautiful, and can be justified on no canons of taste of which that is the end.' He went on to insist that, admirers of Goethe notwithstanding, in the modern world earnestness in art is incompatible with critical canons of the beautiful. Arnold, in 1848, told Clough that he had 'a growing sense of the deficiency of the *beautiful* in your poems, and of this alone being properly *poetical* as distinguished from rhetorical, devotional or metaphysical.' *Letters to Clough*, p. 66.

54. Pater, *The Renaissance*, p. 230.

55. Mill did concur in Goethe's dictum that, as Mill paraphrased it, 'the Beautiful is greater than the Good; for it includes the Good, and adds something to it; it is the Good made perfect, and fitted with all the collateral perfections which make it a finished and completed thing.' 'Inaugural Address,' in Cavenagh, p. 195.

56. *The Works of Samuel Johnson*, ed. by Arthur Murphy (12 vols., London, 1824), II, 90.

57. *The Works of Jeremy Bentham* (11 vols., Edinburgh, 1838–43), II, 254.

58. *Dissertations and Discussions*, I, 72. In 1840 Mill wrote to Lewes: 'You are certainly a conjurer in finding out my old obscure articles. The only valuable thing in these two [the essays subsequently reprinted as 'Poetry and Its Varieties'] is I think the distinction between poetry & oratory.' *Earlier Letters*, II, 449. For an example of Mill's early espousal of the Benthamite view of poetry, see his attack on David Hume as a historian whose mind 'was completely enslaved by a taste for literature . . . which without regard for truth or utility seeks only to excite emotion.' 'Brodie's *History of the British Empire*,' *Westminster Review*, II (October, 1824), 346.

59. *Essays in Criticism: Second Series*, p. 48.

60. *Ibid.*, p. 95.

61. *The George Eliot Letters*, ed. by Gordon S. Haight (7 vols., London, 1954), III, 111.

62. Tocqueville, II, 173–76.

63. *Dissertations and Discussions*, I, 71.

64. *Early Essays*, p. 261.

65. *Ibid.*, pp. 271, 277–78.

66. *Ibid.*, p. 310.

67. *Ibid.*, p. 279.

68. *Ibid.*, p. 275.

69. Mill criticized Bentham because, although he enjoyed music and the plastic arts all his life, 'his ignorance of the deeper springs of human character prevented him (as it prevents most Englishmen) from suspecting how profoundly such things enter into the moral nature of man, and into the education both of the individual and of the race.' *Bentham and Coleridge*, p. 95.

70. *Ibid.*, pp. 61–62.

71. 'Notes on Some of the More Popular Dialogues of Plato: *The Protagoras*,' *Monthly Repository*, VIII (March, 1834), 211.

72. 'Notes on Some of the More Popular Dialogues of Plato: *The Gorgias*,' *Monthly Repository*, VIII (December, 1834), 841–42. Mill complimented Comte because 'he not only appreciates, but rates high in moral value, the creations of poets and artists in all departments, deeming them, by their mixed appeal to the sentiments and the understanding, admirably fitted to educate the feelings of abstract thinkers, and enlarge the intellectual horizon of people of the world.' *Auguste Comte and Positivism*, p. 117.

73. Article in *Examiner*, June 3, 1832, p. 358.

74. 'Inaugural Address,' in Cavenagh, p. 193.

75. *Three Essays on Religion*, p. 49.

76. *Dissertations and Discussions*, I, 284–85. For other illustrations of Mill's doctrine of the morality of imaginative sympathy, see 'Macaulay's *Lays of Ancient Rome*,' *Westminster Review*, XXXIV (February, 1843), 106; and *Three Essays on Religion*, p. 250.

77. *Dissertations and Discussions*, I, 214–15.

78. 'Writings of Junius Redivivus.' *Monthly Repository*, VII (April, 1833), 263.

79. In 1824, Mill had expressed agreement with Dr. Johnson's belief in the moral purpose of poetry without saying whether he believed in the

effectiveness of the means Johnson chose to that end. 'Periodical Literature
—*Edinburgh Review*,' *Westminster Review*, I (April, 1824), 535.

80. *Classical Tradition*, pp. 188, 136.

81. *Ibid.*, pp. 138–39. To show the efficacy of Homer when spiritual consolation is needed, Arnold repeated an account of the way in which Lord
Granville, on his death-bed, was recalled to his sense of duty by remem-
bering a speech from Homer.

82. *Essays in Criticism: Second Series*, pp. 141–43. Mill, too, insisted on a
'broad' definition of moral ideas. He said that moral precepts, such as those
of Jesus, are to be considered not as laws laid down for the precise regulation of conduct, 'but as the bodying forth in words of the *spirit* of all morality,
right self-culture, the principles of which cannot change, since man's
nature changes not, though surrounding circumstances do.' They are intended to inculcate the proper spirit in which man is to contemplate action,
but not to prescribe a particular mode of action. *Earlier Letters*, I, 101.

83. *Letters to Clough*, pp. 101, 146.

84. *Mixed Essays*, p. 258.

85. *Ibid.*, pp. 257–59.

86. *Essays in Criticism: Second Series*, pp. 61–64.

87. *Lectures and Essays*, p. 132.

88. *Essays in Criticism: Second Series*, pp. 183–84.

89. *Ibid.*, p. 5.

90. *Ibid.*, pp. 16–17.

91. *Discourses in America*, pp. 126–27.

92. *Works*, II, 254.

93. *Dissertations and Discussions*, I, 64–65. In his Essay Supplementary to
the Preface of 1815, Wordsworth wrote: 'The appropriate business of
poetry, . . . her appropriate employment, her privilege and her *duty*, is to
treat of things not as they *are*, but as they appear; not as they exist in themselves, but as they *seem* to exist to the senses, and to the passions.' *Poetical
Works*, ed. by E. de Selincourt and H. Darbishire, 2nd ed. (5 vols., Oxford,
1952), II, 410.

94. *Dissertations and Discussions*, I, 69–70.

95. M. H. Abrams, *The Mirror and the Lamp* (New York, 1953), p. 322.

96. *Earlier Letters*, I, 113. Mill said of Plato's dialogues that they 'afford an
example, once in all literature, of the union between an eminent genius
for philosophy and the most consummate skill and feeling of the artist.'
Dissertations and Discussions, III, 330.

97. *Earlier Letters*, I, 163.

98. *Ibid.*, I, 219. See *Autobiography*, pp. 124, 132.

99. *Early Essays*, p. 278.

100. *Letters of Mill*, II, 358.

101. *Autobiography*, pp. 106–7.

102. *Works*, V, 386–87.

103. See, e.g., the reasons Mill gave Huxley for refusing to support his
educational program. *Letters of Mill*, II, 43–44.

104. 'Inaugural Address,' in Cavenagh, p. 138.

105. *Essays in Criticism: Second Series*, p. 3.

106. *Poetical Works*, II, 396–97.

107. *Letters of Arnold*, I, 285–86, 313, 364–66. Mill, on the contrary, when asked by a clergyman for his advice on educating the working classes, recommended all that 'which relates to human life and the ways of mankind; geography, voyages and travels, manners and customs, and romances, which must tend to awaken their imagination and give them some of the meaning of self-devotion and heroism, in short, to unbrutalise them,' *Letters of Mill*, I, 165.

108. *Poetical Works*, II, 396.

109. *Lectures and Essays*, p. 330.

110. *Ibid.*, p. 13.

111. *Ibid.*

112. *Essays in Criticism: Second Series*, p. 55.

113. *Discourses in America*, pp. 107–12. In his essay 'On the Modern Element in Literature,' Arnold attributed the survival of Aristophanes' comedies rather than Menander's to 'the instinct of self-preservation in humanity.' *Classical Tradition*, pp. 29–30.

114. *Essays in Criticism: Second Series*, pp. 1–2. For a staunch defense of Arnold against critics of this pronouncement, see F. R. Leavis, 'Arnold as Critic,' *Scrutiny*, VII (December, 1938), 323.

115. *Works*, ed. by J. Spedding, R. L. Ellis, and D. D. Heath (14 vols., London, 1857–74), IV, 316.

116. *Discourses in America*, pp. 116–18.

117. *Literature and Dogma*, p. 3.

118. *God and the Bible*, pp. xi–xii.

119. *Letters of Arnold*, II, 41.

120. *J. S. Mill and Harriet Taylor*, pp. 195–96.

121. *Three Essays on Religion*, pp. 103–4.

122. *Ibid.*, pp. 104–5. In the essay in this volume called 'Theism' Mill wrote, p. 250, that one of the most important functions of the imagination is its familiarity 'with the conception of a morally perfect Being, and the habit of taking the approbation of such a Being as the *norma* or standard to which to refer and by which to regulate our own characters and lives. This idealization of our standard of excellence in a person is quite possible, even when that person is conceived as merely imaginary.'

123. *Dissertations and Discussions*, I, 284–85.

124. *Essays in Criticism: Second Series*, p. 149.

125. Bain, *J. S. Mill*, p. 154.

CHAPTER SIX

1. *On the Classical Tradition*, p. 22.

2. *Culture and Anarchy*, p. 48. See *Letters of Arnold*, II, 220.

3. *Culture and Anarchy*, p. 49.

4. *Friendship's Garland*, p. 146.

5. David Thomson, *England in the Nineteenth Century* (Aylesbury, 1950), p. 32.

6. *Culture and Anarchy*, p. 161.

7. *Ibid.*, pp. 157–58.

8. *Democratic Education*, p. 24.

9. *Discourses in America*, p. x.

10. *Culture and Anarchy*, pp. 57–58.

11. *Mixed Essays*, p. 80.

12. *Culture and Anarchy*, p. 6.

13. *Lectures and Essays*, pp. 283–84.

14. Arnold suggested the link between certain nations and the various powers of human nature in the Preface to *Mixed Essays* when he said: 'That the aim for all of us is to make civilisation pervasive and general; that the requisites for civilisation are substantially what have been here enumerated, that they hang together, that they must all have their development, that the development of one does not compensate for the failure of others; that one nation suffers by failing in this requisite, and another by failing in that: such is the line of thought which the essays in the present volume follow and represent.' *Mixed Essays*, p. ix.

15. *Culture and Anarchy*, pp. 43–44. See *Democratic Education*, p. 313.

16. *Dissertations and Discussions*, I, 290.

17. 'Inaugural Address,' in Cavenagh, pp. 191–92.

18. *Ibid.*, p. 193.

19. *Bentham and Coleridge*, pp. 66, 93.

20. *Auguste Comte and Positivism*, p. 100.

21. *Utilitarianism*, p. 19.

22. *Dissertations and Discussions*, II, 70.

23. *Autobiography*, pp. 41–42.

24. *J. S. Mill and Harriet Taylor*, pp. 142, 301, n. 58.

25. *Earlier Letters*, I, 37. Armand Carrel, the French journalist, was Mill's example of a man who could combine the practicality 'of which in England we have too much' with nobler qualities of mind and spirit. He called Carrel 'a human being complete at all points, not a fraction or frustum of one.' *Dissertations and Discussions*, I, 217, 281.

26. 'The Negro Question,' *Fraser's Magazine*, XLI (January, 1850), 27.

27. 'Inaugural Address,' in Cavenagh, pp. 145–47.

28. *Ibid.*, pp. 189–91.

29. *Earlier Letters*, II, 438–39.

30. Mueller, pp. 22–23.

31. *Apologia Pro Vita Sua*, p. 30.

32. *In Memoriam*, CIX.

33. *Letters and Memories* (2 vols., New York, 1900), I, 202.

34. G. D. H. Cole, *The Life of William Cobbett* (London, 1924), p. 16.

35. 'Scott's *Life of Napoleon*,' *Westminster Review*, IX (April, 1828), 257.

36. *Dissertations and Discussions*, II, 220.

37. *Letters of Arnold*, I, 10.

38. *Letters to Clough*, p. 147.

39. *Lectures and Essays*, pp. 245–52.

40. *Letters of Mill*, I, 203.

41. *Autobiography*, pp. 165, 188–89.

42. *Lectures and Essays*, p. 276.
43. *Ibid.*, p. 42.
44. *J. S. Mill and Harriet Taylor*, p. 223.
45. *Autobiography*, p. 43.
46. *Classical Tradition*, p. 92. See *Letters of Arnold*, I, 115.
47. *Dissertations and Discussions*, III, 161, 177–78.
48. *Lectures and Essays*, p. 284. See also *Essays in Criticism: Second Series*, p. 126.
49. *Lectures and Essays*, p. 376.
50. *Ibid.*, pp. 297–98.
51. *On Liberty*, p. 80. See also *Considerations on Representative Government*, pp. 363–64.
52. *Literature and Dogma*, pp. 55–56.
53. *Mixed Essays*, pp. 62–64.
54. *Democratic Education*, p. 16.
55. *Ibid.*, pp. 29, 17.
56. See Hugh Trevor-Roper, 'A Question of Nationality,' *New Statesman*, March 2, 1962, pp. 303–4; and J. R. Levenson, *Confucian China and Its Modern Fate* (London, 1958).
57. *Fox*, pp. 114–15.
58. *Halévy*, p. 149, 298.
59. *Bentham and Coleridge*, pp. 72–73. See *Earlier Letters*, II, 712.
60. *Bentham and Coleridge*, pp. 82–83. See also *System of Logic*, pp. 567, 586, 591; *Considerations on Representative Government*, p. 197 and *passim*.
61. See Mill's remarks on centralization in *Letters of Mill*, I, 235; *Autobiography*, pp. 134–35; and 'Centralization,' *Edinburgh Review*, CXV (April, 1862), 323–58.
62. See *Considerations on Representative Government*, pp. 177, 196.
63. 'Age of Chivalry,' *Westminster Review*, VI (July, 1826), 62–63.
64. *Lettres Philosophiques ou Lettres Anglaises* (Paris, 1956), pp. 53, 36.
65. *Earlier Letters*, II, 713–14.
66. *Friendship's Garland*, pp. 134–36. See also *Classical Tradition*, p. 84.
67. *Uncollected Essays*, p. 90.
68. Letter to H. S. Chapman in James McCrimmon, *Studies Towards a Biography of John Stuart Mill* (Evanston, 1936), p. 387.
69. *Lectures and Essays*, p. 120.
70. 'Comparison of the Tendencies of French and English Intellect,' *Monthly Repository*, VII (November, 1833), 802.
71. 'Taylor's Statesman,' *London & Westminster Review*, XXVII (April, 1837), 3.
72. *Dissertations and Discussions*, II, 221–22.
73. *Democratic Education*, p. 11.
74. *Friendship's Garland*, pp. 149, 153. See also *Letters of Arnold*, I, 360.
75. *Letters to Clough*, pp. 72–73.
76. *Lectures and Essays*, pp. 264–65. Although Arnold and Mill persistently used the average Englishman's dislike for political theories dependent upon notions of divine or natural right as a sign of his unintelligence, they presented their own outright and vehement rejection of the same theories—

in place of which they asserted expediency—as a sign of high intellectual sophistication. See, e.g. Arnold's remarks in *Mixed Essays*, pp. 58–60; and Mill's in *Autobiography*, p. 74.

77. 'Scott's *Life of Napoleon*,' *Westminster Review*, IX (April, 1828), 255.

78. *Letters of Mill*, I, 167. See also I, 172.

79. *Classical Tradition*, pp. 78–79.

80. *Mixed Essays*, pp. 65–67. See also *Uncollected Essays*, p. 78.

81. *Lectures and Essays*, pp. 392–94.

82. *Autobiography*, pp. 56, 76, 40–41.

83. *Lettres Philosophiques*, pp. 43–44.

84. Woodward, p. 28.

85. *Principles of Political Economy*, p. 110.

86. *Mixed Essays*, p. 81.

87. *Dissertations and Discussions*, II, 360.

88. *Principles of Political Economy*, p. 286.

89. *Earlier Letters*, I, 192.

90. 'Taylor's Statesman,' *London & Westminster Review*, XXVII (April, 1837), 22.

91. *Principles of Political Economy*, p. 258.

92. *Dissertations and Discussions*, I, 258–59.

93. See, e.g., Tocqueville, I, 254.

94. *Dissertations and Discussions*, II, 7–9, 14–21.

95. *Subjection of Women*, p. 259.

96. *Mixed Essays*, pp. 319, 320–21.

97. Quoted in *Democratic Education*, p. 9n.

98. *Ibid.*, pp. 8–9.

99. *Mixed Essays*, pp. 60, 92–93. Yet when Arnold returned to the subject in 1885, he seemed to have lost his patience and become ready to enter the realm of practice: '. . . One would wish, if one set about wishing, for the extinction of title after the death of the holder, and for the dispersion of property by a stringent law of bequest. Our society should be homogeneous, and only in this way can it become so.' *Uncollected Essays*, p. 42.

100. Arnold said that the modern problem was how 'to make human life . . . more natural and rational; [and how] to have the greatest possible number of one's nation happy.' *Friendship's Garland*, p. 140. See Mill's remarks on the primacy of equality in *Dissertations and Discussions*, II, 395.

101. *Mixed Essays*, pp. 159–60. See *Irish Essays*, pp. 113–14.

102. *Mixed Essays*, p. 75.

103. *Democratic Education*, p. 23.

104. *Ibid.*, p. 282.

105. *Mixed Essays*, pp. 141–43, 156–58.

106. *Ibid.*, pp. 166–69.

107. *Letters of Arnold*, I, 132.

108. In 1848 Arnold bemoaned the failure of Napoleon's English contemporaries to understand him, and the tragedy implicit in Napoleon's defeat by 'the union of invincibility and speculative dulness in England.' *Ibid.*, I, 12.

109. *Dissertations and Discussions*, I, 220.

110. *Comte*, pp. 181–82.
111. *Mixed Essays*, pp. 174–75.
112. *Comte*, p. 153.
113. *Considerations on Representative Government*, p. 375.
114. *Letters of Mill*, II, 86.
115. *Autobiography*, p. 128.
116. *Dissertations and Discussions*, I, 27–31.
117. *Ibid.*, IV, 12.
118. *Ibid.*, IV, 14.
119. *Ibid.*, II, 68.
120. *Ibid.*, III, 365, 372.
121. *Ibid.*, IV, 19.
122. *On Liberty*, p. 161.
123. *Letters of Mill*, II, 106. See *Liberty*, pp. 161–62.
124. *On Liberty*, p. 161.
125. The French Academy is an excellent example. For Arnold's opinions on the subject, see *Lectures and Essays*, pp. 232–57; *Uncollected Essays*, pp. 97–98. For Mill's, see *Dissertations and Discussions*, I, 191–92; *Bentham and Coleridge*, p. 146; *Comte*, pp. 97–98; and *Letters of Mill*, I, 252–53.
126. *Considerations on Representative Government*, pp. 346–47.
127. *Dissertations and Discussions*, II, 65.
128. *Considerations on Representative Government*, p. 214.
129. *Dissertations and Discussions*, III, 179.
130. *Letters of Arnold*, I, 287.
131. *Uncollected Essays*, p. 6.
132. *Dissertations and Discussions*, II, 76.
133. *Considerations on Representative Government*, p. 289.
134. *Essays in Criticism: Second Series*, p. 57. See also *Letters of Arnold*, I, 133.
135. *Democratic Education*, p. 18.
136. *Ibid.*, pp. 11, 15–16, 18.
137. *Culture and Anarchy*, pp. 17–19, 36.
138. *Considerations on Representative Government*, p. 278.
139. *Dissertations and Discussions*, II, 22–24, 35.
140. *On Liberty*, p. 167.
141. The Mill-Taylor Collection in the British Library of Political and Economic Science, Vol. III, MS letter from Mill to Henry Fawcett, February 5, 1860.
142. *Dissertations and Discussions*, II, 38–42.
143. *Considerations on Representative Government*, pp. 269–70. Mill's view of simple, majority rule is comparable to that of John C. Calhoun, who opposed the idea of government based on a 'concurrent majority' to what he thought the ultimately undemocratic conception of government by a numerical majority.
144. *J. S. Mill and Harriet Taylor*, p. 144.
145. Arnold said that Scott and Macaulay could not hope to apply ideas to life as Homer had done because Homer belonged 'to an incomparably more developed spiritual order than . . . Scott and Macaulay.' *Classical Tradition*, p. 211.

146. *Democratic Education*, p. 25.
147. *Dissertations and Discussions*, II, 283.
148. *Considerations on Representative Government*, pp. 216–17.
149. *Democratic Education*, p. 314. See also *Classical Tradition*, p. 23.
150. *Dissertations and Discussions*, II, 534–35, 526.
151. *Democratic Education*, p. 314.
152. Young, p. 6.

CHAPTER SEVEN

1. Tocqueville, I, 7.
2. *Dissertations and Discussions*, II, 6–7.
3. *Democratic Education*, p. 19.
4. Tocqueville, I, 255.
5. *Early Essays*, pp. 317–18.
6. *Letters of Arnold*, I, 97.
7. *Democratic Education*, pp. 11–12.
8. *Earlier Letters*, II, 712.
9. *Mixed Essays*, pp. 87–88.
10. *Autobiography*, p. 120. See also *On Liberty*, p. 70.
11. *Autobiography*, pp. 120–21. Cf. Ruskin, *Works*, XVIII, 437.
12. *Dissertations and Discussions*, III, 16–18.
13. *Irish Essays*, p. 141.
14. *Discourses in America*, p. 7.
15. *Principles of Political Economy*, p. 757.
16. *Democratic Education*, p. 300.
17. *Ibid.*, p. 8.
18. *Bentham and Coleridge*, pp. 83–84.
19. *Autobiography*, p. 134.
20. *Bentham and Coleridge*, pp. 87–88.
21. *Ibid.*, pp. 86–87.
22. *Democratic Education*, p. 13.
23. *Ibid.*, pp. 13, 18–19.
24. *Ibid.*, pp. 18, 24.
25. *Ibid.*, pp. 26–27.
26. *Ibid.*, p. 28.
27. In the lecture called 'Numbers,' Arnold attempted to reconcile his allegiance to the political principle of popular government with the ethical maxim, sanctioned by Plato and Isaiah, that the majority of a people is always unsound. *Discourses in America*, pp. 7–8, 14–16, 21–26.
28. Tocqueville, II, 387. See also I, 434; II, 13, 307–9.
29. *Democratic Education*, pp. 28–29.
30. *Bentham and Coleridge*, pp. 122, 136, 128.
31. *On Liberty*, pp. 66–67. In 1837 Mill himself had entertained this argument. See 'Taylor's Statesman,' *London & Westminster Review*, XXVII (April, 1837), 19–20.
32. *Democratic Education*, p. 28.

33. *Autobiography*, pp. 178–79.
34. *On Liberty*, p. 62.
35. *Culture and Anarchy*, pp. 126–27.
36. Humboldt, pp. 11, 21, 65, 200–201.
37. *On Liberty*, pp. 74–76.
38. *Ibid.*, pp. 70–71.
39. *Letters of Arnold*, I, 372. See also *Culture and Anarchy*, p. 50.
40. *On Liberty*, p. 115.
41. *Ibid.*, pp. 88–90.
42. *The Constitution of Liberty* (London, 1960), p. 68.
43. *J. S. Mill and Harriet Taylor*, p. 217.
44. *On Liberty*, p. 87.
45. *Ibid.*, p. 88.
46. *Ibid.*
47. *Ibid.* See *The Amberley Papers*, I, 119.
48. *On Liberty*, p. 88.
49. *Letters of Arnold*, I, 111. Carlyle, on the contrary, is said to have become violent upon reading the book, about which he wrote to his brother: 'As if it were a sin to control, or coerce into better methods, human swine in any way; . . . ach Gott im Himmel!' *New Letters of Thomas Carlyle*, ed. by Alexander Carlyle (2 vols., London, 1904), II, 196.
50. *Lectures and Essays*, pp. 133–36.
51. *Letters of Arnold*, I, x.
52. *Poetical Works*, p. 168, l. 2.
53. *Lectures and Essays*, pp. 140–41.
54. *Ibid.*, p. 143.
55. *Ibid.*, pp. 144–45.
56. *Ibid.*, p. 145.
57. *On Liberty*, pp. 99–100.
58. *Culture and Anarchy*, p. 29.
59. *Lectures and Essays*, pp. 145–46.
60. *On Liberty*, p. 147.
61. *Culture and Anarchy*, p. 112.
62. *On Liberty*, pp. 114–15.
63. *Ibid.*, pp. 116–17.
64. *Ibid.*, pp. 121, 125. See also *Auguste Comte and Positivism*, pp. 141–42.
65. *Culture and Anarchy*, p. 120.
66. *On Liberty*, p. 115.
67. *Bentham and Coleridge*, pp. 86–87.
68. *On Liberty*, p. 128.
69. *Ibid.*, p. 75.
70. *Culture and Anarchy*, p. 82. In the *Autobiography*, pp. 45–46, Mill wrote about Bentham's *Introduction to the Principles of Morals and Legislation:* 'What . . . impressed me was the chapter in which Bentham passed judgment on the common modes of reasoning in morals and legislation, deduced from phrases like 'law of nature,' 'right reason,' 'the moral sense,' 'Natural rectitude,' and the like, and characterized them as dogmatism in disguise, imposing its sentiments upon others under cover of sounding expressions

which convey no reason for the sentiment, but set up the sentiment as its own reason.' See *A Fragment on Government and An Introduction to the Principles of Morals and Legislation,* ed. by Wilfrid Harrison (Oxford, 1948), p. 141.

71. *Culture and Anarchy,* pp. 94–95.
72. *Ibid.,* pp. 95–96.
73. *Ibid.,* pp. 202–3.
74. *Bentham and Coleridge,* p. 87.
75. *Democratic Education,* p. 29.
76. *Culture and Anarchy,* p. 204.
77. *Ibid.,* p. 205.
78. *Ibid.,* p. 125.
79. *On Liberty,* p. 139. See *Comte,* pp. 143, 145–46.
80. *On Liberty,* p. 170. See Tocqueville, II, 347.
81. *Works,* XXX, 1–2.
82. *Letters of Arnold,* I, 389–90, 438.
83. *Culture and Anarchy,* p. 97.
84. *Autobiography,* pp. 204–5.
85. *Ibid.,* p. 204.
86. *Daily News,* July 31, 1866.
87. *Autobiography,* p. 205.

BIBLIOGRAPHY

WORKS OF MATTHEW ARNOLD

Culture and Anarchy. Edited with an introduction by J. Dover Wilson. Cambridge, 1932.

Democratic Education. Vol. II of *The Complete Prose Works of Matthew Arnold*. Edited by R. H. Super. Ann Arbor, 1962.

Discourses in America. New York, 1896.

Essays in Criticism: Second Series. New York, 1896.

Essays, Letters, and Reviews by Matthew Arnold. Edited by Fraser Neiman. Cambridge, Mass., 1960.

Five Uncollected Essays of Matthew Arnold. Edited by Kenneth Allott. Liverpool, 1953.

A French Eton. London, 1904.

Friendship's Garland. 2nd ed. London, 1897.

God and the Bible. London, 1904.

Irish Essays. London, 1904.

Lectures and Essays in Criticism. Vol. III of *The Complete Prose Works of Matthew Arnold*. Edited by R. H. Super. Ann Arbor, 1962.

Letters of Matthew Arnold. Edited by G. W. E. Russell. 2 vols. in 1. New York, 1900.

The Letters of Matthew Arnold to Arthur Hugh Clough. Edited with an introduction by H. F. Lowry. London and New York, 1932.

Literature and Dogma. London, 1904.

Mixed Essays. London, 1904.

The Note-Books of Matthew Arnold. Edited by H. F. Lowry, Karl Young, W. H. Dunn. London, New York, and Toronto, 1952.

On the Classical Tradition. Vol. I of *The Complete Prose Works of Matthew Arnold*. Edited by R. H. Super. Ann Arbor, 1960.

Poetical Works. Edited by C. B. Tinker and H. F. Lowry. London, 1950.

St. Paul and Protestantism. London, 1904.

Unpublished Letters of Matthew Arnold. Edited by Arnold Whitridge. New Haven, 1923.

WORKS OF JOHN STUART MILL

'Age of Chivalry,' *Westminster Review*, VI (July, 1826), 62–103.

Auguste Comte and Positivism. Ann Arbor, 1961.

Autobiography of John Stuart Mill. Edited by Roger Howson with a preface by John Jacob Coss. New York, 1924.

'Brodie's *History of the British Empire,*' *Westminster Review,* II (October, 1824), 346–402.

'Centralization,' *Edinburgh Review,* CXV (April, 1862), 323–58.

'Chapters on Socialism,' *Fortnightly Review,* XXV (January–June, 1879), 217–37, 373–82, 513–30.

'Comparison of the Tendencies of French and English Intellect,' *Monthly Repository,* VII (November, 1833), 800–804.

Considerations on Representative Government. (See *Utilitarianism* below.)

Dissertations and Discussions: Political, Philosophical, and Historical. Reprinted chiefly from the *Edinburgh* and *Westminster Reviews.* 2 vols. London, 1859. 3 vols. London, 1867. 4 vols. London, 1875.

The Earlier Letters of John Stuart Mill: 1812–1848. Edited by Francis E. Mineka. 2 vols. Toronto and London, 1963.

The Early Draft of John Stuart Mill's Autobiography. Edited by Jack Stillinger. Urbana, 1961.

Early Essays by John Stuart Mill. Edited by J. W. M. Gibbs. London, 1897.

England and Ireland. 5th ed. London, 1869.

An Examination of Sir William Hamilton's Philosophy. London, 1865.

Examiner, June 3, 1832, pp. 358, 361.

'Inaugural Address at St. Andrews,' in *James & John Stuart Mill on Education.* Edited by F. A. Cavenagh. Cambridge, 1931.

John Mill's Boyhood Visit to France. Edited with an introduction by Anna Jean Mill. Toronto and London, 1960.

John Stuart Mill and Harriet Taylor: Their Friendship and Subsequent Marriage. Edited by F. A. Hayek. Chicago, 1951.

The Letters of John Stuart Mill. Edited by Hugh S. R. Elliot. 2 vols. London, 1910.

'Macaulay's *Lays of Ancient Rome,*' *Westminster Review,* XXXIX (February, 1843), 105–13.

Mill on Bentham and Coleridge. Edited with an introduction by F. R. Leavis. London, 1959.

'The Negro Question,' *Fraser's Magazine,* XLI (January, 1850), 25–31.

'Notes on Some of the More Popular Dialogues of Plato,' *Monthly Repository,* VIII (February–December, 1834), 89–99, 203–11, 404–20, 633–46, 691–710, 802–15, 829–42; IX (February–March, 1835), 112–21, 169–78.

On Liberty. (See *Utilitarianism* below.)

'On the Present State of Literature,' *The Adelphi,* I (October, 1923–January, 1924), 681–93.

'Periodical Literature: *Edinburgh Review*,' *Westminster Review*, 1 (April, 1824), 505–41.
Principles of Political Economy. Edited with an introduction by W. J. Ashley. London, 1909.
'Reorganization of the Reform Party,' *Westminster Review*, XXXII (April, 1839), 475–508.
'Scott's *Life of Napoleon*,' *Westminster Review*, IX (April, 1828), 251–313.
The Spirit of the Age. Edited with an introduction by F. A. Hayek. Chicago, 1942.
The Subjection of Women. London, 1929.
A System of Logic. 8th ed. London, 1959.
'Taylor's Statesman,' *London & Westminster Review*, XXVII (April, 1837), 1–32.
Three Essays on Religion. London, 1874.
Utilitarianism, On Liberty, and Considerations on Representative Government. With an introduction by A. D. Lindsay. London, 1910.
'Writings of Junius Redivivus,' *Monthly Repository*, VII (April, 1833), 262–70.

GENERAL WORKS

ANSCHUTZ, R. P. *The Philosophy of J. S. Mill*. Oxford, 1953.
ARNOLD, THOMAS, D.D. *Introductory Lectures on Modern History*. Oxford, 1842.
—— *Miscellaneous Works*. London, 1845.
BAIN, ALEXANDER. *James Mill: A Biography*. London, 1882.
—— *J. S. Mill, A Criticism*. London, 1882.
BAMFORD, T. W. *Thomas Arnold*. London, 1960.
BATE, WALTER JACKSON. 'Matthew Arnold,' in *Victorian Literature: Modern Essays in Criticism*. Edited by Austin Wright. New York, 1961.
BONNEROT, LOUIS. *Matthew Arnold, Poète: Essai de Biographie Psychologique*. Paris, 1947.
BURSTON, W. H. 'James Mill on the Aims of Education,' *Cambridge Journal*, VI (October, 1952–September, 1953), 79–101.
CARLYLE, THOMAS. *The Works of Thomas Carlyle*. Edited by H. D. Traill. 30 vols. London, 1896–99.
CAVENAGH, F. A., ed., *James & John Stuart Mill on Education*. Cambridge, 1931. Includes James Mill's article on Education reprinted from 5th ed. of Encyclopaedia Britannica and J. S. Mill's Inaugural Address as Rector of St. Andrews in 1867.
CHRISTIE, W. D. 'Mr. John Stuart Mill for Westminster,' *Macmillan's Magazine*, XII (May–October, 1865), 92–96.

CLOUGH, ARTHUR HUGH. 'Recent English Poetry,' *North American Review*, LXXVII (July, 1853), 1–30.

COURTNEY, W. L. *Life of John Stuart Mill*. London, 1889.

CULLER, A. DWIGHT, ed., *Poetry and Criticism of Matthew Arnold*. Boston, 1961.

FAIN, J. T. 'Ruskin and Mill,' *Modern Language Quarterly*, XII (June, 1951), 150–54.

FEUER, LEWIS S. 'John Stuart Mill and Marxian Socialism,' *Journal of the History of Ideas*, X (April, 1949), 297–303.

FOX, CAROLINE. *Memories of Old Friends*. Edited by H. N. Pym. Philadelphia, 1882.

HAINDS, J. R. 'J. S. Mill's *Examiner* Articles on Art,' *Journal of the History of Ideas*, XI (April, 1950), 215–34.

HAINES, L. F. 'Mill and "Pauline": The "Review" that "Retarded" Browning's Fame,' *Modern Language Notes*, LIX (June, 1944), 410–12.

HALÉVY, ELIE. *The Growth of Philosophic Radicalism*. Translated by Mary Morris. With a preface by A. D. Lindsay. Boston, 1955.

HARRISON, FREDERIC. 'Culture: A Dialogue,' in *The Choice of Books*. London, 1886.

HAYEK, F. A. 'J. S. Mill's Correspondence,' *Times Literary Supplement*, February 13, 1943, p. 84.

—— *John Stuart Mill and Harriet Taylor: Their Friendship and Subsequent Marriage*. Chicago, 1951.

HOLYOAKE, GEORGE JACOB. *John Stuart Mill, as some of the Working Classes knew him*. London, 1873.

HOUGHTON, WALTER. *The Victorian Frame of Mind: 1830–1870*. New Haven, 1957.

HUMBOLDT, WILHELM VON. *The Sphere and Duties of Government*. Translated by Joseph Coulthard, Jr. London, 1854.

HUNT, E. L. 'Matthew Arnold and his Critics,' *Sewanee Review*, XLIV (October, 1936), 449–67.

HUXLEY, THOMAS H. *Science and Education*. London, 1893.

JAMES, HENRY. 'Matthew Arnold,' *English Illustrated Magazine*, (January, 1884), 241–46.

JONES, HOWARD MUMFORD. 'Arnold, Aristocracy, and America,' *American Historical Review*, XLIX (April, 1944), 393–409.

LASKI, HAROLD J., ed., *Autobiography of J. S. Mill, with an Appendix of Hitherto Unpublished Speeches*. London, 1924.

LEAVIS, F. R. 'Arnold as Critic,' *Scrutiny*, VII (December, 1938), 319–32.

—— ed., *Mill on Bentham and Coleridge*. London, 1959.

LEVI, A. W. 'The "Mental Crisis" of John Stuart Mill,' *The Psychoanalytic Review*, XXXII (January, 1945), 86–101.

LUCAS, F. L. '*Matthew Arnold*' in *Victorian Literature: Modern Essays in Criticism*. Edited by Austin Wright. New York, 1961.

MACMINN, NEY, J. R. HAINDS, and JAMES MCCRIMMON. *Bibliography of the Published Writings of John Stuart Mill*. Evanston, 1945.

MILL, ANNA JEAN. 'John Stuart Mill's Visit to Wordsworth,' *Modern Language Review*, XLIV (July, 1949), 341–50.

MILL, JAMES. 'Ecclesiastical Establishments,' *Westminster Review*, V (April, 1826), 504–48.

—— 'Education,' in *James & John Stuart Mill on Education*. Edited by F. A. Cavenagh. Cambridge, 1931.

—— *Essays*. London, 1828.

—— 'Formation of Opinions,' *Westminster Review*, VI (July, 1826), 1–23.

—— *The History of British India*. 5th ed. 10 vols. London, 1858.

—— 'Southey's *Book of the Church*,' *Westminster Review*, III (January, 1825), 167–212.

MORLEY, JOHN. *Critical Miscellanies*. 4 vols. London, 1886–1908.

—— 'Matthew Arnold,' *Nineteenth Century*, XXXVIII (July–December, 1895), 1041–55.

—— *Recollections*. 2 vols. London, 1917.

MUELLER, IRIS W. *John Stuart Mill and French Thought*. Urbana, 1956.

NEFF, EMERY. *Carlyle and Mill: An Introduction to Victorian Thought*. 2nd ed. rev. New York, 1926.

NESBITT, GEORGE L. *Benthamite Reviewing: The First Twelve Years of the Westminster Review, 1824–1836*. New York, 1934.

NEWMAN, JOHN HENRY. *Apologia Pro Vita Sua*. Edited by C. F. Harrold. New York, London, and Toronto, 1947.

—— *The Tamworth Reading Room*. London, 1841.

ONG, WALTER J., S.J. 'Mill's Pariah Poet,' *Philological Quarterly*, XXIX (July, 1950), 333–44.

PACKE, MICHAEL ST. JOHN. *The Life of John Stuart Mill*. New York, 1954.

'Prophet of European Unity,' *Times Literary Supplement*, April 16, 1938, pp. 257–58.

REES, J. C. *Mill and his Early Critics*. Leicester, 1956.

ROBBINS, WILLIAM. *The Ethical Idealism of Matthew Arnold*. London, 1959.

ROBSON, JOHN M. 'J. S. Mill's Theory of Poetry,' *University of Toronto Quarterly*, XXIX (July, 1960), 420–38.

—— 'Mill and Arnold: Liberty and Culture—Friends or Enemies?' *The Humanities Association Bulletin*, XII (Fall, 1961), 20–32.

RUSKIN, JOHN. *The Works of John Ruskin*. Edited by E. T. Cook and Alexander Wedderburn. 39 vols. London, 1905.

RUSSELL, BERTRAND. 'John Stuart Mill,' *Proceedings of the British Academy*, XLI (1955), 43–59.

RUSSELL, BERTRAND, and PATRICIA RUSSELL, eds., *The Amberley Papers*. 2 vols. London, 1937.

SELLS, IRIS E. *Matthew Arnold and France: The Poet*. Cambridge, 1935.

STANLEY, ARTHUR PENRHYN. *Life of Thomas Arnold, D.D.* London, 1904.

STEPHEN, FITZJAMES. 'Mr. Matthew Arnold and his Countrymen,' *Saturday Review*, December 3, 1864, pp. 683–85.

STEPHEN, LESLIE. *The English Utilitarians*. 3 vols. London, 1900.

—— 'Some Early Impressions,' *The National Review*, XLII (October, 1903), 208–24.

STRACHEY, LYTTON. *Eminent Victorians*. London, 1928.

TOCQUEVILLE, ALEXIS DE. *Democracy in America*. Translated by Henry Reeve (as revised by Francis Bowen). Edited by Phillips Bradley. 12th ed. 2 vols. New York, 1956.

TRILLING, LIONEL. *Matthew Arnold*. 2nd ed. New York, 1949.

—— 'Wordsworth and the Rabbis,' in *The Opposing Self*. New York, 1955.

WELLINGTON, SAMUEL. 'John Stuart Mill—the Saint of Rationalism,' *Westminster Review*, CLXIII (January–June, 1905), 11–30.

WHITE, HELEN C. 'Matthew Arnold and Goethe,' *Publications of the Modern Language Association of America*, XXXVI (September, 1921), 436–53.

WICKELGREN, F. L. 'Matthew Arnold's Literary Relations with France,' *Modern Language Review*, XXXIII (April, 1938), 200–214.

WILLIAMS, RAYMOND. *Culture and Society: 1780–1950*. New York, 1958.

WILSON, J. DOVER, ed., *Culture and Anarchy, by Matthew Arnold*. Cambridge, 1932.

WOODS, MARGARET. 'Matthew Arnold,' *Essays and Studies by Members of the English Association*, XV (1929), 7–19.

WOODS, THOMAS. *Poetry and Philosophy: a Study of the Thought of John Stuart Mill*. London, 1961.

YOUNG, G. M. *Victorian England: Portrait of an Age*. London and New York, 1936.

INDEX

Tennyson, Hallam, 23
Teufelsdröckh, 133-34
'Theism' (Mill), 289 n.
Thirty-Nine Articles, 81, 116, 124-125, 127
Thomson, David, 289 n.
Thoughts on French Affairs (Burke), 46
'Thoughts on Parliamentary Reform' (Mill), 235
Thucydides, 80, 84-86, 88
'Thyrsis' (Arnold), 23
Time Stream, 69
Times, The (London), 197, 199
'To a Gipsy-Child by the Sea Shore' (Arnold), 123
Tocqueville, Alexis de, 67-68, 82, 114, 169, 172, 176, 197, 217, 228, 233, 237-38, 241
Tolstoy, Leo, 150, 283 n.
Tom Brown's Schooldays (Hughes), 82, 99
Tories and Toryism, 5, 8, 41-42, 44, 89, 262
'Touchstones,' 177
Toynbee, Arnold (the elder), 71
Tractarians, 75, 116, 124; *see also* Oxford Movement
Traité de Législation (Bentham), 104
Transcendentalism, 9
Transitional periods, 27-40, 42-43, 50, 64, 114; *see also* Organic periods; Concentration, epochs of; Expansion, epochs of
Trevelyan, G. M., 192
Trevor-Roper, Hugh, 291 n.
Trilling, Lionel, 7, 25, 26, 118, 123, 149, 151
Truth, 38, 43, 46, 50, 128-29, 131, 133, 140, 179-86, 246
Turgot, A. R. J., 223
Tyranny, 228-29

United States, *see* American democracy; American institutions; Federal constitution in the U.S.

Universal suffrage, 236
University College (London), 90-91
Upper class, *see* Aristocracy
Utilitarianism (Mill), 55, 149
Utilitarians and Utilitarianism, 5, 24, 27, 56, 75, 87-88, 89, 91, 111, 114, 126, 147, 197, 231, 236
Utilitarian Society, 214
Utility, 83, 91, 104, 245
'Utility of Religion' (Mill), 55, 131, 190

Vigny, Alfred de, 32, 131, 145
Virgil, 194
Virtue, 172
Voltaire, F. M. Arouet, de 15, 20, 23, 44, 76, 138, 175, 209, 210, 213, 215

Walpole, Spencer, 262, 263, 265
Ward, W. G., 116, 267 n.
Ward, Wilfrid, 274 n.
Weber, Max, 194
Westminster Review, 26, 27, 44-46
Whewell, Dr. William, 66
Whigs, 5, 44-45
Whitman, Walt, 2
Wilde, Oscar, 25
Winchester, 80
Wiseman, Nicholas, Cardinal, 282 n.
Women suffrage, *see* Female suffrage
Wordsworth, William, 6, 24, 26, 87, 109-10, 112, 144-49, 151-54, 157-158, 175, 178-79, 182, 186, 232, 288 n.
'Wordsworth and the Rabbis' (Trilling), 26
Work, 96, 110, 134, 140-41, 197-98
Working class, *see* Lower class

Young, G. M., 50, 82, 88, 97, 140, 231

Zeitgeist, 12, 62, 64, 67-68, 69, 73, 122, 273 n.